Herbs

Growing & Using
The Plants of Romance

By Bill and Sylvia Varney
Photography by Scott Millard

IRONWOOD PRESS

IRONWOOD PRESS

Editor and Publisher
Scott Millard

Associate Publisher
Eric A. Johnson

Business Manager
Michele V. M. Millard

Printing 10 9 8 7 6 5 4 3 2 1

Printed in China through
Palace Press International

Library of Congress Cataloging-in-Publication Data

Varney, Bill.
Herbs: Growing & Using the Plants of Romance/written by Bill & Sylvia Varney; photography by Scott Millard.
p. cm.
Includes index.
ISBN 0-9628236-7-8
1. Herbs. 2. Herb gardening.
3. Herbs—Utilization. I. Varney, Sylvia. II. Millard, Scott. III. Title.
SB351.H5V37   1998
635'.7—dc21
98-6643
CIP

Address inquiries to:
IRONWOOD PRESS
2968 West Ina Road #285
Tucson, Arizona   85741

Dedication

This book is dedicated with gratitude and love in honor of my grandparents, Quitman and Pauline Adams, and Roy and Thelma Varney, who, by example, taught me to love every leaf.

Contributing Writer,
Gallery of Herbs
Jacqueline A. Soule

Cover Photograph
Scott Millard

Additional Photography
Lynn Herrmann, page 12, top right. Texas Department of Transportation, page 13, center. Michael Skott, page 152, page 160, top; page 164, top left and top right.

Illustrations
Don Fox

Editorial Consultant
Mary Campbell

Design Consultants
Ed Allard
Paul Fitzgerald

Indexing
Sara Smith

Important Notice
The information in this book is true and accurate to the best of our knowledge. It is offered without guarantees on the part of the authors and the publishers, who disclaim any liability in connection with the use of this information. Be aware that if herbs are misused, they can be harmful. This book is not to be used as a medical reference. The advice it contains is general, not specific, and neither the authors or the publishers can be held responsible for any adverse reaction to the recipes, formulas, recommendations or instructions contained herein. Do not try self diagnosis or attempt self-treatment for serious or long-term problems without consulting a qualified medical herbalist. Do not take herbal remedies if you are undergoing any other course of medical treatment without seeking professional advice.

Special thanks to the Fredericksburg Herb Farm staff

Barbara H. Avery
Yavonna M. Bailey
Carissa Ballard
Rebecca L. Black
Anita Burg
Chelsea Cline
Dan S. Harper
Shirley T. Keyser
Vickki Lopez
Imelda Luycx
Priscilla K. Martin
Guillermina Neri
Raphael Ortega
Randal G. Rankin
Maricella Robles
Lucy J. Sim

Thank you to the following individuals for their support

David and Esthermae Rooke, Kerrville, Texas
John and Karen Haebig, Fredericksburg, Texas
Dick and Rosemary Estenson, Fredericksburg, Texas
Ellison Phelps, San Antonio, Texas
Carol Luckenbach, Corpus Christi, Texas
Luis Robles, Fredericksburg, Texas
Martin Ortiz, Fredericksburg, Texas
Brian and Jan Bailey, Fredericksburg, Texas
Taylor and Myra Starkey, Victoria, Texas
Tricia Foley, New York, New York
Lana Robinson, Cranfill Gap, Texas
Emelie Tolley, New York, New York
Michael Skott, Seattle, Washington
Gene and Paula Varney, Nixon, Texas
Carleton Varney, New York, New York
Walter and Margaret Ann White, Tryon, North Carolina

Additional thanks to

Charles and Lou Ann Basham, Huntington Beach, California
Helen Chandler, San Diego Wild Animal Park, Escondido, California
Huntington Botanic Gardens, San Marino, California
Rogers Gardens, Costa Mesa, California
San Antonio Botanic Gardens, San Antonio, Texas
Rudy Vis, River Ridge Farms, Oxnard, California

Foreword

Sylvia and Bill Varney approach life with passion: Family, friends, community, church and herbs all excite their enthusiasm and commitment. This commitment, paired with vision and lots of hard work, has made the Fredericksburg Herb Farm a special place. There visitors are welcomed warmly and given the opportunity to enjoy the fruits of the Varneys' labors and absorb some of their wisdom.

I first visited the Fredericksburg Herb Farm many years ago when I was searching for gardens and food to photograph for an herb book I was writing. Even then, when the garden was contained in the space around the shop on Main Street, it was clear that the Varneys' interest in the subject of herbs was deep and sincere. Bill had a particular talent for gardening and perfumery; Sylvia was a whiz in the kitchen and was fascinated with the history and healthful properties of herbs. As they walked me through the garden, waved a new fragrance beneath my nose, or seduced me with one of Sylvia's luscious desserts, their enthusiasm and kindness enhanced the experience and surely, had I not already been captivated by these wonderful plants, I would have been a convert.

Over the years I've watched with pleasure as their garden has grown and their business has expanded in new herbal directions. Fortunate enough to be a friend, I've enjoyed Sylvia and Bill's ebullience and kindness first hand. I am so glad that this book will now enable everyone to experience their enthusiasm and partake of their vast knowledge of growing and using herbs.

Emelie Tolley, Herbalist and Author

New York, New York

Table of Contents

Making Sense of Herbs 8

The Fredericksburg Herb Farm 10

Glossary..14

Who's Who in the Herb Garden 16

Mainstay Culinary Herbs 18

Mainstay Medicinal Herbs...20

Mainstay Cosmetic Herbs 22

Mainstay Decorative Herbs 24

Herbs in the Landscape . . . A Landscape of Herbs 26

Gallery of Herbs 30

Complete descriptions of how to grow and use more than 100 herbs

Framework for a Garden **124**

Planning Your Herb Garden 126

Herb Gardens For Fragrance 131

Color Sense with Herbs and Flowers 134

Adding Personality to Your Garden 135

Putting Down Roots **136**

The Big Picture of Gardening 138

The Scoop on Soil 139

Ready, Set, Plant 142

Watering 142

Propagating Herbs 143

Growing Herbs in Containers 146

Garden Maintenance 147

Pests in Your Herb Garden 147

Winter Protection 151

Reaping and Keeping Your Harvest 151

Herbal How-to Recipes **152**

Herbs in the Kitchen 154

Herbs in the Home 167

Sources and Resources **173**

Index **174**

Preface

Herb. What's in a name we cherish? The plants we call "herbs" come from the Latin word *herba,* meaning "green crops." This all-encompassing definition is evident in the *Book of Genesis,* where God caused the earth to "bring forth grass, the herb yielding seed, and the fruit tree yielding fruit." The 4th-century Greek philosopher and student of Aristotle, Theophrastus, narrowed the field of greenery a little further by dividing the plant world into trees, shrubs and herbs, mainly by size. The category he created and labeled *herb* included plants similar to the large group now classified botanically as *herbaceous.*

Botanists further refined and altered what is called an herb, defining it as a plant whose soft or succulent stems (herbaceous)—as opposed to stems that are persistently woody—die down to the ground after flowering and return the following season (perennial).

This definition was certainly not followed by past generations, who used plants to meet many of life's necessities. In order to survive, trees, shrubs, weeds, flowers and even fungi were put to use.

The same approach to utility holds true today. Whether you are a novice gardener or experienced with herbs, we recommend that you not overlook selected trees and shrubs that have woody and persistent stems but are definitely herbal in character—hyssop, sweet bay, rosemary, thyme and winter savory, to name a few. And the herbs we've known and loved and grown on the Farm have been annuals, biennials and bulbs as well as perennials.

As gardeners, we have come to a different understanding of which plants are herbs based on our changing relationship with nature. Today, *herb* has an expanded definition that includes plants, generally aromatic or fragrant, whose parts, whether leaf, flower, seed or root, are useful to mankind for food, flavoring, medicine, household and cosmetics. Whew! By contrast, *spices,* with their many uses for flavoring and fragrance, primarily are harvested from the bark, root, seed, berry or pod of vines, shrubs or trees grown mostly in tropical climates.

> "If the day and night are such that you greet them with joy and life emits a fragrance like flowers and sweet scented herbs—that is your success. All nature is your congratulations."
>
> —Henry David Thoreau

The Plants of Romance

Almost 2,000 years ago Ovid lamented, "Alas, there are no herbs to cure love." This may well have been true, but the addition of herbs certainly enhances many sweet pleasures that are important to a well-lived life.

On a personal level, Bill and I have reached an understanding of herbs that reflects our changing relationship with each other—in who we once were, who we are and who we will become. We call herbs *the plants of romance.* As we've come to know herbs, they have twined around our hearts' qualities and preferences. Herbs grow up close and personal. They are not just flowers, but calendulas, nasturtiums and roses. They are not garnishes, but cinnamon and lemon basil, apple mint and chocolate mint, parsley and lavender thyme. They are not bulbs, but garlic and chives, dill and fennel. That is why we encourage you to try your hand at growing savory, reputed to have earned its name from the satyrs who found it essential to their amorous activities. Consider, too, the advice of Nicholas Culpeper, herbalist of the 17th century, who suggested a garden of mustard, onion and prickly asparagus for sparking an enchanted evening. Even earlier, the Greek physician Dioscorides in A.D. 40 counseled that a species of sage, *Salvia horminum,* "doth revoke to conjunction." Cumin retained love along with basil and vervain. Partial to roses? Their sweet breath and delicate petals have long been considered the essence of romantic encounters. And small wonder that a secret garden aids and abets our romantic impulses so effectively.

Growing the plants of romance will be different for every individual, a distinction that's important to recognize. That's because it's easy to become limited in our thinking about what is romantic. Many people define romance as hearts and flowers, only pink satin and lace. Others may think only of physical love. A person who dares to try something new, who makes the choice to work at an herb garden that he or she loves, who makes time for little sprigs and blossoms of beauty and grace, we believe, speaks our language. We hope that as you read this book, you will discover, as we have, ways to use herbs to make your meals more flavorful, your work more enjoyable and your life more pleasurable.

> "There is a garden in every childhood, an enchanted place where colors are brighter, the air softer, and the morning more fragrant than ever again."
>
> —Elizabeth Lawrence

The Garden Is Growing Us

The longer we're involved with herbs, the more we appreciate that we are not just growing a garden, the garden is growing us. We realize we are not the first gardeners to discover herbs leave us heirlooms that reach far beyond the borders of the garden. Far from it. It was around the Nile that the ancient Egyptians learned the lessons of watering and fertilizing. The students of Plato and Socrates learned philosophy in the groves around Athens. And Jesus advised his followers to "consider the lilies of the fields..." and to learn from them.

The garden truly is a school for higher learning, and herbs and flowers become our beautiful visual aids. Theophrastus, the father of botany, wrote down the observations that influenced gardeners and scientists for centuries to come. The 9th-century monk Walafrid Strabo patiently recorded his herbal discoveries in the monastery of St. Gallen; his writings continue to amaze our medical community. Winter-weary pilgrims learned from their Native American hosts to plant corn, with pieces of fish as fertilizer, to survive. Fearless 19th-century plant collectors explored dark continents to collect new and unheard-of specimens that have benefited us all. And we started our life as newlyweds by putting down roots for an herb farm. Planting trees, herb and flower beds in the courtyard of our Main Street shop as well as in the front yard of our home, growing antique roses, and seeding pots of flat-leaf parsley, sweet basil and cilantro. (How happy Bill was one morning when he exclaimed, "I've finally found the trick to growing lavender!")

Later we collected and hauled the granite for what was to become our Star Garden at the Herb Farm. Our gardens have given us so much to learn, so much growing to do, together.

Prune the Faults

Throughout this book, we have attempted to embrace each of the senses: sight, hearing, touch, taste and smell. We believe it is our senses that allow us to reconnect with nature, both physically and emotionally. We've also provided glimpses of many time-honored methods of using herbs. We hope you will borrow freely from these traditions as you create your own garden for personal expression.

In *Hortulus*, A.D. 840, Walafrid Strabo wrote, "And I offer this, that as you read what I gladly dedicate to you, you may know of my labors. And, please, as you read, prune the faults and approve what is good."

We encourage you to do the same.

Bill and Sylvia Varney, Fredericksburg, Texas

Making Sense of *herbs*

*W*hat is it about herbs? What gives these plants their universal appeal? Ask a dozen gardeners this question and you'll probably get a dozen different answers. But from their responses you will discover some common ground, so to speak, about why herbs are important to them and why herbs are included in their gardens. For many, it is what herbs can do. For these gardeners the philosophy is, "Why grow it if you can't use it?" Nothing wrong with that. Herbs certainly fill the bill for utility. Since the dawn of civilization, herbs have been pharmacy and spice rack rolled into one. They have been a bouquet for the eyes and the nose, and have stimulated, relaxed, flavored, scented, soothed, preserved, attracted or discouraged, depending on the need. And many botanists believe we have only scratched the surface as to the medicinal and healing properties of herbs.

For other gardeners, the appeal may be the herbs themselves. Many are superior landscape plants, blessed with unique qualities. Herbs are available to rival the finest perennials (many also fall into this plant category), providing seasonal flowers as well as year-round texture and foliage color.

It doesn't matter why you are attracted to this broad group of plants, or the essential nature of their appeal. But to get the most out of all that herbs offer, it takes some time and experience in growing and using them. And that is what this book is about: learning which herbs are best for you and how to use the herbs you grow. As you will see, your choices are varied. To get started we suggest you read the chapter Who's Who in the Herb Garden, pages 16 to 29. It will guide you in selecting herbs for a particular purpose, be it culinary, medicinal, cosmetic, decorative, crafts or landscape.

Welcome to the world of herbs. Whether your goal is a formal herb garden or a few pots of basil and thyme by the back door, the plants of romance beckon.

"We can never have enough of nature. We must be refreshed by the sight of inexhaustible vigor."

—Henry David Thoreau

Left: Chamomile and pansies surround a garden sundial at the Fredericksburg Herb Farm.

Above: *Salvia officinalis*, garden sage, in bloom.

The Fredericksburg Herb Farm

Drive out of Austin, the capital of Texas, and head due west. Within minutes you're traveling deep in the heart of Texas—into the Hill Country. Pass through Johnson City, hometown of President Lyndon Johnson, then after 30 miles or so, tucked into the rolling farmland, amid groves of oaks and peach tree orchards, you'll come to the storybook town of Fredericksburg. It is home to Bill and Sylvia Varney, founders and owners of the Fredericksburg Herb Farm, and authors of this book. It is here they are growing their dream.

The Varneys' love affair with herbs also has a storybook beginning. In 1985, they moved from Houston, seeking the quiet refuge and slower pace of small-town life. Bill remained true to his lifelong love of plants and managed a local nursery. Sylvia opened a small apothecary shop on Fredericksburg's Main Street, offering natural soaps, lotions and other toiletries. To everything there is a season: Demand for such natural products was high, and the business grew at a Jack-and-the-Beanstalk pace. Within a year, Bill quit the nursery to work full time at the store.

The shop expanded and live herbs and herb crafts were offered for sale. More space was needed, so in 1991, the Varneys took a gamble and purchased a long-vacant, four-acre farm just south of Main Street. The focus of their business changed when the Varneys began to make their own natural herb products. That same year, their Edible Flowers Herb Vinegar received the Outstanding Condiment Award at the International Fancy Food Show in New York City. It was an honor for the Varneys, and fueled interest in the fledgling company. Sales of their herb products tripled, and the couple has never looked back.

Today, the farm spreads comfortably over 14 acres, with space allotted for future gardens. An 1880s limestone farmhouse that was once a cannery operation for World War II Victory Gardens has been restored and now serves as the hub of the farm. Herbal experiences are as varied as the guests who visit. You can stroll around the grounds, select from herb-based necessities and niceties in the Farm's apothecary and enjoy an herb-enhanced luncheon at the Tea Room. Or join the tour groups that explore this scratch-and-sniff playground, while Bill Varney advises visitors how to select and grow herbs in their own gardens. If one day is not enough to absorb all the sights and smells, visitors can spend the night at the Farm's bed-and-breakfast, the Herb Haus.

Five Gardens to Explore
Of the Farm's five gardens, shown throughout this book, the Star Garden (a bird's-eye view can be seen on page 13) is the largest and was the most challenging to create. An antique windmill was brought in from nearby Johnson City and installed in the center of the garden, which forms a circle 180 feet in diameter. To form the planting beds, Bill, Sylvia and son Roy worked an entire summer to place more than 36 tons of limestone rock. Each of the planting-bed "points" flourishes with herbs grown for a purpose—*medicinal, cosmetic, culinary, crafting* or *ornamental.*

The neighboring Working Garden is a no-frills minifarm that supplies much of the Tea Room's fresh produce. Farm staff are busy almost year-round with planting and harvesting fresh salad greens, herbs, peppers, onions and edible flowers. Vegetables and herbs are picked at peak flavor and walked to the kitchen to become part of the daily fare.

Sylvia Varney

The Farm's Cross Garden and Ichthus Garden, designed in the fish-shaped Greek symbol of Christianity, lend a sense of faith and harmony to the Varneys' handiwork. See photos of each garden on page 12 and page 133.

Tucked behind the farmhouse shop, visitors can find sanctuary in the Secret Garden. Strategically placed benches at the ends and junctures of paths allow views of the resident ducks as they paddle lazily across the creek that flows through the grounds. Ducks and guinea hens are more than rural trappings; they consume their share of insect pests, so are part of the Varneys' "organic only" approach to pest and disease controls. (See photo, page 149.) A unique herb meadow blends into native oaks just beyond the Secret Garden, created over the years when herb seeds borne by wind and birds set root in the fertile soil. The nature of the meadow is most evident after a mowing, when the sweet, fragrance of dozens of different herbs perfume the air.

Indoors, culinary and cosmetic uses of herbs are showcased at the Farm's apothecary and in the adjacent Tea Room restaurant. Recipes for Cheddar and Chive Corn Chowder, Rosemary Foccaccia Bread and Sylvia's Spicy Kahlua Chocolate Cake rate high on the menu. They appear in this book's Herbal How-to Recipes, pages 152 to 172.

Recently the Varneys discovered that most-Texan of endeavors—oil—aromatic oil, that is. It's put into practice at their Quiet Haus day spa as an integral part of *aromatherapy*. This ancient healing art combines plant-based oils with touch and smell. A massage therapist kneads away at aching muscles and rubs tired feet with fragrant essences. A facialist applies custom-made mud masks to complexions.

A Family Affair
In the course of coming to the farm year after year, many customers have become friends too. They have seen the Varneys and their farm grow. And, at some point during a visit, they are likely to run into the Varneys' young son, Roy, who has grown up on the farm. They have comforted him when he was stung by a bee, laughed at his muddy dance in the sprinklers and applauded him and his friends when the Fredericksburg Children's Chorale sang at the farm. Roy is a friendly touchstone for children visiting, and a bright potential resource whom Bill and Sylvia call "the Farm's future herbalist."

Cultivating an Herbal Experience
The Varneys are ever mindful that individuals' lives can be enriched through the experience of herbs: in their gardens, kitchens, baths, medicine chests, homes and places of worship. Plants like basil, dill, oregano and thyme allow people to ingest less sodium, sugar and fat without sacrificing the delight of flavorful food. Lavender, lemon verbena, santolina, bay and roses decorate homes as fragrant living artistry.

In a sense, Bill is the farmer and Sylvia the cook in a modern-day version of our American heritage. The farm they've created endures as a quiet slice of Eden, a place to stop and smell, touch and nibble the rosemary. What better way to learn how to grow and use herbs than from these folks? As keepers of these lovely plantings, the Varneys bring us into their world, a place to sow and cultivate fresh ideas for a bountiful and useful harvest.

"What a lovely place to come and relax and enjoy God's good gifts! The herb gardens are quite an inspiration for our own little garden. The bed of lavender was especially wonderful."

—Guest book entry, the Herb Haus Bed-and-Breakfast

Bill Varney

Above: At the Fredericksburg Herb Farm it's a family affair, with Sylvia Varney and son Roy at entrance to the original farmhouse.

Right: Cosmetics and candles on display at one of the Farm's shops, dressed up for the holidays.

Below: An overview of the Farm's Cross Garden, with bed-and-breakfast in the background.

Left: Bill Varney collects herbs that will become part of the daily fare at the Farm's restaurant.

Below left: A bird's-eye view of the Star Garden. Photo: Texas Department of Transportation.

Bottom left: Growing up on an herb farm can be a lot of fun. For Roy Varney, a Star Garden path makes a perfect bicycle track.

Bottom right: Herb plants for sale at the Farm.

Glossary

Herbs have their own terminology. Use this glossary as a reference guide to these terms, used throughout this book.

Absolute—Highly concentrated, viscous, semisolid or solid obtained by alcohol extraction.

Acid [soil]—Having a pH value below 7.

Air Layering—Propagation method. Portion of stem is induced to root by enclosing it in a rooting medium while attached to the parent plant.

Alkaline [soil]—A pH value above 7. See pH.

Alternate [leaves]—Borne singly at each node, on either side of a stem.

Angiosperm—Any plant that has its seeds enclosed in an ovary.

Annual—Plant that completes its life cycle in one season.

Anther—Part of a stamen that produces pollen, usually borne on a filament.

Apex—Tip or growing point of an organ such as a leaf or shoot.

Aphrodisiac—Increases or stimulates romantic desire.

Apothecary—Person who makes, sells and prescribes herbal medicines.

Aquatic—Plant that grows in water.

Architectural—Plants that have strong and often spectacular shapes.

Aromatherapy—Therapeutic use of essential oil.

Aromatic—Materials having pungent, spicy scent and pleasing taste. Mildly stimulating fragrances. Many aromatic herbs were thought to heal or prevent disease.

Axil—Upper angle between a leaf and stem, between a main stem and a lateral branch or between a stem and a bract.

Balm—Soothing ointment obtained from a variety of herbs and trees. Derived from the word *balsam*. Applied to several mint family plants.

Biennial—Plant that completes its life cycle in two years, usually flowering and fruiting the second year.

Bitter—Tonic component that stimulates the appetite and promotes the secretion of saliva and gastric juices by exciting the taste buds.

Blender—A perfumer's term referring to a secondary, complementary fragrance in a perfume blend.

Bolt—To produce flowers and seed prematurely, such as *bolt to seed*. Occurs most often when plants are set out too late in the year or when unseasonably hot weather accelerates their growth.

Botany—Science of plants, including their growth, form, function and classification.

Bouquet Garni—Bundle of several herbs tied in cheesecloth, added to soups, stews and sauces for flavoring, then removed when desired.

Bract—Modified leaves that can take on the appearance of flowers. Bracts are usually green but can be conspicuous and colorful. Examples include bougainvillea and poinsettia.

Bruise—To lightly pound plant stems and leaves.

Bud—Rudimentary or condensed shoot containing embryonic leaves and or flowers.

Caliche—Soil condition found in some areas of the arid Southwest. It is a deposit of calcium carbonate beneath the soil surface.

Calmative—A sedative.

Calyx—All of the sepals, considered collectively as one unit.

Compost—Mixture of decomposed vegetative matter, useful for amending the soil, mulching and fertilizing.

Condiment—Sauces and relishes to add to food at the table.

Cream—To blend butter, usually softened, with a granulated or crushed ingredient until the mixture is light and fluffy.

Culpeper, Nicholas—English apothecary, astrologer and herbalist, 1616-1654. Wrote *The Complete Herbal* and *English Physician*.

Cultivar—Cultivated variety of a plant, rather than a variety that occurs naturally in the wild. Designated in this book with single quotation marks.

Cuttings—Portions of stem or root, sometimes called "slips," that can be induced to form roots and develop into new plants.

Deciduous—Losing leaves or other plant parts during dormant season of year. Plant seems to die but regrows in the spring.

Decoction—Herbal preparation made by boiling an herb, usually seed, root or bark, in a covered container for 15 minutes. The liquid is strained and the herb residue is discarded.

Dioscorides, Pedanius—Greek pharmacologist and physician to the Roman army, A.D. 40-90. Wrote *De Materia Medica*.

Division—Propagation by dividing a clump into several parts, often while plant is dormant.

Dormant—Alive but not actively growing.

Elixir—A distillation of tincture.

Enfleurage—Process of preparing perfumes by exposing odorless fixed oils to the exhalations of certain flowers.

Essence—Solution of one ounce essential oil to one pint of alcohol.

Essential Oil—Volatile and fragrant substance produced by many herbs.

Evergreen—Plants that have green leaves throughout the year.

Everlastings—Flowers that hold their shape and color when dried.

Extract—A strong decoction.

Family—A biological classification. All members of a plant family share certain characteristics that are not found in other families. See *Genus*.

Fixative—Perfumer's term that refers to substances added to a perfume or potpourri blend to absorb and preserve the delicate fragrances.

Floret—Small, individual flower in the flowerheads of the *Compositae* family, or a cluster of flowers.

Flower—Reproductive unit of an angiosperm. The basic flower forms are *single*, with one row of usually 4 to 6 petals; *semidouble*, with more petals, usually in two rows; *double*, with many petals in several rows and few or no stamens; *fully double*, usually rounded in shape, with densely packed petals and with stamens obscured.

Garnish—To add a decorative touch to food, as

with edible flowers, parsley or croutons.

Genus—Most important subdivision of a plant or animal family, designated by the first word in the botanical name. In *Salvia elegans,* (pineapple sage), *Salvia* is the genus, *elegans* is the species. See the listing, *Species.*

Gerard, John—English botanist, barber-surgeon, 1545-1612. Author of the still-famous *Herbal* or *General Historic of Plants.*

Hardy—Describes a plant's resistance to, or tolerance of, frost or freezing temperatures (as in "hardy to 20F"). The word does not mean tough, pest resistant or disease resistant. See *Tender.*

Herbaceous—Plants that die down at the end of the growing season. In a general sense, plants having nonwoody tissues.

Herbal—Book of herb information and lore.

Herbalism—The study of herbs.

Herbalist—One skilled in the identification and use of herbs.

Hippocrates—Greek physician known as "The Father of Medicine," 460-377 B.C. Wrote 87 medical treatises.

Homeopathy—A system of medical treatment consisting in part of the administration of herbs.

Humus—Soft, moist, dark brown to black content of soil, mostly derived from decaying plant matter.

Hybrid—Offspring of genetically different parents, usually produced accidentally or artificially in cultivation, occasionally occurring in the wild.

Infusion—Solution made by pouring boiling water on dried or fresh herbs, allowing them to steep several minutes, then straining off the herbs.

Leader—In a single-trunked shrub or tree, the central, upward-growing stem.

Leaven—To cause batters and doughs to rise, usually by means of a chemical agent. May occur before or during baking.

Lift—To take out of the ground for transplanting or harvesting.

Loam—Well-structured, fertile soil that is moisture retentive and well drained.

Mince—To cut or chop into very small pieces for cooking.

Mulch—A layer of matter applied to the soil around a plant's root zone to conserve moisture, protect the roots from frost, reduce weed growth and enrich the soil.

Parkinson, John—London apothecary and king's herbalist. Author of *Theatrum Botanicum,* an herbal containing descriptions of 3,800 plants.

Perennial—Living for at least three seasons, normally flowering every year. May die down during the winter season.

Petiole—In botany, the stalk to which a leaf is attached.

pH, pH Scale—A measure of soil acidity or alkalinity.

Pliny (the Elder)—Roman scholar, A.D. 23-79. Author of *Historia Naturalis.*

Pomade—Prepared perfume material obtained by the enfleurage process.

Potion—An herbal drink.

Potpourri—A French term meaning "rotten pot." Mixture of fragrant flowers, herbs and spices.

Poultice—Crushed herb or plant extracts heated and applied to bruised or inflamed skin.

Rhizome—Underground stem that lives for more than one season.

Runner—Horizontally spreading, usually slender stem that forms roots at each node; often confused with stolon.

Self-Seed, Self-Sow—Dropping or freely distributing its seed, from which new plants grow the following season.

Sepals—Individual segments of the calyx that surrounds the petals.

Sieve—To pass dry or liquid ingredients through a closely meshed utensil so as to separate liquid from solid and fine from coarse in cooking.

Simple—Medicinal plant or herb.

Skim—To ladle or spoon off excess fat or scum from the surface of a liquid in cooking.

Species—Plants having certain differences from other plants within the same genus. The second word in a plant's latin name. See *Genus.*

Spice—A strongly flavored, aromatic substance, usually obtained from tropical plants.

Sprig—Small, 2- to 3-inch twig or section of stem and leaves cut from the tip of a plant.

Stolon—Stem that creeps along the surface of the ground, taking root at intervals and forming new plants where it roots.

Strewing Herb—In ancient times, herbs scattered (strewn) on floors so that when walked upon they produced a pleasant scent to mask odors.

Tender, Cold Tender—Susceptible to cold temperature damage, as contrasted to Hardy.

Tincture—Herbal remedy or perfumery material prepared in an alcohol base.

Tisane—French term for herb tea.

Topiary—Technique of shaping shrubs and trees into formalized shapes, often in geometric or animal forms.

Torte—A rich cake, high in egg content, usually covered and layered with thick frosting, cream sauce or meringue, often made with nuts or crumbs.

Tuber—Thick underground stem, from which a plant grows. Similar to a rhizome but is usually shorter and thicker.

Tussie-Mussie—Also known as *nosegay.* A cluster of flowers, usually with at least one rose in the center, kept fresh by a "mussie"—a moistened piece of moss.

Umbel—Flower cluster sometimes resembling an umbrella supported by pedicels (small stems) that seem to rise from the same point.

Variegated—Marked with patches or streaks of different colors.

Variety—Naturally occurring variation of a species. Sometimes abbreviated as var.

Volatile—Unstable, evaporating easily. Example: Volatile oils are used in perfumery.

Whip—In cooking, to beat a mixture until air has been thoroughly incorporated and the mixture is light and frothy.

Wort—Herb or plant. From Old English *wyrt,* "root," but later applied to the entire plant. Wort persists in many word compounds (mugwort) and combinations (louse wort).

Who's Who in the

herb garden

ere we provide an overview of herbs at their most functional, organized by use. If you are looking for guidance as to which herbs are among the most practical to grow, this chapter is a good place to begin. Consider herbs for the following uses:

Culinary . . . Herbs enhance the foods we eat, capturing the lure of uplifting fragrances and the hint of romance. They give us an appreciation of subtle foliage, flowers and flavors. Although the vitamins and minerals herbs provide may be minute in quantity, it is the taste, mood-enhancement and health benefits they give foods that make them so valuable.

Medicinal . . . "You may consider yourself happy when that which is your food is also your medicine," wrote Thoreau. He was far from being the first to claim health from the garden. For thousands of years, physicians of the body and spirit—today's doctors and priests—were gardeners and botanists first, healers of aches and pains second.

Cosmetic . . . Our concern for health is inseparable from our pursuit of beauty. What is it that makes us want to squeeze or slather or pat on our outsides the things that cause us to feel good on our insides? This impulse isn't all that illogical. The oldest cosmetic formulas offer advice on the virtues of fruits, vegetables and herbs in enhancing and preserving our appearance.

Decorative . . . Want to extend the life of your garden? Utilize herbs for their decorative qualities—fresh in bouquets, dried in wreaths and potpourris, or use them to enhance candles and oils. Simple bundles of fresh herbs suspended to dry from ceiling or windowsill bring the sharp fragrances and colors of your garden indoors.

Landscape . . . When it comes to herbs in the landscape, Virgil said it best: "Admire a large estate, but work a small one." We admire herbs as we do other quality landscape plants: for their flowers, forms, textures and ease of growth. Herbs can be be companions in existing flower beds or cozied up alongside vegetables to boost their flavor and vitality.

"A life of retreat offers various joys, none, I think, will compare with the time one employs in the study of herbs, or in striving to gain some practical knowledge of nature's domain."

—Abbott Walafrid
Strabo

Left: A mass planting of basil takes on an ornamental effect. Above: Purple coneflower, also known by its genus name, *Echinacea.*

Mainstay Culinary Herbs

Herbs are the aphrodisiacs of the culinary world. Most of us can chop, stir and sauté, but the real romance of cooking comes from exciting the flavors of your ingredients so they will taste their very best.

Our strategy for learning how to use herbs in the kitchen? Learn to grow them. A ready supply will be conveniently on hand when the need arises. Freshly picked herbs have an enticement far more precious than dried herbs. Plus, when dried, homegrown herbs are pure, unprocessed and pungently pleasing.

On the opposite page is a list of herbs we find indispensable for our own culinary use. We recommend you include a wide selection of these stimulating herbs in your garden. Begin with fresh herbs, add in a little imagination and you'll always be able to prepare a decent meal. See pages 150 to 166 to learn how to prepare some of our Tea Room's favorite dishes.

Below: Herb-flavored vinegars and oils in the kitchen. For recipes on how to make your own herb vinegars, see page 158.

Basic Herb Butter

The flavors of most herbs are more fully drawn out when the herbs are first blended with butter and then added to your recipe.

Allow 1/2 cup of unsalted butter to reach room temperature. Add 1 to 3 tablespoons of your choice of a finely chopped fresh herb, or 1 to 3 teaspoons of dried herb and 1 tablespoon minced fresh parsley. Blend well. You may also add lemon juice, salt and pepper to taste. Wrap with plastic and refrigerate overnight before using.

Herbs for a Culinary Garden

Basil—This herb has a grassy, sweet-clove flavor and fragrance. It adores tomatoes and is an essential ingredient in pesto. Sprinkle it on pasta, fish, chicken and salads. Page 35.

Chives—This petite member of the onion family adds a ladylike onion kick to salads, potatoes, egg and cheese dishes and dips. Its pompon pink or white flowers do double duty as an edible garnish. Page 51.

Coriander (Cilantro)—This herb is the Don Juan of Indian, Chinese and Mexican cuisines. Its pungent leaves and spicy seeds are valued in many dishes. Page 55.

Dill—The tickle-feather leaves of this herb add a memorable touch of anise, parsley and celery flavors to salads, fish dishes and sauces. Page 58.

Fennel—Use with salmon, greens, in salad dressings and breads. It's even pleasant in apple pie. Page 62.

Garlic—We revel in its glories, adding garlic to breads, fresh and cooked vegetables, meats, fish, chicken and sauces. Cooking transmutes its tough-guy essence to addictively piquant and subtle. Page 66.

Lemon Balm—The gentle lemon perfume of this herb blends well with a range of foods, including green salads, fresh and cooked fruits, baked sweets, juices and teas. Page 79.

Mint—This fresh-kiss herb is available in many varieties. Our favorite? Definitely chocolate mint. A classic companion to lamb, we also add it to fruits, sweets and drinks. Page 86.

Oregano and Sweet Marjoram—These two different herbs have a similar flash-and-dash flavor. They are compatible together or with basil, parsley, chives, sage or thyme. Well suited for Italian, Greek, Mexican and Provençal cuisines. Page 93 and page 113.

Parsley—Some like it curly, some like it flat-leaved and Italian. Both are ideal garnishes, blessed with vitamins A and C, perking up salads, cooked vegetables and soups. Page 94.

Rosemary—The leaves of this bristly evergreen have a pungent, pinelike scent. Enlivens meats, chicken, fish, potatoes and wine. Makes a suitable hangover tea, too. Page 102.

Sage—This silver-leaved herb makes fatty meats, sausages, poultry and cheese more digestible. Page 105.

Scented Geraniums—Many people grow them just for the touchable, fragrant leaves. But cakes, cookies and pies, as well as strawberries, peaches and pears, benefit from the sweet, fragrant flavors. Page 66.

French Tarragon—This anise-scented herb elevates sauces, egg and cheese dishes and chicken to heavenly heights. Popular as flavoring in vinegars for salads and sauces. Page 115.

Thyme—A piny-peppery herb that socializes with parsley in dishes from chicken and pork to zucchini and tomatoes. Consider the many other thymes, including lemon, caraway and lavender thyme. Page 117.

More Culinary Herbs

Arugula, page 35.

Sweet Bay, page 39.

Borage, page 40.

Salad Burnet, page 42.

Chervil, page 50.

Epazote, page 59.

Lovage, page 83.

Mexican Mint Marigold, page 85.

Nasturtium, page 91.

Winter and Summer Savory, page 119.

Left: Some important culinary herbs to consider for your garden. Top row, left to right: chives, parsley, hyssop, sweet marjoram and oregano. Bottom row, left to right: basil, rosemary, mint and sage.

Mainstay Medicinal Herbs

Herbs have been used to treat ailments and injuries since the dawn of creation. Thousands of years ago, the Chinese, Egyptians and Greeks were known to take advantage of herbs' curative properties. Today, alternative medicine, which uses herbs in massage, meditation, acupuncture and aromatherapy, is experiencing a rebirth of enormous proportions.

Using medicinal herbs requires making responsible choices. Have the information at hand to know which herb is best for a particular problem. Use common sense and and realize that diagnosing and dosing yourself with herbs can be dangerous.

The information here is intended to stimulate your thinking about the curative power of herbs. To learn more, read books by respected researchers with credentials in medicine or *pharmacognosy*—the science of discovering medicinal products in nature. Herbs can indeed prevent and effectively treat certain health conditions, but do not presume that because herbs are plants they are necessarily safe. If you're new to trying an herbal remedy, start with the lowest dose, increase it gradually, and don't take more than the recommended amount or exceed the recommended duration. If you feel worse after taking an herb, stop using it. Always err on the side of caution. Be especially cautious if you are pregnant, nursing or taking prescription medications.

Below: These common medicinal herbs are also excellent landscape plants, and are especially effective in this naturalistic grouping. Shown are lavender, top left and center, blue-flowering rosemary, center, and aloe vera, foreground.

Opposite page: Some important medicinal herbs include, from left: valerian, anise hyssop, chamomile, yarrow and horsetail reed.

Herbs for a Garden Medicine Chest

Calendula—Treat minor cuts and burns with a poultice. Steep equal parts fresh petals and boiling water until soft, squeeze petals and apply as a compress. Page 43.

Chamomile, Roman—We still rely on this apple-scented tea to help comfort upset stomachs and cramps. Soaking an external injury reduces swelling. Page 47.

Comfrey—An external application of the roots or leaves shredded and pounded into a gluey mass is believed to help speed the healing of external injuries and sores. Page 51.

Fennel—Licorice-flavor seeds reduce appetites for weight-watchers. A tea made from its crushed seeds treats overindulgences of many kinds. Page 62.

Garlic—Either raw or taken as a syrup (made by boiling cloves and water for half a day), garlic is a potent antiseptic for colds, sore throats and coughs. Page 66

Lavender—Its sedative-inducing essential oil is said to decrease anxiety. Taken internally, a water-diluted drop is believed to relieve intestinal gas. Page 78.

Lemon Balm—Tea from leaves relieves feverish colds and headaches, menstrual cramps and nervous stomachs. Crushed leaves soothe insect bites. Page 79.

Parsley—As a tea it's said to treat high blood pressure, heart failure, allergies and fever or to induce labor. Use 2 teaspoons dried leaves or root per cup of boiling water. Page 94.

Peppermint—Tea helps relieve nausea and vomiting. For fast relief of painful sores, burns, scalds and herpes, apply a few drops of its essential oil directly to the problem area. Page 86.

Rosemary—Calming aromatic tea settles stomachs and helps clear stuffy noses. Page 102.

Sage—Originating from the Latin words "to heal," sage has been used for so many maladies it's gained a reputation as a cure-all herb. Leaves also provide a convenient band-aid for garden cuts and scrapes before washing. An infusion settles stomachs and soothes sore throats. Page 105.

Thyme, Lemon Thyme—Long history of use as an antiseptic, cough remedy and digestive aid. Crush leaves and place onto a wound on the way to washing. Its faint clovelike tea settles stomach upheavals, coughs and menstrual complaints. Page 117.

Yarrow—This herb's ferny leaves have been found so effective in stopping bleeding in brawls on and off the battlefield, it earned the name "bad man's plaything." Its calming benefits make it the tangy thing to sip for indigestion and menstrual cramps, or to soak in for wounds and inflammations. Page 123.

More Herbs from Nature's Pharmacopoeia

Aloe Vera, page 33.

Angelica, page 33.

Anise, page 34.

Basil, page 35.

Sweet Bay, page 39.

Bee Balm, Bergamot, page 39.

Borage, page 40.

Caraway, page 43.

Chervil, page 50.

Chives, page 51.

Dill, page 58.

Horehound, page 74.

Hyssop, page 75.

Lemon Verbena, page 83.

Lovage, page 83.

Sweet Marjoram, page 113.

Mullein, page 90.

Nasturtium, page 91.

Rose, page 99.

Salad Burnet, page 42.

Southernwood, page 111.

Spearmint, page 86.

Summer Savory, page 119.

Sweet Annie, page 111.

Sweet Woodruff, page 113.

Valerian, page 118.

Herbal Home Remedies

Acne: After washing, rinse the skin with a strong tea made from one of the following: lavender, chamomile, yarrow, catnip or thyme. Treat pimples with lemon juice and then apply a calendula balm or lotion.

Colds and Flu: Fight cold and flu symptoms with hot tea made of yarrow and peppermint. Add lemon and honey to taste.

Coughs: Eating raw garlic helps fight bronchial infections. Chew on parsley afterward to freshen breath.

Hangover: Steep peppermint and thyme leaves in a cup of boiling water, covered, for five minutes. Strain and sip.

Insomnia: A cup of hot chamomile tea at bedtime helps promote sleep. Teas made from marjoram and lavender can be effective in this way, too.

Mainstay Cosmetic Herbs

Calendula, lemon verbena, rose and yarrow: Their names alone summon up heady aromas, luscious flavors and lavish possibilities. These common herbs and flowers are also skin-care essentials, and can enhance or soothe skin, hands, hair, nails, eyes, teeth and feet.

Growing a selection of annual and perennial herbs from the list, opposite, will allow you to create a surprising quantity of cosmetics throughout the year. Harvest and dry cold-tender herbs at the end of the growing season to store for winter skin care. You'll find our cosmetic recipes are as easy to prepare as a great dessert. As a bonus, their cost is less than half the price of an over-the-counter treatment. Also see Beauty and the Bath, pages 171 to 172.

Below: Herbs can add their unique fragrances to a wide range of cosmetic products.

Opposite page: Some herbs and flowers commonly grown for cosmetic use. From left: poppy, carnation, rue, dianthus and calendula.

Natural Body Scrub

Helps heal minor skin irritations. Soothes and smoothes the skin.

    4 ounces white sugar
    1 ounce finely ground fresh rosemary
    4 ounces sea salt
    1 ounce finely ground fresh thyme
    4 ounces ground oatmeal

Blend all ingredients in a mini-food processor and bottle in an attractive jar. In the shower or tub, rinse body with water. While skin is damp pour small amount of Natural Body Scrub into your hands and massage into skin. Gentle enough for use on face and for acne. Rinse thoroughly.

Bette Davis Eyes Tonic

An eye-opening classic that renews and smoothes skin around tired eyes.

    4 tablespoons chamomile tea
    2 teaspoons castor oil
    4 tablespoons witch hazel
    4 drops rosewood oil

Brew cup of chamomile tea and allow to cool. Add 4 tablespoons of tea to witch hazel, then add castor oil and rosewood oil. Pour in small jar and shake well. Dip cotton pads into tonic, squeeze out excess and place pad over eye area. Relax and leave in place for 15 minutes, then remove. Do not apply to open eyes.

Herbs for a Backyard Spa

Calendula—Soothe tired and swollen feet with an infusion made from fresh petals and leaves. An oil or ointment made from the petals treats sunburn, helps battle blemishes and soften skin stressed by bruises, burns and rashes. Tea sweetened with honey aids poor circulation and dehydrated, tired complexions. Page 43.

Chamomile—Daisylike flowers from German chamomile and Roman chamomile have the same gentle healing substance, *azulene.* An infusion soothes irritated or puffy skin, highlights blonde hair, and invigorates bath water and body lotions. Page 47.

Comfrey—We must give thanks for this large hairy-leaved herb: It provides the rejuvenating cosmetic ingredient *allantoin.* Add it to any herbal bath mixture for its emollient and astringent properties. Page 51.

Fennel—As a facial steam it deep cleanses. As a compress it reduces puffiness around the eyes. As a hair rinse it's a body-builder for lifeless manes. Put it in the bathtub and it spells relief for tired, aching muscles.

Tea made from its seeds is said to inhibit wrinkles. Page 62.

Lavender—The stimulating astringent action derived from its flower's essence makes a superior after-shave lotion, extracting facial cleanser or topical application for blemishes. Its sensual scent receives high scores from both men and women. Page 78.

Lemon Verbena—This herb is prized for the lilting citrus scent it adds to perfume. Spritz an infusion of witch hazel and fresh lemon verbena sprigs to stimulate circulation of your face and body. Page 83.

Rose—This flower's cosmetic legacy is its divine tonic water. Rose water is a mild astringent and cleansing skin toner. We like it as an after-shave lotion or after-bath splash. A small spray bottle of rose water in the refrigerator provides a cooling, fragrant mist. Page 99.

Rosemary—Use the leaves as an invigorating bath soak, steam or hair rinse. As an ancient herbal promised, "Make thee a box of the wood of rosemary and smell it and it shall preserve thy youth." Page 102.

Sage—Its antiseptic and antibacterial essential oil makes it an ideal aftershave lotion. Add strong sage tea to invigorate the bath. Cleansing sage facial steam aids oily skin. Page 105.

Thyme—To "smell of thyme" was to have virtue, style, grace and elegance. Include this skin-bracing botanical in your bath, body lotions and splashes for its disinfectant and antioxidant properties. Page 117.

Yarrow—A tea of its flowers and leaves offers an astringent, cleansing and mildly aromatic splash. Facial pores tighten and skin appears firmer and smoother. Make a batch to keep in the refrigerator for a last-minute facial energizer. Page 123.

More Herbs for Natural Cosmetics

Bee Balm, page 39.

Scented Geranium, page 66.

Ginger, page 70.

Lemon Balm, page 79.

Mint, page 86.

Patchouli, page 95.

St. John's Wort, page 106.

Violet, page 119.

Mainstay Decorative Herbs

A vase, a pitcher, a pretty bowl or vintage bottle. Some fresh herbs and flowers. Scissors. A deft hand, a critical eye and a sensitive nose. Combine the above to cast a decorative spell. The art of containing and preserving plants is as much an art of subtraction as it is of addition. Depending on the mood, the season, the room, the garden and you, the resulting bouquet can be profuse and lush, or elegantly simple.

Your pleasure in gathering herbs from the outdoor garden shouldn't be limited to a vase. Herbs are among the best and most decorative accessories, fresh or dried, offering visual and fragrant rewards in a range of textures and soft colors. Consider, for example, that almost all cultures use herbal wreaths and garlands to grace important occasions: sacrificial, honorary, nuptial, sociable and festive. Aromatic herbs give potpourris their exotic and lasting touch. Sage, basil, marjoram, costmary, bay, lemon balm, eau de cologne mint, peppermint, bergamot, myrtle, rosemary, and lemon verbena leaves are popular choices. Herbs can also be made to scent and color candles, giving the creative gardener an opportunity to preserve and enjoy some of the summer's harvests.

The herbs listed opposite are some of the best to use for crafts. Also refer to pages 167 to 172 for more simple ideas on using herbs in and around the home.

Below: Wreaths and bundles of dried herbs add fragrance and charm to the Herb Haus bed-and-breakfast at the Fredericksburg Herb Farm.

Below right: Herb flowers can rival the finest floral bouquets. This arrangement features yellow and red yarrow, hot pink cosmos, purple coneflower and purple-leaved basil.

Herbs To Scent Your Home

Silver King and Silver Queen Artemisia, page 87.

Calendula, page 43.

Feverfew, page 63.

Geraniums, Scented, page 66.

Lamb's Ears, page 78.

Lavender, page 78.

Lemon Balm, page 79.

Lemon Verbena, page 83.

Rosemary, page 102.

Rose. Antique roses, especially the apothecary's rose, floribundas, yellow-blooming and red-blooming, page 99.

Yarrow, page 123.

Herbs for Crafts

Basil, page 35.

Sweet Bay, page 39.

Bee Balm, page 39.

Chamomile, page 47.

Hyssop, page 75.

Lemongrass, page 82.

Lemon Thyme, page 117.

Mint, page 86.

Nigella, Love-In-A-Mist, page 93.

Pennyroyal, page 98.

Sage, page 105.

Sweet Annie, page 111.

Sweet Marjoram, page 113.

Also consider these flowers for crafts: baby's breath, bachelor's button, jasmine and strawflower.

Ten Tips on Preserving Herbs

1. Harvest herbs early in the morning or late in the evening on a dry day.

2. Harvest herb leaves just before flower buds break into bloom. This is when leaves are most flavorful and fragrant.

3. Allow some of your herbs to reach flowering stage to attract butterflies, bees and hummingbirds, and to use for indoor decorations.

4. Cut stems as long as possible, but try not to remove too many unopened buds at one time.

5. Use scissors or a sharp knife to recut stems under clear warm water soon as you bring them indoors to prevent them from drying out. Cut at a deep angle to provide as much surface as possible to draw up water.

6. To help keep the fresh-cut stems of roses, honeysuckle and dahlias free of blockage, dip cut ends into peppermint oil. Or briefly dip cut stems of most flowers and herbs into gin.

7. Coax long stems to curve a bit after floating them overnight in deep water.

8. Want to force a bud to open early? Choose ones that feel a bit soft to the touch. Blow hard into the top and the flower will unfold.

9. Preserve the scents and colors of your garden by air drying. Rubber-band small bundles together, large stems individually. Hang bundles upside down in a warm, well-ventilated place out of direct sunlight.

10. In moist, humid climates, dense, heavy flowers such as roses, tend to stay damp and can mold. Highly fragrant flowers such as magnolias, which tend to turn brown, are best dried in a desiccant such as cornmeal, borax, sand or silica gel. See page 167.

Below left: A collection of decorative herbs and flowers. Top row from left: tansy, Russian sage, statice, rosemary and curry. Bottom row from left: basil, globe amaranth, lavender and yarrow.

Below: Drying made simple: A wire coat hanger makes an instant and portable drying rack for herbs and flowers.

Herbs in the Landscape. . .
A Landscape of Herbs

Herbs are among the most versatile landscape plants. They can be mixed with shrubs, flowers or vegetables, or planted as edgings or ground covers. Most are suited to grow in containers on terraces, balconies or decks. They can become the landscape themselves as formal and informal *herb gardens*. When pruned and controlled, they will adhere to a classic shape or style; left largely to their own devices they create their own version of a naturalistic garden.

If you're just getting started, consider a small border garden, the easiest of all. Set aside a rectangle about three or four feet wide in a sunny spot, ideally located against a wall or fence. (No paths to worry about here.) Tall plants go in back, short ones in front, and middle-sized in between. Consider color combinations. Try background plants of tall-growing gray sage and silver artemisias alternating with bright green and yellow yarrow or tansy, and feathery bronze fennel. Middle plants could include lavender, lovage, pineapple sage, calendula, basil, sweet marjoram or lemon balm. Along the front, place shorter plants such as parsley, chives, chervil, violets, thyme or nasturtiums.

Include a selection of annuals, biennials and perennials. Annuals grow rapidly, so a first-year garden will have substance. By the second year, perennials and biennials will have matured enough to fill in some of the space, but enough room will remain to tuck in a few more annuals.

Below: Inviting pathways, angled planting beds, benches and focal points such as the garden crystal ball make a landscape of herbs that much more interesting. This is the Secret Garden at the Farm.

Opposite page, left: The Cross Garden at the Farm is planted in the shape of a Celtic cross. See planting plan, page 131.

Opposite page, right: A path lined with red valerian, *Centranthus ruber*, adds color to the garden.

PERENNIAL HERBS

These are plants that live year after year. Most can be used as a permanent part of the landscape.

Artemisias, page 35.

Bee Balm, page 39.

Salad Burnet, page 42.

Catnip, page 46.

Chives, page 51.

Comfrey, page 51.

Costmary, page 57.

Dittany of Crete, page 59.

Fennel, page 62.

Feverfew, page 63.

Garlic, page 66.

Geranium, Scented, page 66.

Germander, page 70.

Ginseng, page 71.

Hops, page 72.

Horehound, page 74.

Hyssop, page 75.

Lady's Mantle, page 77.

Lamb's Ears, page 78.

Lavender, page 78.

Lemon Balm, page 79.

Lemongrass, page 82.

Lemon Verbena, page 83.

Lovage, page 83.

Mexican Mint Marigold, page 85.

Mint, page 86.

Oregano, page 93.

Patchouli, page 95.

Pennyroyal, page 98.

Poliomintha, page 98.

Rosemary, page 102.

Rue, page 103.

Sage, page 105.

St. John's Wort, page 106.

Santolina, page 107.

Soapwort, page 107.

Society Garlic, page 110.

Sorrel, page 110.

Sweet Marjoram, page 113.

Sweet Woodruff, page 113.

Tansy, page 114.

French Tarragon, page 115.

Thyme, page 117.

Valerian, page 118.

Violet, page 119.

Winter Savory, page 119.

Yarrow, page 123.

ANNUAL HERBS

These plants grow, flower, set seed and die in one growing season. Many reseed and regrow as new plants the following year. Prepare the soil and plant after the last frost, or start seeds indoors and transplant when danger of frost has passed. In mild-winter regions, many herbs can be planted in fall.

Anise, page 34.

Arugula, page 35.

Basil, page 35.

Borage, page 40.

Calendula, page 43.

Chamomile, Roman, page 47.

Chervil, page 50.

Coriander, page 55.

Dill, page 58.

Epazote, page 59.

Lavender, French, page 78.

Mustard, page 90.

Nasturtium, page 91.

Nigella, page 93.

Parsley (biennial), page 94.

HERBS FOR FULL SUN

Artemisias, page 35.
Basil, page 35.
Bee Balm, page 39.
Borage, page 40.
Salad Burnet, page 42.
Butterfly Weed, page 42.
Catnip, page 46.
Chives, page 51.
Coriander (Cilantro), page 55.
Dill, page 58.
Epazote, page 59.
Fennel, page 62.
Garlic, page 66.
Germander, page 70.
Hoja Santa, page 72.
Hops, page 72.
Horehound, page 74.
Lamb's Ears, page 78.
Lavender, page 78.
Lemongrass, page 82.
Lemon Verbena, page 83.
Mexican Mint Marigold, page 85.
Mint, page 86.
Mullein, page 90.
Nasturtium, page 91.
Nigella, page 93.
Oregano, page 93.
Rosemary, page 102.
Sage, page 105.
St. John's Wort, page 106.
Soapwort, page 107.
Society Garlic, page 110.
Sweet Marjoram, page 113.
Thyme, page 117.

HERBS FOR SHADE

Salad Burnet, page 42.
Chamomile, Roman, page 47.
Chervil, page 50.
Comfrey, page 51.
Costmary, page 57.
French Tarragon, page 115.
***Ginseng, American,** page 71.
***Lady's Mantle,** page 77.
Lemon Balm, page 79.
Lemon Thyme, page 117.
Lovage, page 83.
***Mint,** page 86.
Nigella, page 93.
Oregano, page 93.
Parsley, page 94.
***Pennyroyal,** page 98.
Sorrel, page 110.
Tansy, page 114.
Violet, page 119.
***Sweet Woodruff,** page 113.
*Accepts deep shade

HERBS FOR BACKGROUNDS

Locate these plants in the rear of large planting beds. Dense herb plantings controlled by clipping serve as chaperones for fine, pale or vividly colored herbs. During winter, backgrounds can lend texture and definition to an otherwise dreary garden.

Artemisias, page 35.
Dill, page 58.
Fennel, page 62.
Hoja Santa, page 72.
Lemongrass, page 82.
Pineapple Sage, page 105.
Tansy, page 114.

HERBS FOR BORDERS AND LOW HEDGES

Consider combining a variety of long-lived flowers, herbs and shrubs in an eye-catching mixture of sizes, textures and colors along the edge of your lawn, path, building or fence.

Chives, page 51.
Germander, page 70.
Lamb's Ears, page 78.
Rosemary, page 102.
Santolina, page 107.
Society Garlic, page 110.
Southernwood, page 111.
Thyme, page 117.
Violet, page 119.
Winter Savory, page 119.

HERBS TO PLANT NEAR PATHS

These low-growing herbs create an aromatic walkway in the garden. They lighten your step, cover and add interest in and around paths and help decrease mowing time.

Salad Burnet, page 42.
Chamomile, page 47.
Germander 'Prostratum', page 70.
Mint (Corsican), page 86.

The casual growth habits of many herbs make them excellent plants for a naturalistic landscape. Include rocks and boulders with herbs to make the scene even more interesting. Featured plants include bright green curly parsley, left, silver *Artemisia* species, white-flowering chives and purple-flowering catmint.

Left: At the Huntington Botanic Garden in southern California, a silver-leaved *Artemisia* species brightens a shady corner and contrasts with black wrought-iron bench.

Below left: Many herbs do double-duty as flowering perennials. These are purple coneflower, *Echinacea purpurea*.

Below: A half-barrel planter is ideal for herb gardeners having little or no space to garden, or as a means of controlling invasive herbs. Shown are lemon balm (left) and lemon verbena (right).

Oregano (creeping), page 93.
Pennyroyal, page 98.
Rosemary (prostrate), page 102.
Thyme, page 117.
Violet, page 119.

HERBS BY COLOR

Blue
Borage, page 40.
Lavender, page 78.
Rosemary, page 102.
Rue (leaves), page 103.
Sage (many varieties), page 105.
Violet, page 119.

Yellow to Orange
Calendula, page 43.
Chamomile, page 47.

Mullein, page 90.
Nasturtium, page 91.
Santolina, page 107.
Tansy, page 114.
Yarrow, page 123.

Yellow to Green
Dill, page 58.
Fennel, page 62.
Lady's Mantle, page 77.
Lovage, page 83.
Rue, page 103.

Pink to Purple
Basil (purple), page 38.
Chives, page 51.
Comfrey, page 51.
Hyssop, page 75.
Soapwort, page 107.

Sweet Marjoram, page 113.
Thyme, page 117.
Yarrow, page 123.

Red to Burgundy
Apothecary's Rose, page 99.
Bee Balm, page 39.
Hyssop, page 75.
Nasturtium, page 91.
Pineapple Sage, page 105.

White to Cream
Chamomile, Roman, page 47.
Comfrey, page 51.
Feverfew, page 63.
Garlic Chives, page 27.
Sweet Woodruff, page 113.
Valerian, page 118.
Yarrow, page 123.

Gallery of
herbs

*O*ur "Gallery of Herbs" is a field guide for gardening well, but sensibly. It's for those who want to become acquainted with growing and maintaining the healthiest, most personally relevant and pleasurable of plants.

Certain things should be known about herbs, particularly if you are a vegetable or hybrid flower-garden transplant and just beginning to scratch the surface of herbal soil. We have tried to penetrate the labyrinth of confusion that sometimes surrounds this subspecies of horticulture by studying more than 100 herbs. We've admired their appearance, learned their growing habits and become familiar with their common uses and individual personalities. Herbs are plants that come in all sizes and descriptions, and reach far beyond the tidy cupboard stocked with good things to make our cooking more exciting.

Those who know them well consider herbs one of the great natural resources of this world, for they have charm and purpose like no other. For the record, we adore our botanical beaux, but also acknowledge that, like a properly made mint julep, they take some getting used to.

The information in this chapter is based on 28 years of growing experience in the Texas Hill County and Gulf Coast regions, and the Oklahoma Panhandle, as well as invaluable knowledge grafted over the years from gardeners across the world. Each growing environment we've experienced was completely different, from moisture conditions to temperature, elevation, planting and harvesting seasons. As you consider the advice and recommendations in these pages, be aware of the climate of your own area—seasonal high and low temperatures, rainfall, humidity and wind patterns. Exposure of the sun, including how sunlight is affected by buildings, trees and walls, and the kind of soil you have to work with, play important roles in how your herbs will grow.

"The man who has planted a garden feels that he has done something for the good of the whole world."

—Charles Dudley Warner

Left: Pineapple sage, *Salvia elegans*, is a free-flowering herb with edible leaves and flowers.

Above: The fresh new growth of apple mint.

Right: Angelica plants are highly ornamental with large, robust, brilliant green leaves that are divided into many leaflets, each with a serrated edge.

Below right: Propagate aloe vera from suckers or offshoots called *pups.* Remove these small plants from the parent plant and replant where desired.

Below: Aloe vera is an attractive accent plant in the landscape.

Aloe Vera

Aloe barbadensis
(Aloe vera)

Tender herbaceous perennial
Cosmetic, Medicinal, Ornamental
2 feet high, 1-1/2 to 2 feet wide
Full sun to light shade
Neutral soil with good drainage

For many Americans, aloe vera is the first encounter with a medicinal herb. Aloes have been used medicinally since prehistoric times and have spread with human migrations through Africa, Persia, Arabia and into India. Cosmetics containing aloe have been found in ancient Egyptian tombs, and the original Bible mentions the bitterness of aloe.

There are almost 300 *Aloe* species. Some are toxic or induce blisters. If unsure what species you have, ask your county extension service to identify your plants before use. Aloe vera produces yellow flowers on 2-foot stalks in spring if plants are grown outdoors. Flowers are rich in nectar and may attract hummingbirds.

Planting and Care—Propagate aloes from pups—suckers or offshoots. Remove these small plants from the parent plant and replant where desired. Make sure you get a portion with roots. Seeds are like onion seeds in size, shape and requirements. Aloes do best in full sun, developing robust, greyish green leaves and a compact, upright form. In partial shade leaves lose some of their green coloring and are more susceptible to pests. Fertile soil with neutral pH is preferred, but aloes are tolerant of soils low in organic matter and alkaline or even limestone soils. Planting in well-drained soil is perhaps the most critical requirement for success. Standing water or excessive watering will rot roots and kill plants. Allow soil to dry between waterings.

Aloes do well in containers indoors or out. If your plant is indoors, it will enjoy a summer vacation outdoors, but do not place in full sun immediately or it will sunburn. All indoor plants must be allowed to gradually become accustomed to direct sun.

Harvesting and Use—Sap of fresh leaves used in moisturizing creams is believed to be helpful for dry skin and burns caused by heat. Do not use on chemical burns.

Caution: Some people are sensitive to aloe and develop a rash. Many people grow or collect *Aloe saponaria*, thinking it is *Aloe barbadensis*. *A. saponaria* is smaller, has pale spots on the leaves and coral-colored flowers. Occasional cases of dermatitis from contact with aloes have been traced to this species. Test a small area of healthy skin prior to medicinal use. Do not use aloe for poison ivy rashes. Seek medical help for serious burns.

Angelica

Angelica archangelica

Hardy herbaceous perennial or biennial
Aromatic, Craft, Culinary, Dye,
Medicinal, Ornamental
4 feet high, 4 feet wide; flowering stalks
to 8 feet high
Full sun to partial shade
Moist, slightly acid soils

Native to Europe and Asia, angelica has been used by humans since before recorded history. Plants were believed to ward off evil spirits. In some areas angelica is used in Christian feast day celebrations for St. Michael, the archangel, hence its name.

Angelica plants are highly ornamental. They are large and robust with bold brilliant green leaves that are divided into many leaflets, each with a serrated edge.

Planting and Care—In late summer or fall, sow newly ripe (pale yellow) seeds in moist fertile soil, or divide offsets to 3 feet apart. Plant in a cool, lightly shaded location. Sited along the edge of a line of trees, this herb provides a striking backdrop for smaller-stature plants. Because of its large central taproot, angelica does not typically do well in containers. If an angelica plant flowers, it dies. You can avoid this by removing the flowering stalk before blooms develop. A single plant can be grown for many years, and divided like a perennial. If you decide to let your angelica reach flowering stage, it usually blooms in early summer. In mild-winter areas, it may flower in spring. Occasionally it flowers its first year. Flower stalks grow 6 to 8 feet high and are crowned with a flattened, spreading mass of

Aloe Hair Treatment

This solution works great on oily hair. Add 1/4 cup aloe vera gel to 1 cup shampoo. Mix well and massage into wet hair. Leave on 3 to 5 minutes. Rinse in tepid water.

Angelica Tea

Pick a few fresh angelica leaves and put them in a porcelain teapot. Pour boiling water over them, cover and leave to infuse for 5 minutes.

Artemisia

Named for Artemis, the Greek goddess of the moon and the hunt, this group of herbs was believed to be imbued with her magical powers of protection for those who carried or used them.

In this spirit, a wreath of artemisia on your door marks a warm welcome to a safe haven.

tiny white flowers called an umbel. Each umbel can be 2 to 6 inches across. Flowers have a pleasant, honeylike fragrance.

Harvesting and Use—All of angelica's parts are strongly anise-aromatic and edible. Its naturally sweetish stems can be candied for tasty treats and used for pungent cake decorations. Green stems glorify fruit pies, cheese dishes (including cheesecake!) with a just-picked sweetness. Cook the celerylike leaf stalks or eat them raw for a healthy, side-serving crunch. The seeds taste very different from the leaf or stem; enjoy them as a *tisane*—tea for health—as the seeds contain *carminative* qualities—that is, they relieve flatulence, colic and general digestive complaints. The seeds usually require some simmering to extract their full flavor. Essential oils distilled from the seeds and roots are popular today in fragrances for perfumes and as flavorings for gin, vermouth, white wine and liqueurs such as Chartreuse.

Potpourri requires a fixative for long-lasting scent. Before orris root was used as a fixative for potpourri (see page 170), angelica gum was the fixative of choice.

Caution: There is some preliminary evidence that indicates angelica may be carcinogenic if used excessively. Further studies are under way. At this time, the U.S. Food and Drug Administration (FDA) has cleared angelica for culinary use.

Anise
Pimpinella anisum

Tender annual
Aromatic, Culinary, Medicinal, Ornamental
2 feet high, 2 feet wide
Full sun
Accepts almost any well-drained soil

Anise is native to the dry, rocky soils of the eastern Mediterranean, including Israel and Egypt, where, based on archaeological evidence, it has been cultivated for more than 10,000 years. The Greeks know the plant as *anison,* while the name in modern Hebrew and Arabic is *anysum.*

In the Middle Ages, anise was used in mousetraps, as a spice, for medicine and in several aphrodisiac mixtures. More recently, wolf and cougar trappers would try to hide the steel scent of their traps with oil of anise.

The extract from anise, called oil of anise, has different secondary components than licorice and thus a different flavor quality. Oil of anise is used in perfumery, soaps, beverages and to bolster the flavor of the more expensive oil of licorice in some cough medicines and lozenges.

The anise plant is an annual growing to 2 feet high, with almost lacy foliage on the stalks and larger leaves near the base. The tiny, yellowish white flowers are borne in umbels to 3 inches across.

Planting and Care—Anise and many other herbs in the *Umbelliferae,* or carrot, family respond to similar growth conditions much as carrots do. Due to the large and sensitive taproot, seeds must be sown directly where you want plants to grow. Thin to 18 inches apart. Does best in poor, well-drained soil. Anise responds well to richer soils but good drainage is required. Prefers cool-summer regions; can be difficult to grow where summers are hot. For best flavor with no bitter aftertaste, maintain a regular irrigation schedule. Anise can grow in a large tub but needs bright sunlight for best flavor.

Harvesting and Use—Leaves, flowers and seed are edible. Spice uses vary by ethnic origin. The seed is used in many Moroccan and Arabic dishes; the French consume anise in the liqueur anisette. The Austrians use anise to flavor beef dishes, the Germans to season pork. East Indians spice their curries with anise, and Swedes and Norwegians use it to flavor their bread when caraway is not available. Anise is also tasty in eggs, cheeses, baked goods, pastries and fish dishes and with many types of steamed vegetables, in pickles, or in fruit dishes such as compote, applesauce and some chutneys. Vegetarian stir-fry and sautéed tofu benefit from anise seed or leaves for a pleasantly different flavor. Others use the leaves raw in either green or fruit salads, or in soups and stews. Leaves may also be dried for tea or use as a spice.

Medicinally, anise is used to promote digestion or relieve stomach upsets. To use as a home cold remedy, prepare it as an *infusion*. Pour boiling water over the seeds. Don't confuse with *decoction*—boiling the seeds in water. There is no indication of toxicity, but because all plants contain defensive compounds to deter pests, it is best consumed in small doses or for short periods of time.

The Artemisias

There are more than two hundred *Artemisia* species, and many of them are used as aromatic plants. Most are cold-hardy shrubby perennials. The following are described in this book:

A. abrotanum, southernwood, also called lad's love, old man, page 111.

A. absinthium, wormwood, also known as absinthe, common wormwood, green ginger, old woman wormwood, page 122.

A. annua, sweet Annie, page 111.

A. dracunculus, French tarragon, page 115.

A. dracunuloides, Russian tarragon, page 115.

A. frigida, fringed wormwood, page 122.

A. lactiflora, white mugwort, page 87.

A. ludoviciana var. *albula*, silver king mugwort, page 87.

A. pontica, Roman wormwood, page 122.

A. stellerana, dusty miller, also known as old woman wormwood or beach wormwood, page 122.

A. vulgaris, mugwort, also called St. John's plant, moxa herb, page 87.

Arugula, Roquette

Eruca vesicaria sub. *sativa*

Annual
Culinary, Ornamental
3 feet high, 1 foot wide
Full sun to partial shade
Prefers rich, moist soil

A member of the mustard family, arugula is also known in France as *roquette*. It is one of the choicest Southwest-style salad greens to grow and to eat. The young tender leaves of arugula in salads and cold dishes are something to be experienced. When young, leaves have a crispy, crunchy texture combined with a nutty-peppery taste, which some describe as garliclike. Fully grown, its ruffly green leaves are similar to oak leaf lettuce or radish leaves, only darker, reaching to 3 feet high.

Planting and Care—Like lettuce, spinach and chard, arugula grows best as a cool-weather crop. Plant from seed or transplants in spring or fall. Arugula germinates similarly to radishes, in thoroughly moist, cool soil, usually within a few days. It thrives in a rich, moist, well-drained soil with full sun or some shade. Tolerates mild freezes. Warm temperatures cause arugula to go to seed quickly. It reseeds readily so expect to see it again.

Harvesting and Use—Harvest young tender leaves as often as possible to maintain a regular supply before the onset of hot days or prolonged cold weather. The longer the leaves remain on the plant the stronger their taste.

As the season progresses older leaves become inedible and tough, acquiring a bitter, fiery taste along with a faintly skunky aroma. At this point the herb bursts into clusters of small, four-petaled, creamy white flowers, penciled with deep, brown-red veins. They make a lovely filler for bouquets or as garnish for salads and soups.

The key to enjoying arugula is to use it in moderation. Mix with other salad greens such as red leaf, bibb, or Boston lettuce, radicchio or endive. Make a special spinach salad by tossing spinach and arugula leaves, crisp bacon pieces, slices of hard-boiled egg, red pepper slices and garlic croutons with your favorite dressing. Add a few arugula leaves with lettuce to spice up sandwiches. To savor arugula's special flavor, try the salad recipe shown on this page.

Basil

Ocimum basilicum

Annual
Culinary, Ornamental
2 to 2-1/2 feet high, 2 feet wide
Full sun
Prefers well-drained soil

If you like basil, one pot of it won't be enough. And each pot can house a

Arugula Salad with Pistachios

4 teaspoons balsamic vinegar
1/4 cup olive oil
3 bunches arugula, torn into bite-sized pieces
1/3 cup shelled husked pistachios, coarsely chopped
Salt and fresh-ground pepper to taste

Combine vinegar, salt and pepper in small bowl. Slowly whisk in oil in thin stream. Adjust seasoning. Toss vinaigrette with arugula in medium bowl. Divide among plates. Sprinkle with pistachio nuts and serve.

Serves four.

Above: A sweet basil and purple basil hybrid.

Right: Use the tender young leaves of arugula to add a crisp, nutty flavor to salads.

Below: Silver king, one of the many *Artemisias* described in the Gallery of Herbs. Here it is used in combination with iris and upright rosemary. See description, page 87.

Left: A garden of basils. From right: purple basil, sweet basil, cinnamon basil and licorice basil.

Below: Cinnamon basil (foreground) and sweet basil planted in combination. Basils can be attractive plants in the landscape, with striking flowers and foliage that add color and interest throughout the growing season.

Chile-Peach Pesto

2 cups fresh cinnamon
  basil
4 cloves garlic, minced
1/4 cup minced sun-dried
  peaches
1/2 cup freshly grated
  Parmesan cheese
2 teaspoons freshly minced
  rosemary
1/2 teaspoon crushed red
  chile pepper
3/4 cup olive oil
1/4 cup chopped pecans,
  toasted

In a food processor, grind
the basil, garlic, peaches,
cheese, rosemary and chile.
While machine is running,
slowly add the oil. Add
pecans and pulse briefly. We
love to stuff this under the
skin of chicken breasts, or
use in a cheese torta (see
page 105) with cinnamon
basil sprigs.

different variety, with about 150 varieties available. The large selection is due to the range of essential oils that give basils their characteristic fragrances. In most instances their fragrance and flavor difference is distinct. Sometimes flavors vary between each plant's leaves, flowers and seeds.

For gardeners and cooks, fresh, aromatic basil leaves are one of the most indispensable flavors. Basil is a traditional companion plant with tomatoes. Some gardeners believe basil helps keep tomato plants free from insects, and imparts a richer flavor to the tomato fruits.

Best of the Basils

Sweet Basil—This is the most commonly known, and its large green leaves have a sweeter, more delicate flavor than many basils. A gourmet necessity for tomatoes and garlic, it's the one preferred for pesto. Of several strains, three are often recommended:

Basil napolentano has large, light green leaves, with a mellow-sweet aroma and rich, buttery flavor. A great appetizer wrapper.

Basil genova profumatissima has long, pointed, shiny leaves with a distinctively strong perfume flavor. This one is the most prolific leaf producer.

Basil fino verde compatto has thick clusters of sweet mini-leaves that cause it to look more like a pretty shrub. Its 12-inch height make it the most suitable for containers or with low-growing flowers in a border.

Lemon Basil—Shrubbier, to 2 feet high and 2 feet wide, with longer white flowering spikes than other types. Its delicate pale-green leaves have a pronounced citrus scent, making it a pucker-up favorite for fish, vegetables and pasta. Combine it with mint to create a delicious iced libation. Refreshing in potpourri.

Cinnamon Basil—An attractive purplish plant to 2 feet high. Glossy leaves and pink flower spikes have a definite herb and spice fragrance. We devour it in sweets with toasted pecans or fresh fruits, as well as in savory chicken and seafood dishes.

Anise Basil—Any tomato-based dish that would benefit from the flavor of fennel can be accommodated by this licoricelike basil. Add a touch of Asian mystery to mild vegetables such as squash, potatoes and eggplant with a minced fresh leaf or creamy flower cluster.

Purple (Opal) Basil—Has a bite that's as intense as its purple leaf color. It's too sharp for many palates, yet for those with a preference for the robust, add as a light garnish to pasta, seafood or poultry. Its deep purple leaves lend an amethyst cast to basil vinegar, oil or jelly. It's also a dramatic filler in a bouquet of bright flowers.

Purple Ruffles Basil—It's less prone to color loss, damping off and bacterial wilt than dark opal basil. Although it grows to just over 1 foot high and as wide, its strong growth habit and dark, frilly, folding leaves are eye-catching in the garden. Indoors, its soft flavor and color are welcome in salad greens and bouquets.

Holy (Perfume) Basil—Sacred to the Hindus, who use it in their religious ceremonies. Its free-spirited growth causes it to become lanky, so don't delay controlling it. The jagged leaves are coarse and sweet smelling. Add sparingly to fruits, jellies and breads, as well as to potpourris. Its essential oil often refines luxury fragrances and soaps.

Lettuce-Leaf Basil—Looking more like a mounded, 18-inch salad bowl in the garden, this basil's shiny, crinkled, 4-inch leaves and greenish white blossoms define a true kitchen herb. Use to wrap cheeses, rice melanges, grilled mini-meat cuts and vegetable chunks.

Spicy Globe Basil—A superior landscape selection. Minimal clipping required to keep its compact sphere shape. Decorate as a low border or plant in a pot. This basil adds soft fragrance to a garden.

Planting and Care—Seeds germinate quickly—usually 7 to 10 days after planting in rich, moist warm soil. Basils do best in full sun when day and night temperatures are above 60F. If grown indoors in a sunny south window, basils make handsome and fragrant house plants. See page 146 for care on growing herbs indoors.

Basils are usually classified as annuals. New plants are germinated from seed. However, in mild, frost-free climates, such as in Hawaii, a basil plant can develop into a semi-woody perennial shrub.

Harvesting and Use—Basil is a vigorous herb, producing abundant leaves. For the best flavor and to prolong its productive season, pinch off blossoms as soon as they appear.

The smell of basil is said to be "good for the heart and the head," so we recommend including it in more than spaghetti sauce. Basil lends an unforgettable spicy flavor and aroma to herb butters and vinegars.

A basil tea is claimed to quiet the nerves. Add basil stems and flower stalks to stews and soups. Throw basil stalks on the coals when grilling for a wonderful, permeating aroma. The sweet flowers can be used to make a delicious marinade.

To preserve basil, bundle sprays together and hang-dry in a dark place, or wrap individual stalks and freeze in plastic bags or seal in plastic containers.

Sweet Bay, Grecian Laurel
Laurus nobilis

Tender long-lived shrub or small tree
Culinary, Ornamental
Tree form grows to 40 feet high or more.
As shrub, can be maintained at 2 to 8 feet high with equal spread
Full sun to partial shade
Almost any well-drained soil

Although not technically an herb, bay is often described by herbalists as the *most* beautiful, the *most* fragrant and the *most* versatile, due to its many uses. Bay was first an herb of the poets, but later associated with oracles, warriors, statesmen and doctors.

Over time, bay gained the reputation of protecting against natural and human disasters. It was once believed that lightning would not strike where bay was planted.

The medicinal uses of the herb have always been important. Bay was used to protect against epidemics. Culpeper, the English 17th-century medical astrologer, said that bay berries were "effectual against the poisons of all venomous creatures and the sting of wasps and bees." Oil from the berries was rubbed on sprains and used as ear drops. Perhaps because the tree is resistant to diseases and pests, and supposedly protects nearby plants as well, its leaves are reputed to repel fleas, lice, moths and even bugs that hatch in flour and grains.

In the Mediterranean region where it is native, sweet bay grows in dense stands in canyons and along slopes below 2,000 feet. Plants typically grow 15 to 25 feet high but can reach to 40 feet. Leaves are oval, leathery, without sheen, bright green when young, becoming dull with time. Clusters of small yellow flowers are followed by purple berries that attract birds.

Several plants are called *laurel*. It is important to distinguish the sweet bay, which has leaves used in cooking, from the poisonous mature mountain laurel. Sweet bay has a delicious spicy aroma when leaves are crushed. Leaves of mountain laurel are not fragrant. If in doubt, do not use in foods.

Planting and Care—Plant from containers available at the nursery. Sweet bay accepts almost any soil and tough conditions but prefers well-drained soils and regular moisture. Locate in a sunny, sheltered spot. In regions where temperatures reach much below 40F in winter, grow in a container and move to a protected location until spring.

Harvesting and Use—Most herbs give off their flavor in a short cooking time, whereas bay leaf enriches a soup, stew or slow-cooking dish over a period of hours. That is why bay leaves go in at the start of a spaghetti sauce, and basil or oregano are added near the end. Use the leaves whole, then remove when the dish is served. Leaves do not reduce in volume, and if chopped can be unpleasantly tough to chew. Use leaves in stews, roasts, casseroles and patés. A delicious, easy-to-make dessert is Bay Rum Custard, recipe at right.

Bay leaves add a traditional touch to herb wreaths. See pages 169 to 170.

Bee Balm, Bergamot
Monarda didyma

Hardy herbaceous perennial
Craft, Culinary, Ornamental
3 to 5 feet high, 3 to 4 feet wide
Partial shade
Prefers moist, rich soil

One of the few native American herbs, bee balm is a beautiful, must-

Bay Rum Custard

1-1/2 cups milk
1 cup half-and-half cream
2 large bay leaves, preferably fresh
4 egg yolks
1/2 cup light honey
Large pinch of salt
2 tablespoons dark rum

Scald milk and cream in saucepan with the bay leaves. When the mixture has cooled about 10 minutes, remove bay leaves and slowly whisk in egg yolks, honey and salt. Stir in the rum. Preheat oven to 350F.

Pour custard into 6 lightly buttered custard cups or a 1-quart soufflé dish. Place the dishes in a pan of very hot water and bake. The individual custards take about 25 to 30 minutes; the souffle dish takes about 45 to 50 minutes. Test custard by shaking the dish slightly to see if custard is set.

Remove dishes from hot water and cool to room temperature. Chill custard 3 to 4 hours or overnight. Serves 6.

Borage

Modern research indicates that borage tea stimulates adrenaline, the "fight or flight" hormone, which primes the body for action in moments of danger.

To make an infusion, use 1 teaspoon dried flowers or 2 to 3 teaspoons dried leaves with 1 cup boiling water. Steep for 5 minutes then strain before drinking.

Oswego Tea

A citrus-scented tea, good for sore throats and colds. Use 3 teaspoons fresh or one teaspoon dried bee balm leaves per cup. Place in a glass or china pot, cover with boiling water and steep for 10 minutes. Sweeten with honey.

have flower for your herb garden. The scientific name, *Monarda didyma,* comes from Monardes, a 16th-century Spanish medical botanist who wrote about herbs used by the early settlers.

Interest in bee balm skyrocketed after the Boston Tea Party. Indians of the Oswego tribe showed the colonists how to make a substitute "freedom tea" from its fragrant leaves. Thus another common name, Oswego tea. With time, bee balm began to be included in potpourris, jellies, fruit salads and iced drinks.

Bee balm is not a refined plant, but what it lacks in grace it makes up in vibrant flower colors that attract butterflies and hummingbirds. Plants have square stems and aromatic, toothed, opposite leaves alternating in pairs, characteristic of the mint family. Plants become small shrubs, reaching to 3 feet or more high. The most fragrant parts are the large, 6-inch, oval-pointed leaves. When brushed, the leaves emit a pleasant citrus scent.

From midsummer to fall, flowers bloom in vivid clusters of scarlet, pink or purple on top of hollow, brittle, erect stems 2-1/2 to 4 feet high. Looking something like a fireworks display, flowers appear in whorls of frilly tubes and have a lemony mint fragrance and taste. Bees and hummingbirds are attracted to the flowers. After blooming, cut back foliage in the fall to keep plants healthy.

'Alba' has large white flowers. 'Cambridge Scarlet' has brilliant red flowers on 2-1/2- to 3-foot stems. 'Croftway Pink' produces rosy pink flowers on 2-1/2-foot stems. If mildew is a problem in your area, try growing 'Marshall's Delight', which is said to be resistant.

Planting and Care—Start from seeds or divide existing plants in spring. Select a site with moist, fairly rich soil that receives sun or partial shade. Bee balm's root system is shallow and invasive, so space new transplants 18 inches apart to allow for spread. When plants are about 12 inches high, support with wire hoop or stakes to help keep flowers upright. Susceptible to rust disease in high-humidity regions. To prevent, space plants well apart and remove debris from planting area. Avoid watering at night and keep moisture off the foliage.

Plants tend to be short lived in hot, dry climates, so be prepared to replace them. *M. fistulosa* var. *menthifolia* is more heat and drought tolerant.
Harvesting and Use—Bee balm's fresh crimson blooms give color and a delicious lemon zest when sprinkled on fruit, cold dishes and fish.

For a relaxing nightcap or a soothing drink for a sore throat, try a cup of Oswego tea, recipe on this page.

Borage
Borago officinalis

Hardy annual
Culinary, Ornamental
2 to 3 feet high, 1 foot wide
Full sun to partial shade
Prefers almost any well-drained soil

During the Middle Ages, borage flowers were embroidered on scarves and presented to warriors before battle as an emblem of courage. Taken as a tonic by competitors before tournaments and jousts in England, borage was believed to exhilarate the mind. Its popular names are indicative of its other attributes: herb of gladness, cool tankard, bee bread and burrage.

Plants grow up to 3 feet high. Gray-green leaves are covered with bristly whitish hairs that can reach to 6 inches long. During summer, lovely, blue, star-shaped flowers droop downward. Foliage and flowers do not emit a fragrance but produce a fresh, cucumberlike flavor.
Planting and Care—Seeds are large and easy to sow in place. Accepts any well-drained soil. After seedlings are up and growing keep on the dry side; overwatering will kill plants. Borage will grow in sun or partial shade and self-sows. Allow at least two feet of space between neighboring plants. Once you plant borage, you'll likely have volunteer seedlings for years to come.
Harvesting and Use—Good companion plant with tomatoes and strawberries, repelling tomato worms. Honeybees are attracted to the flowers, which helps increase pollination of surrounding plants.

In the kitchen, tender young leaves and stems are chopped and added to green salads, spreads and fruit and wine drinks, imparting a cool cucum-

Above left: Sweet bay typically grows 15 to 25 feet high but can reach up to 40 feet. Leaves (above right) are leathery, bright green when young, becoming dull with time.

Left: The gray-green leaves of borage are covered with long, bristly, whitish hairs. The profuse, blue, star-shaped flowers bloom spring into summer.

Below: Bee balm has square-shaped stems and aromatic, toothed leaves alternating in pairs, characteristic of the mint family.

Salad Burnet Sour Cream

Chop 1/2 cup salad burnet greens and mix with one pint sour cream. Refrigerate overnight or longer for best flavor. Use as vegetable dip or topping for baked potatoes.

Calendula Vinaigrette

6 yellow pear tomatoes
1/3 cup calendula petals
1/3 cup white wine
   vinegar
2 tablespoons balsamic
   vinegar
Freshly ground white
   pepper and salt
1 cup olive oil

Quarter tomatoes and sprinkle petals on top. Combine remaining ingredients except olive oil and puree in blender. Now add olive oil slowly with blender running. Pour mixture over tomatoes and petals. Cover and marinate at room temperature several hours before adding to your favorite tossed salad.

ber flavor. Scrape long hairs from large stems and chop before adding to salads or steeping in beverages.

Floating borage flowers in punch bowls and summer drinks is a tradition, and they are especially striking frozen in ice cubes. For an unusual, striking cake decoration, dip borage flowers in egg white, coat with sugar and dry.

Caution: Borage is high in potassium and calcium. However, when consumed in large quantities over a long period of time, it can cause liver damage. Use in moderation.

Salad Burnet
Poterium sanguisorba

Hardy herbaceous perennial
Culinary, Ornamental
Grows 1 to 2 feet high, 2 feet wide
Full sun
Prefers light, well-drained, alkaline soil

Symbolizing a merry heart, this wonderful salad herb is usually one of the first herbs ready for cutting in early spring. From Elizabethan times, salad burnet has cooled tankards and wine cups—this use perhaps accounts for its merry sentiment. As a cordial, it was taken to promote perspiration. As an infusion with wine and beer, it treated gout and rheumatism.

Today, salad burnet is valued for its astringent properties. Its tea is useful as a facial tonic or steam bath. An infusion of leaves can cool sunburn.

This hardy evergreen perennial reaches 1 to 2 feet high. Small, serrated leaves look like wild rose leaves. They grow close to the ground with a fountain shape, making salad burnet an attractive edging in herb gardens and flower gardens, or a lacy-textured ground cover.

Pale crimson flowers are unusual, thimblelike tufts that appear in spring and summer. Some gardeners remove them to encourage additional new leaf growth from the crown.

Planting and Care—For year-round greens, seeds may be sown in early spring and late fall. Plant in well-drained alkaline soil in a sunny, sheltered spot.

Harvesting and Use—Salad burnet's tender leaves are a delicious addition to salads. The nutlike, cucumber taste

adds flavor to raw vegetables, vinegars, cream cheese and drinks. Use for seasoning herbal butters and as a garnish to iced drinks and soups. Leaves are best used in the spring and fall and can be added generously without overpowering the flavor of a dish. For a dip for raw vegetables, crackers, chips or as a topping for baked potatoes, try the recipe for Salad Burnet Sour Cream, at left.

Butterfly Weed
Asclepias tuberosa

Spreading hardy perennial
Craft, Ornamental
2-1/2 to 3 feet high, 1-1/2 feet wide
Full sun to partial shade
Poor to improved well-drained soil

(Canada Root, Wind Root, Pleurisy Root, Silkweed)
If you think herb gardens must always be a sea of green and gray foliage, you're in for a pleasant surprise. Besides its usefulness as an ornamental and in crafts, butterfly weed offers colorful, eye-catching flowers, ornamental foliage and a safe haven for wildlife. Its umbels of pumpkin orange flowers are choice sources of nectar for bees and swallowtail and monarch butterflies. Covered with beating wings, it is one of the showiest of summertime herbs.

This native to the U. S. is suited to a range of soils and climates. You may have seen it growing along a sunny roadside or field in the heat of midsummer. It is drought tolerant with a preference for sandy or gravelly welldrained soil. This is not an herb for heavy clay conditions.

Uncomplaining of wind, the arching branches never need staking. Its super-stout taproot makes it difficult to transplant, but once established it's hard to kill. This herb grows thicker and bushier with each season, lasting for years. The more branches it produces, the more it flowers.

'Gay Butterflies' flowers bloom in reds, yellows and oranges.

Planting and Care—Start from nursery transplants set out in spring or fall in a lawn or meadow open to full or dappled sun. If propagating by seed, be patient. Butterfly weed breaks dormancy and shows new leaves in the spring much later than other plants, so don't give up. Mark the spot so you won't dig it up by mistake. It may take two or three years to be mature enough to produce its vibrant clusters of 2- to 3-inch flowers, poised atop solid green, lance-shaped leaves. The spectacular flowers are followed by equally entertaining long, pointed seedpods called *follicles.* As other milkweeds, the pods open in fall to reveal rows of silky seeds that drift with the wind. Unlike most milkweeds, this one contains a watery juice instead of the characteristic milky sap.

Harvesting and Use—In the garden, the destinies of butterfly weed and butterflies are uniquely intertwined. Blooming as large, flat, terminal clusters, flowers create a hospitable landing pad for pollinating winged creatures. The orange and black monarch butterfly not only gains sustenance from these nectar-rich flowers but also lays its eggs on the plant.

Butterfly weed dries easily, retains its shape and color and can be incorporated into wreaths and arrangements. Native Americans ate its tender shoots like asparagus and made a meal of the boiled young seedpods with buffalo meat. Roots were powdered and mixed into a paste to treat sores. Brewed into a tea, leaves induced vomiting in certain rituals. *Caution:* Now known to contain toxic cardiac *glycosides,* butterfly weed could be lethal in large doses.

Calendula, Pot Marigold
Calendula officinalis

Hardy annual
Cosmetic, Culinary, Medicinal, Ornamental
1 to 1-1/2 feet high, 1 foot wide
Full sun
Rich, well-drained soil

As cooler weather approaches in the fall and many herbs stop flowering, calendula is a special plant to have in the garden. Plants have long been cherished for the long periods of color they add late in the season, the flavor they add as a seasoning and the relief they provide as medicine.

Calendulas originated in India where the Hindus used them to decorate their temple altars. It takes its botanical name from the Latin word *calendae,* which means "throughout the month," referring to its long bloom season.

Flowers are single or double, and definitely live up to their name, "flowers of the sun." They close up at night and occasionally on dark days, then reopen with sunshine. Flowers are borne on top of sturdy stems, framed by large, oblong, pale green, aromatic leaves. This herb's neat growth and cheerful color make it a lovely indoor container plant.

Planting and Care—Easy to grow from seed. Sow in light, well-drained, rich soil in a sunny location in spring. For fall bloom, sow in early summer. These hardy annuals reseed freely. With the right conditions new plants come up year after year. To encourage new blooms on existing plants, pick and enjoy flowers frequently.

Harvesting and Use—Flower petals have many medicinal and cosmetic values. They are an excellent source of vitamin A and phosphorus. Drinking an infusion of the petals has been recommended to help poor circulation and varicose veins. Use it for bathing to relieve tired swollen feet, for cleansing and softening skin and for soothing tired eyes. An ointment made from the petals can treat acne, relieve sunburn and minor burns and help fade old scars.

Petals give food a delicate, tart flavor, which some claim is similar to tarragon. Chopped blooms impart a strong color to eggs, cheeses and soups, and can be used as an inexpensive substitute for saffron in rice and pasta dishes, biscuits and breads. The petals make a colorful and nutritious addition to salads. To experience this edible flower, try the recipe for Calendula Vinaigrette, page 42.

Caraway
Carum carvi

Hardy herbaceous biennial
Cosmetic, Culinary
2-1/2 feet high, 2 feet wide
Full sun to partial shade
Almost any well-drained soil

To herbalists, caraway seeds are believed to strengthen vision and con-

Biennial Herbs
Caraway is a biennial, meaning that in the first year it grows only foliage, then dies back to the roots, resprouting in the second year. The plant then flowers, sets seed and dies. Many members of the umbel family share this habit.

Above and above right: Salad burnet grows as a hardy evergreen perennial, reaching 1 to 2 feet high. Small, serrated leaves look like wild rose leaves. They grow in a fountain shape close to the ground.

Right and below: Butterfly weed offers colorful, eye-catching flowers and ornamental foliage. Its pumpkin orange flowers are choice sources of nectar for swallowtail and monarch butterflies, as well as bees.

Above and above left: Calendulas show why they are called *flowers of the sun*. They close up at night and occasionally on dark days, then reopen with sunshine. Flowers bloom on top of sturdy stems that are framed by large, oblong, pale green, aromatic leaves.

Left: Catnip 'Six Hills Giant' combines beautifully with *Rudbeckia* 'Indian Summer'. White to lavender-blue flowers typically bloom late spring to early summer.

Catnip Tea

Use one teaspoon per cup, plus one for the teapot. Pour boiling water over catnip in the pot and let the mix brew for three to five minutes. Sweeten as desired.

Caraway Apple Muffins

1/4 cup butter
1/3 cup sugar
1 egg
2-1/2 cups cake flour
1/2 teaspoon salt
4 teaspoons baking powder
1 cup milk
1 cup peeled, finely diced apple
1/2 teaspoon nutmeg
1 teaspoon cinnamon
2 teaspoons caraway seeds
1/4 cup sugar

Cream butter with 1/3 cup sugar. Stir in egg. Sift together flour, salt and baking powder and add to butter mixture. Mix in milk and the diced apple. Fill greased muffin cups two-thirds full. Mix the nutmeg, cinnamon, caraway seeds and 1/4 cup sugar together and sprinkle on muffin batter. Bake in preheated 400F oven for 20 minutes or until brown and puffy.

fer the gift of memory to those who eat them. Superstition holds that the presence of caraway is as good as a bank; thieves cannot steal anything that contains the seeds.

For romantics, caraway provides another kind of insurance. Seeds were once given to engaged couples to bring and keep them together, and to serve as a cure for the fickle-hearted. Caraway seeds were slipped into a husband's pockets when he traveled to bring him safely back home.

Caraway is a hardy biennial herb. This means it needs two seasons to complete its life cycle. The first year, glossy, bright green, feathery leaves resembling those of a carrot form a mound 1 to 3 feet high. Branching stems are slender, hollow and ribbed. Leaves die to the ground with the first heavy frost. A thick, tapering, pale root remains, similar to that of a parsnip, only smaller. The caraway root is considered by many to be a sweet vegetable delicacy and can be boiled and eaten like carrots.

The following spring (the second year), leaves regrow from the root and are followed by tiny white to pinkish flowers in summer. Caraway seeds, which are actually the plant's fruit, become ripe about a month after flowers appear. The seeds develop into two, tiny, brown, nutlike seeds shaped like a half-moon.

Planting and Care—Plant in average, well-drained soil in full sun. If starting from seed, sow in fall in mild-winter regions for an early spring crop of leaves. Seeds will be ready to harvest after flowering the following summer. Or sow seed in spring.

Harvesting and Use—After bearing fruit the plant begins to die. Hang plants upside down in paper bags to collect the brown, crescent-shaped seeds. Harvest before seeds fall to the ground and before birds begin to eat them—usually mid- to late summer.

Caraway is cultivated as a commercial crop in England, Holland and Germany. Caraway oil is extracted from the herb's leaves and seeds and used in perfume, soap, the German liqueur Kümmel and as an ingredient in gin.

Caraway remains an everyday ingredient in Middle Eastern cooking. It also adds flavor to a variety of continental dishes—salads, soups and vegetables—

especially cabbage, potatoes and pickles. Its fresh leaves can accent the taste of breads and baked apples; its seeds can flavor wine. Sample this herb in Caraway Apple Muffins. See our recipe at left.

Catnip
Nepeta cataria

Hardy perennial
Medicinal, Ornamental
2 to 3 feet high, 2 feet wide
Full sun to partial shade
Sandy to rich loam soil

According to ancient legend, those who chewed catnip roots were awarded extraordinary courage. Hangmen were believed to have relied on catnip to face up to their gruesome task. In the past, it has been used to treat hysteria, nervousness, headaches and insomnia.

Catnip has a penetrating, mintlike odor that cats find stimulating. They bite off the leaves and roll and rub against plants. It's common to see cats run up and down trees and stalk imaginary prey before collapsing into a sleepy "drunk." Catnip is also reputed to repel rats and insects.

Shrubby plants with small, heart-shaped, scalloped leaves bear white or lavender-blue flowers in late spring to early summer. The gray leaves look attractive tumbling down among boulders in a rock garden or draping over walls or raised beds. An excellent ground cover for small areas, space plants 1-1/2 to 2 feet apart for a continuous cover. The aromatic foliage delights humans and, of course, cats.

Nepeta mussinii, catmint, grows to 1-1/2 feet high and as wide. It is sometimes confused with the hybrid *N. X faassenii*, which has a more open and sprawling growth habit. *N. X faassenii* 'Blue Wonder' forms neat, soft mounds to 2 feet high and flowers over a long season. Hardy to cold.

Planting and Care—Easy to grow from seed. Sow directly where you want plants to grow when the soil is warm in spring or fall. Plant in light, rich soil in full sun. Plants are generally available in containers at nurseries for fall or spring planting. Shear plants after first flowering to promote a second flush of blooms later in the year. If cats damage plants, selectively prune to repair. To propagate, take cuttings of nonflowering shoots in midsummer or divide in spring or fall. Plants self-sow readily if some flowers are allowed to go to seed.

Harvesting and Use—Catnip makes a relaxing and soothing bedtime tea. The herb acts as a mild sedative for humans—quite the opposite effect it has on cats. Europeans use it regularly for a nightcap, often combined with chamomile, and as a treatment for feverish colds. Its generous amounts of vitamins C and A make this latter use noteworthy.

Locate plants where you can touch the leaves and enjoy their fragrance. Makes a fine cut flower for casual arrangements and bouquets. The soft gray leaves serve as a good color harmonizer in the landscape, combining well with brightly colored flowers.

Chamomile, German
Matricaria recutita
(Matricaria chamomilla)

Annual
Aromatic, Cosmetic, Culinary,
Medicinal, Ornamental
1-1/2 to 2 feet high, to 6 inches wide
Full sun to light shade
Light, well-drained soil

(Also called Sweet Chamomile, False Chamomile, Hungarian Chamomile, Wild Chamomile, Annual Chamomile, Scented Mayweed)

This northern European annual is not as well-known as its perennial cousin, Roman chamomile. Carried by explorers, it is now found naturalized across Asia and cooler regions of India. North American pioneers brought seeds with them, tucked away as valued ingredients in their medicine chests. Today, German chamomile is widely sold throughout Europe as a bedtime tea to promote restful sleep.

With finely divided, lacy foliage, and many stems crowned with white and yellow daisylike flowers, this annual is a princess in the garden. Flowers appear in late spring and last through late summer.

Plants are tolerant of tough conditions and can often be seen growing wild along railroad tracks or up through cracks in parking lots. Grows well in a sunny window box or large pot on a sunny porch. Indoors, plants become leggy and may not flower due to inadequate sun.

Planting and Care—Plant from seed, which you can start indoors and transplant after danger of frost has passed. Or sow seed directly where you want plants to grow in fall or spring. Thin seedlings to 6 inches apart. Accepts almost any light, well-drained soil with a neutral pH. For best growth and flavor, water regularly, but do not allow soil to remain wet.

Harvesting and Use—See Roman Chamomile, below.

Chamomile, Roman
Chamaemelum nobile
(Anthemis nobilis, A. chamaemelum)

Hardy herbaceous perennial
Aromatic, Cosmetic, Medicinal,
Ornamental
6 to 12 inches high, spreading to form
dense mat
Full sun to partial shade
Light, well-drained soil

(Also called Common Chamomile, English Chamomile, True Chamomile, Perennial Chamomile, Russian Chamomile)
Roman chamomile is a native of western and southern Europe. It is an herb with a long history of medical use. In ancient Egypt, priests dedicated it to the sun and used its flowers to treat fevers. The Greeks named it *khamaimelon*, which loosely means "ground apple," referring to its creeping growth and the applelike scent of the crushed flowers. They used chamomile tea to soothe upset stomachs, as an anti-inflammatory to reduce swelling after injury and to reduce menstrual cramps.

Anthemis tinctoria, dyer's chamomile, is used for dye and also makes a lovely ornamental plant. It has lacy foliage and yellow daisylike flowers. *Anthemis cotula*, mayweed, is one of the so-called "false chamomiles." It has flowers like true chamomile but contains a potent allergen that can cause allergic reactions. Flowers appear in late spring and last through late summer.

Other varieties include *Chamaemelum nobile* 'Flore-pleno', a

"For though the camomile, the more it is trodden on, the faster it grows, yet youth, the more it is wasted, the sooner it wears."
—Shakespeare

Right: *Nepeta mussinii,* catmint, grows to 1-1/2 feet high and as wide. It is sometimes confused with the hybrid *N.* X *faassenii,* which has a more open and sprawling growth habit.

Below: Catnip is a shrubby plant with small, heart-shaped, scalloped leaves, bearing white or lavender-blue flowers in late spring or early summer. It is attractive tumbling down among boulders in the rock garden or draping over walls or raised beds.

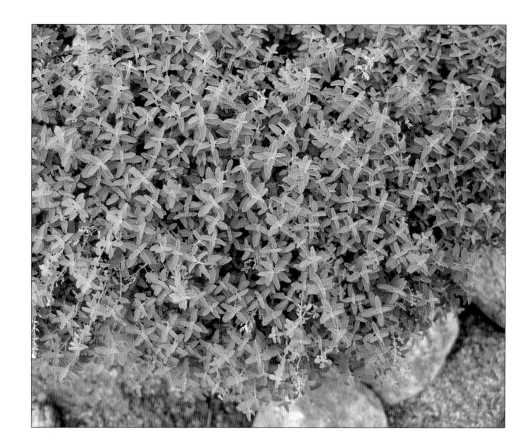

Above: Fresh or dried flowers and leaves of chamomile make a calming tea and are also used in cosmetics.

Left: Sylvia Varney gathers German chamomile for use in the Farm restaurant.

Chervil Herb Popovers

Unsalted butter for
 greasing
3 eggs
1 cup milk
2 tablespoons unsalted
 butter, melted
3/4 cup unbleached all-
 purpose flour
Pinch of salt
1 tablespoon chopped
 fresh chives
1 tablespoon chopped
 fresh chervil

Liberally butter a muffin tin.
Lightly beat eggs. Whisk in
milk and melted butter, and
then whisk in flour and salt
until blended. Do not over-
mix. Stir in the fresh herbs
and half-fill the prepared tin
with the batter. Place in a
cold oven. Turn the oven on
to 425F and bake for 30
minutes. Do not open the
oven while the popovers are
baking. Serve at once.
Makes 12 popovers.

double form with showy flowers. *C. nobile* 'Treneague', a nonflowering, mat-forming clone, grows to 2 inches high. Excellent for planting in walkways or as a mowable chamomile lawn. When stepped on or mowed, they release a delightful, green apple scent.

Planting and Care—Perennial chamomiles are smaller than annual forms but they have similar, fine, fern-like foliage and a pleasant, applelike scent when crushed. Grows as a flat mat of spreading leaves. Best grown by dividing runners in spring or fall. Take cuttings from nonflowering side shoots in summer and root in moist sand. Or sow seed directly in place fall or spring. Thin seedlings 8 to 10 inches apart. All chamomiles prefer full sun to light shade. Once established, all self-sow.

Harvesting and Use—Gather leaves in spring to early summer for best scent. Dried flowers can be added to potpourri but do not retain much scent. Harvest flowers for drying any time. A rinse for lightening blonde hair can be made by gently boiling flowers and leaves. Use this same solution to treat acne and other skin ailments.

A calming tea is made with an infusion of fresh or dried flowers or leaves. There is no known toxicity, but the tea has demonstrated mildly laxative properties. Avoid excessive use. Also useful as a remedy for upset stomach and cramps. A decoction, made by gently boiling leaves and flowers, can be used as a topical antiseptic on burns and painful scrapes. Cool before applying to injuries.

Chervil
Anthriscus cerefolium

Hardy annual
Aromatic, Cosmetic, Craft, Culinary,
Medicinal, Ornamental
1 to 2 feet high and 1 foot wide
Light shade
Light, organic, well-drained soil

(Also called Beaked Parsley, French Parsley, Gourmet Parsley)
A native of the Caucasus Mountains, chervil has a long history of culinary, cosmetic, medicinal and ritualistic use. Its flavor is similar to mild anise

and parsley. Because of chervil's alleged powers of rejuvenation, many Europeans serve chervil soup on Holy Thursday to symbolize Christ's resurrection.

In the Middle Ages, chervil was used to relieve hiccups, aid in digestion, strengthen the blood and treat joint inflammation. It is also one of the traditional ingredients French *fines herbes* seasoning.

Chervil is a charming plant for a shady location. Leaves are lacy, fernlike, pale green, gaining a magenta tinge with age. Delicate white flower clusters reach to 3 inches across. If plants overwinter indoors, blooms may appear in late spring. Otherwise, flowering begins two to three months after sowing.

Planting and Care—Although plants are annuals, they reseed so readily that you can have a perennial supply. Grow chervil from seed. As with many members of the carrot family, the fragile taproot makes transplanting difficult. Best to sow seed in place. Thin seedlings 6 to 9 inches apart. Prefers some shade, especially in summer. In the North, the best place to plant chervil is under a deciduous shade tree. When the leaves drop in fall, seedlings receive the sunlight they need to become established for winter. In the South and Southwest, chervil is often included in the early spring or winter garden because it readily *bolts*—goes to seed—in warm weather. We're vigilant in cutting back sprigs to keep plants producing. Accepts any light, well-drained soil. Prefers soil high in organic matter and slightly acidic (pH 6.5). Chervil, like many herbs, develops the most sprightly flavor with regular water.

Harvesting and Use—Always pick leaves from the outside—the same as for parsley. This allows the plant to continue growing from the center. An infusion can be used to cleanse skin, maintain suppleness, and discourage wrinkles. Flowers are attractive in fresh and dried bouquets. Sprinkle leaves and minced stems over salads and steamed vegetables. Chervil is especially flavorful with green beans, spinach and potatoes. Enhances casseroles, soups, sauces, chicken, fish and egg dishes. Add freshly chopped chervil near the end of cooking for best flavor. Unfortunately, much of its flavor is lost when dried. Chopped frozen chervil leaves may be added just prior to serving a warm dish. Flowering stems and leaves are also well suited to herb vinegar preparations. Try chervil in our herb popover recipe, page 50.

Chives
Allium schoenoprasum

Herbaceous perennial
Craft, Culinary, Ornamental
6 to 9 inches high, spreads 6 inches wide
Full sun to partial shade
Average, moist, well-drained soil

One of the pleasures of growing herbs is sharing them with friends. Chives, the smallest cultivated member of the onion family, are among the best of the "pass-along plants." They're a good choice for new herb growers because they develop quickly and produce abundantly. A small bed typically yields more than one family can handle.

Chives were discovered in China almost five thousand years ago. They produce fountains of thin, hollow, bright green leaves. Growing in clumps, the herb is referred to in the plural.

Garlic chives, *Allium tuberosum*, are similar to chives but leaves have a mild, garlic flavor. Plants grow to 1 to 1-1/2 feet high and produce white flowers.

Planting and Care—Start from seed, division or containers. Divide existing clumps in midspring and set 6 inches apart in your garden or large container. Provide ample space to allow plants to produce lush, upright leaves. They require no special care other than soil that drains well and a sunny location. Plants can be grown in partial shade but tend to develop floppy growth.

Chives are perennial growers both indoors and out. Leaves regrow rapidly after clipping. To prevent their spikes from becoming tough and to help the small bulbs develop, harvest the outer leaves, clipping down to the base. Unless your goal is to put the pretty lavender flowers to use (they make a flavorful vinegar and salad seasoning), harvest before flowers begin to develop.

Harvesting and Use—The delicate, onion flavor of chives (without the legacy of onion breath) has many culinary uses. Add chopped leaves to soups and salads. Use to spice up cottage or cream cheese, omelets, casseroles and mashed or baked potatoes. Or simply sprinkle over sautéed fresh vegetables. Chives can substitute for scallions or onions in most recipes. Single pink florets are pretty and delicious when scattered in a green salad. The flowers also dry well for winter bouquets and wreaths.

In the landscape, chives make an attractive low edging. Tuck them into crannies in rock gardens to provide fresh green accents. They are also one of the best herbs for containers.

Comfrey
Symphytum officinale

Hardy herbaceous perennial
Cosmetic, Edible Flowers, Medicinal, Ornamental
3 to 5 feet high, spreading 2 feet wide
Full sun to partial shade
Nutrient-rich soil high in organic matter

(Also called Boneset, Knitbone, Blackwort, Slippery Root, Bruisewort)
Comfrey is a stately plant with a long history as a healing herb. It has been used to stop heavy bleeding, relieve bronchial problems, close wounds and promote healing of broken bones. A 1978 study determined that comfrey caused liver cancer in laboratory rats, so it is considered controversial when prescribed for internal use.

The names for this member of the borage family come to us from both Greek and Latin. *Conferva*, Latin for "grow together," has evolved to become *comfrey*. Its genus name, *Symphytum*, is Greek for "come together plant."

Comfrey is a hardy herbaceous perennial with pointed, deep green, hairy leaves that grow up to 20 inches long. In full sun, plants may reach 3 feet high, becoming even larger in partial shade. Plants spread via underground rhizomes and can overrun nearby plants, so locate carefully.

Pink or white bell-shaped flowers appear early in spring and last through summer with regular water.

"He who bears chives on his breath is safe from being kissed to death."
—Martise, Roman poet

Chive Butter

A sweet onion spread to serve with steamed vegetables, in scrambled eggs, or on grilled lamb, beef or fish.

1/2 cup unsalted butter, room temperature
4 tablespoons chopped fresh chives
1 tablespoon fresh lemon juice
Pinch of salt and pepper

Cream the chives and salted butter together. Beat in the lemon juice and salt and pepper. Cover and chill until ready to use.
Use within 7 days.

Above and right: Chives are among the easiest herbs to grow, especially in containers. Harvest leaves before flowers begin to develop, or use the pretty lavender blooms to flavor vinegars and salad seasonings.

Below right: Comfrey produces graceful arching clusters of flowers. The structure is called a *scorpioid cyme,* because it curls like a scorpion's tail. Pick flowers carefully so as not to damage the cyme that bears them.

Opposite page
Top left: Coriander produces small clusters of off-white or mauve flowers in early summer.

Top right: Coriander seeds are contained within tiny round fruits that split in half when dried.

Bottom: Purple coneflower produces one the most striking flowers of all herbs.

Comforting Comfrey Masque

A soothing facial masque for dry skin. Pour 1/4 cup boiling water into a blender with 1 cup chopped young comfrey leaves. Blend until the comfrey is well pulped. Strain the pulp through a piece of muslin (cheesecloth), squeezing out as much of the juice as possible. Apply the juice to a clean face and leave for 10 minutes. Rinse with tepid water and follow with a moisturizer.

Coneflower for Colds

At the first sign of cold symptoms, take advantage of coneflower's (echinacea) infection-fighting comfort by capsule, tincture or decoction. To make a decoction, bring 2 teaspoons of dried root per cup of water to a boil, then simmer for 15 minutes. Drink up to three cups a day. Its taste is first mildly sweet, then bitter. Medicate at the onset of cold symptoms or in the early stages of infection for about two weeks, then stop. Echinacea is not to be used continuously to prevent colds, but only to stave them off once symptoms appear.

The genus includes about 35 species. Seven are found in America. The best known are *Symphytum grandiflorum,* with creamy red flowers. Dwarf comfrey, a cultivar of *S. grandiflorum,* has yellow to white flowers. Cream-colored flowers adorn the curving flower stalk of *S. tuberosum. S. asperum,* prickly comfrey, has hairy leaves and brilliant blue flowers. Flowers of Russian comfrey, *S. X uplandicum,* are mauve. *S. X uplandicum* 'Variegatum' has variegated green and cream leaves.

Planting and Care—Take cuttings of rhizomes any time but not when the ground is frozen or during summer heat. Comfrey grows best in a nitrogen-rich soil high in organic matter. Provide with regular water. It is difficult to grow indoors, although it can be grown in a deep container outdoors, which is one way to keep plants under control.

Harvesting and Use—Comfrey contains about three percent protein. This offers considerable benefits to our skin. Add an infusion made from fresh or dried leaves or roots to baths and lotions to heal and soothe rough and damaged complexions.

Comfrey produces a drooping cluster of flowers. The structure is called a *scorpioid cyme,* because it curls like a scorpion's tail. The flowers have a pleasant, spinachlike flavor. Pick them carefully so as not to damage the cyme that bears them. One plant can provide an abundance of flowers all summer. Its fresh leaves and flowers produce a yellow and orange dye.

In cooking, comfrey flowers combine well with legumes such as peas and beans. Float flowers on a thick pea soup before serving. Sprinkle a few flowers on green beans as you serve them, or add flowers to salads for a dash of color. Freeze the flowers in ice cubes for a colorful splash. The plant's rapid growth and ability to absorb useful minerals from the soil give it a special value to organic gardeners: Grow plants for the compost pile, use as a mulch or make into a liquid fertilizer. The minerals become part of the compost, to the benefit of garden plants.

Caution: Due to the suspected carcinogenic activity, it is not advisable to use comfrey leaves internally.

Coneflower, Echinacea
Echinacea purpurea

Hardy herbaceous perennial
Craft, Medicinal, Ornamental
2 to 4 feet high, 3 feet wide
Full sun; tolerates light shade
Almost any well-drained soil; accepts slightly alkaline soil

The Greek name *Echinacea* means "hedgehog," which refers to the spiny cone mass of its flower. In late summer, as the flower develops, the center grows to form a large cone with tiny, yellow, disk flowers between the orange spikes. Flower rays usually curve downward. Cones persist long after the petals have dropped.

This native of the American prairie makes a handsome though somewhat rangy plant 2 to 4 feet high, with dark stems and deep green, slightly hairy leaves. Bumblebees love the flowers, which are marvelous for cutting.

Cultivated varieties include: 'Bright Star', which grows 2 to 2-1/2 feet high with rosy pink flowers (the rays) held outward. 'Alba' is the white form. 'White Lustre' has ivory petals that curve downward and a bright orange cone. 'Magnus', a recent perennial plant of the year recipient, has vivid, true pink blooms that are flatter than the species. In general, plants are the ideal size for the rear of a planting bed or along a fence or wall. Plant in clusters for the best show.

Planting and Care—Easy to grow from seed or root cuttings. In mildwinter regions, sow seed where you want plants to grow in spring or fall. When temperatures are 70F and above, don't cover seeds. Instead, press them into moist, well-drained soil. In cold-winter regions, sow in spring in trays indoors and set out seedlings late spring to early summer. Space plants 2 to 3 feet apart in a full-sun location. Because they are native to the prairie, plants grow fine in poor, rocky, slightly acidic soil. Do not overwater after plants are established. Self-sows readily and can also be divided.

Harvesting and Use—More than any other green medicine, coneflower has been the herb of health for native North Americans. It wasn't until the early 1890s, however, that traditional pharmacies caught on and endorsed its prescription for colds, snakebites and scurvy. With current reports coming fast and furious about the immune-boosting, infection-fighting benefits of this herb, this colossal daisy is beginning to appear more like a cure-all drug. Its roots have won new respect as a potent antibiotic and an immune-system stimulant for healing everything from boils, colds, flu, bladder infections and tonsillitis to arthritis and allergies. Scientists are examining the so-called *phyto-chemicals*—the active compounds in the roots. Researchers want to determine what benefits the compounds might have in cosmetics as an internal cleanser for irritated or blemished skin. Externally, coneflower's anti-inflammatory extract is being incorporated in creams, lotions and gels as defense against wrinkles, acne, athlete's foot, bites and stings. What's new about echinacea is the hope that its potent compounds could offer benefits before people get sick, saving health and health-care dollars.

Putting homegrown echinacea plants to therapeutic use does require planning and patience. It takes three to four years for roots to grow large enough to harvest. Pull up established roots in fall after the plant has gone to seed, and dry roots thoroughly. To avoid molding, roots greater than one inch in diameter should be split before drying. Store in a sealed bottle away from light and heat.

As with any natural substance, moderate use of echinacea is the wisest course.

Coriander, Cilantro
Coriandrum sativum

Annual
Culinary, Ornamental
3 feet high, 1 foot wide
Full sun; partial shade in hot regions
Average well-drained soil

Fresh cilantro, *Coriandrum sativum*, is also called Chinese parsley. Fresh cilantro has an assertive culinary personality. Even in the smallest quantities, it makes its presence felt. No one asks, "What is that subtle flavor?"

Cilantro grows as a slender, upright annual to 3 feet high. Leaves that emerge on its main stem are oval with toothed edges. Leaves growing on upper side branches are more lacy and delicate, resembling those of anise or dill.

As the season warms, a central flower stalk branches into beautiful, umbrella-shaped clusters of small, off-white, mauve or lavender flowers. Seeds are inside tiny round fruit that splits in half when dried. Fresh seeds have an unpleasant, musty, bedbug odor. Dried seeds have a pleasant, orange-spice aroma and flavor that increase with maturity.

Planting and Care—One of the easiest herbs to grow from seed in climates where a March sowing is possible. Prefers relatively dry conditions, evenly distributed moisture and even temperatures. It cannot tolerate constant moisture. A sun-loving herb; locate in partial shade in hot-summer regions. To counter coriander's tendency to go to seed rapidly with the onset of long, warm days, growers have developed 'Long Standing', a slow-to-bolt cultivar. Harvests of fresh leaves are extended about 14 days. Whatever kind you grow, cut leaves frequently and stagger sowings to provide continued harvests.

Plants typically reseed even where temperatures drop below 0F. If the ground isn't turned over where coriander has grown during the summer, seedlings may come up in the fall. Some will live over until spring. Like dill, cilantro should be planted away from fennel, which can adversely affect its flavor. Otherwise, cilantro is an especially friendly companion plant. Its musty odor tends to repel nibbling insects.

Harvesting and Use—Coriander is grown for both its seeds and leaves. Harvest leaves when the plant reaches 6 inches high and gather seedheads when the small fruits are brown. Hang them upside down in a dry, well-ventilated room. Place a paper bag under the heads to catch the seeds. In about two weeks, remove dried seeds and store in an airtight container.

The delicate, nippy taste of the leaves combines well with salads, soups, chicken, meat and sauces. Use one to two teaspoons of fresh leaves per serving. The leaves and seeds are not interchangeable. Commercially

Coriander-Kissed Cookies

3 large eggs
1/4 cup soft unsalted butter
2 cups sugar
3-1/2 cups sifted unbleached all-purpose flour
1 tablespoon baking soda
1/2 teaspoon salt
2 teaspoons ground coriander
1 teaspoon cardamom
Zest of one large lemon
1 12-ounce jar currant jelly
1/2 cup toasted almonds, finely chopped

Beat 2 eggs, butter and 1-1/2 cups sugar until fluffy. Mix in flour, baking soda, salt, coriander, cardamom and lemon peel. Mix thoroughly and refrigerate for one hour. Turn out onto lightly floured board. Roll 1/2 inch thick and cut into strips 1-1/2 inches wide. Press groove down middle of each strip. Transfer strips to greased cookie sheet.

Pipe currant jelly into grooves with decorator. Bake for 15 minutes at 350F. While baking, combine remaining egg, 1/2 cup sugar and almonds. Spread cookies with sugar and nut mixture. Return to oven for 5 more minutes. Cut into diagonal bars to serve. Yields 4 dozen.

Above: Leaves of costmary (right) and French sorrel (left) are similar in appearance.

Above right: Costmary is a hardy herbaceous perennial, growing 2 to 3 feet high.

Below: Purple coneflower makes a handsome though somewhat rangy landscape plant, growing 2 to 4 feet high.

dried cilantro is useful only when you can't get fresh leaves, and it should be used only in recipes where it is to be cooked. Clip fresh leaves just before using; the distinctive flavor and aroma dissipate quickly with heat. The dried seed, which has a warm, nutty, floral aroma when ground, spices up fish, curries, fowl, pork, soups, sauces, breads and cookies. See our recipe for Coriander-Kissed Cookies, page 55.

Costmary
Tanacetum balsamita
(Chrysanthemum balsamita)

Hardy herbaceous perennial
Aromatic, Craft, Cosmetic, Culinary,
Medicinal, Ornamental
2 to 3 feet high, spreading to
2 feet wide
Full sun to light shade
Almost any well-drained soil

(Also called Alecost, Bible Leaf)
Costmary is native to western Asia and southern Europe. Leaves and roots have a strong mixed scent of lemon and balsam. The flavor is tangy, suggesting mint and tansy.

In ancient times, costmary was used as a *strewing herb*. These were herbs that were cast on floors to give off a pleasant scent and to mask unpleasant odors when walked upon. It was also believed to repel insects, a use that may have some validity. A close relative of costmary is the source of the natural insecticide, pyrethrum.

Tanacetum balsamita var. *tomentosum* is a similar variety known as the camphor plant. It has a strong, camphorlike odor and has been used to deter insect pests in closets.

Costmary was once added to ale for a spicy taste, thus the common name *alecost*. It also helped keep the ale from spoiling. The name *Bible leaf* developed when people would slip leaves into their Bibles as a bookmark. The tangy leaves surely came in handy as something to nibble on during a long sermon.

This hardy herbaceous perennial grows 2 to 3 feet high. The long, narrow, light green leaves have toothed edges. In cold-winter areas it dies to the ground in winter and resprouts in the spring. Plants can become leggy and begin to grow more prostrate.

Frequent clipping will keep them looking best. Flowers are not showy so feel free to trim plants frequently.
Planting and Care—Produces few or no seeds but spreads rapidly by underground rhizomes. To propagate, take rhizome divisions in spring or early fall; divide every three years or so to keep them under control.

Accepts full sun to light shade. When grown in some shade it is less likely to flower but foliage is a richer green. Grows well in almost any well-drained soil, even limestone soils, but best in fertile loam. Prefers a pH of 6.2. Costmary is a moderate water user and can withstand some dry periods. Does not do well in containers. Plants are susceptible to disease indoors or out. Small yellow daisylike flowers appear midsummer, with a flowering season lasting into the fall.
Harvesting and Use—Harvest any time although the essential oils are strongest just before the plant flowers. If you plan to dry plants, this is also the best time. Leaves retain their rich green color if dried in the dark. They can then be added to potpourris for fragrance and color accent. A crushed fresh leaf is said to soothe insect stings. Dried leaves can be sewn into cotton bags and added to stored woolens or placed in the linen closet. Add fresh or dried leaves to the bath for a refreshing lemon mint soak. An infusion makes an astringent rinse for hair or skin. Finely chop fresh leaves and sprinkle in vegetable soups and on salads, poultry, game and egg dishes. Costmary tea has been used to ease the pain of childbirth and as a tonic to treat colds, upset stomachs, cramps and coughs.

For a sweet-scented potpourri that discourages bugs but not people, try the Shoo-Fly Potpourri at right.

Datura, Jimson Weed
Datura species

Tender annuals and perennials
Medicinal, Ornamental
4 feet high, 2 feet wide
Full sun to partial shade
Rich soil, fields, waste places

Whether it's called apple-of-Peru, devil's-apple, Jamestown weed, mad apple, stinkweed, thorn apple, yerba

Shoo-Fly Potpourri
2 cups lavender flowers
1/4 cup costmary
1 cup rosemary
1/4 cup tansy
1 cup southernwood
1/4 cup cedarwood chips
1/2 cup spearmint
10 yellow roses
1/4 cup pennyroyal
3 tablespoons orris root mixed with 10 drops each cedar, lemon and lavender oils, for fixative

Gently combine the flowers and leaves, then mix in the fixative of orris root. Seal and store in a warm, dry, dark place for ten days to "cure." Place the mixture in open bowl for display, or in muslin bags for linen sachets.

Cool Cucumber and Dill Soup

4 large cucumbers, peeled, seeded, chopped

1 small white onion, chopped

1 quart chicken stock

3/4 cup sour cream

1-1/2 cups plain yogurt

8 4-inch fresh dill sprigs

Dash of Tabasco

1 cup buttermilk

In a skillet, slowly cook half the cucumbers and onion for about 10 minutes or until tender. Combine with the remaining ingredients, then puree in a blender. Taste, and add salt and more fresh dill if needed. Puree again and chill for several hours. Serve ice cold in chilled bowls garnished with a fresh dill sprig and Johnny-jump-up blossom.

del diablo (devil's weed), or Gabriel's trumpet, datura is an herb with many faces. Farmers see it as an obnoxious weed, herbalists reap it as a medicinal remedy (even though it is poisonous), and gardeners plant it for its quirky blossom. Large, 6-inch, white to pale lavender or yellow funnel-shaped flowers grow profusely on tall, branching stems with unevenly toothed, oval leaves to 8 inches long. Spiny, dark brown to black, kidney-shaped seedpods, the "thorn apples," develop with maturity.

Datura is a member of the large *Solanaceae* family, which contains some 2,400 species. It includes potato, eggplant, tomato, tobacco, chile pepper and petunia. At the farm we are most familiar with *Datura stramonium*, commonly called Jamestown weed or jimson weed.

Planting and Care—Datura is easy to grow from seed. Sow in place in early summer in an open, sunny location. It may be started indoors earlier if it receives sunlight at least half the day, high humidity, moderately low temperatures and good drainage.

Harvesting and Use—Datura is a member of the notorious nightshade family. Like its relatives, datura contains the alkaloid *scopolamine*, which acts as a powerful sedative. Although it has antispasmodic, painkilling and narcotic properties, datura is considered a plant to avoid, especially if you have children. We grow it for its beautiful flowers. The difference between a deadly poison and a medicine is sometimes only one of dosage. In the past, asthma sufferers inhaled the smoke of the burning plant leaves or smoked dried leaves for relief. The 19th-century Shakers bottled and marketed the herb for use as a narcotic, a treatment for chorea, epilepsy and neuralgia, and as an ointment for burns and rheumatism.

A remarkable thing about "plant magic" is its journey through many periods of human experience. Datura's most surprising benefit was recently reported by the U.S. Department of Energy, which discovered that the plant can digest radioactive waste left over from the manufacture of nuclear weapons.

Caution: Every part of this weed is poisonous.

Dill
Anethum graveolens

Hardy annual
Culinary, Medicinal
3 feet high or more, 1 foot wide
Full sun to partial shade
Light, well-drained soil

Early New England settlers grew special plants that would reputedly protect against evil spells and other unsociable activities of witches. Among the most effective of the antiwitch herbs were mugwort, vervain and dill. According to herbal lore, burning sprigs of dill cleared the air and drove away destructive rainstorms.

Cultivated for its charming character, dill develops fine, threadlike leaves with large, yellow, umbrella-shaped flowers in early summer. These are followed by aromatic seeds. For centuries, brides put these seeds and salt in their wedding shoes for good luck, even though it would mean a rather uncomfortable walk down the aisle. As the sole important herb of Jewish chicken soup, dill may deserve credit for the soup's reputed curative powers.

Planting and Care—April to early June, and September to November in frost-free areas, are prime times to sow dill's flat oval seeds. Plant directly in loamy, moderately fertile garden soil in full sun. Cover the seed lightly and keep the seedbed moist. After seedlings emerge (about 12 days in warm soil), water well and apply liquid fertilizer once a week. A 2- to 3-foot row planted each month as soon as the soil can be worked will provide plenty of foliage. Don't worry about thinning the plants unless you want to; begin cutting the foliage about four weeks after germination. Allow about two weeks between harvests. If growing plants to harvest for seeds, do not remove any foliage. Maintain 12 to 16 inches of space between plants.

Harvesting and Use—Perhaps what has made dill eternal in the hearts of Americans is its close association with pickles. Although pickles can be flavored with any number of seasonings, dill is delicious with recipes of any ethnic origin, from sweet gherkins to sour pickle chips to everything in between. Fresh dill's astringent quality can also perk up a healthy appetite and provide a flavor spark to salads, root vegetables such as potatoes, fresh, light-flavored fish, eggs, cream sauces and dips. But dill has much more to offer than an inviting and distinctively green bite. Containing potassium, sodium, sulfur and phosphorus, dill is also good for you.

Dill seed, by contrast, tastes quite different from its leaf. Nutty and mildly peppery, we use the seeds for rich foods such as breads, butters and cheeses, marinated fish, Indian curries and herb salt. Dill seeds also make lovely *tisanes*—teas for health. They possess *carminative* qualities, which means they alleviate flatulence, colic and general digestive complaints. The seeds usually require a little simmering to extract their flavor.

Dill's pale yellow flowerheads and feathery leaves lend an airy appearance and creative country charm, especially when arranged in a vase of home-grown mixed sprigs.

For cooking, dill's feathery leaves should have a bright green color and fresh aroma. Add this heat-sensitive herb to dishes at the completion of cooking. To store, wrap in paper towels and seal in a plastic bag. Dill will keep, refrigerated, for about one week. Leaves may be chopped, sealed airtight in plastic bags and stored in the freezer for up to six months.

When fresh dill is not available, use only small amounts of dried dill as a substitute. Culinary companions include mint, parsley, oregano and chives.

Dittany of Crete
Origanum dictamnus

Tender semiwoody perennial
Aromatic, Medicinal, Ornamental
1 foot high, spreading to 1 foot wide
Full sun
Average, well-drained soil

Dittany of Crete is native to the rocky mountain slopes of that ancient Grecian island. It was considered to have the strongest medicinal properties of all *Origanum* species, and was used to heal soldiers' wounds. It earned such a reputation for its curative properties that it was planted beside shrines and in temples.

Bushy plants reach to 1 foot high and produce thick, round, almost fleshy leaves; the leaf surface is covered with downy hairs. Lovely, small, lavender to pink flowers (they are actually *bracts,* which are modified leaves) appear mid- to late summer. They attract bees and butterflies. The plant is particularly striking cascading from hanging baskets, or as a ground cover.

Planting and Care—Propagate from nonflowering stem cuttings in spring or fall. Seed usually has poor viability. Plant in full sun in soil that is well-drained. Moderate water use. Provide winter protection in regions where temperatures drop lower than 15F. Cut back in late winter to induce fresh, new growth.

Harvesting and Use—Herbal sachets stuffed with dried leaves are said to promote restful sleep. Leaves also add interest and scent to potpourri. Green stems laid on barbecue embers give grilled foods a faint marjoram flavor. Generally considered too pungent for direct culinary use. Flower heads and leaves can be infused as a tea for colds, headaches and simple gastro-intestinal disorders.

Epazote
Chenopodium ambrosioides

Tender, semiwoody perennial
Craft, Culinary, Medicinal
5 feet high, 2 feet wide
Full sun to partial shade
Light, well-drained soil

Certain spices and herbs have a unique ability to counter the effects of gas produced by hard-to-digest vegetable proteins. This gas is most common in foods such as beans, peas and root vegetables. A pinch of cumin, a piece of fresh ginger or a few leaves of epazote cooked in the pot with the potential offender can go a long way in rendering the proteins harmless.

Epazote immigrated from Mexico into the United States and Canada through the advance of Yankee pioneers and European settlers. It's an unassuming, strong-smelling herb with many names: American wormseed, Mexican tea, Jerusalem oak, Jesuit tea and stinking weed. Native

Herbal Salt Mixture

This dried mix will keep through the winter until your herb garden is growing again. Sprinkle in salad dressings and over vegetables, casseroles and soups.

1 cup dried oregano
1 cup dried basil
1/2 cup dried marjoram
1/2 cup dried dill weed
1/2 cup dried mint leaves
1/2 cup onion powder
2 tablespoons dry mustard
2 teaspoons salt
1 tablespoon freshly
  ground black pepper

Mix all ingredients together and store in a sealed jar. Use as needed.

Right and below: Datura produces large, 6-inch, white to pale lavender or yellow funnel-shaped flowers. Oval, unevenly toothed leaves grow to 8 inches long. Be aware that plant parts are poisonous.

Bottom: Dittany of Crete grows as a bushy plant to 1 foot high, producing thick, round, almost fleshy leaves. The leaf surface is covered with downy hairs.

Dill develops fine, threadlike leaves with large, yellow, umbrella-shaped flowers in early summer. These are followed by the popular aromatic seeds. Dill is appealing and easy-to-grow but for best results, keep these few tips in mind:

Don't transplant dill.
Dill roots are shallow, so sow seeds where plants will be grown.

Plant dill. near carrots.
Companion planting encourages healthy growth and wards off pests and disease.

Don't grow dill near fennel.
The mature plants are so similar they can cross-pollinate, adversely affecting appearance and flavor. Dill is a more delicate plant in every way. The stalk is finer and leaves have a more subtle flavor, reminiscent of caraway. Fennel is more like aniseed. Its seedheads are smaller and not as heavy and full as those of dill.

Harvest and use dill often.
Dill is a short-lived annual. Don't expect it to become big and bushy like fennel, which is a perennial.

Epazote Room Freshener

Epazote's dried leaves produce an effective eucalyptus-camphor scent for musty rooms and closets. As epazote matures, cut large bunches and hang them upside down in a dark, well-ventilated room until they are thoroughly dried. Strip and store leaves in muslin bags for fragrant closets, or in open baskets for fresh-air potpourri.

Americans educated their newcomers as to its effectiveness and its reputation rose.

Epazote's wild nature takes it to a height of up to 5 feet, supported by erect, woody stems. Alternate and coarsely toothed, lance-shaped leaves mimic goose feet. In late summer and fall its survival instincts take an aggressive turn. Dense spikes of tiny pealike flowers bloom in the leaf axils. If not pinched back, epazote will reseed all over your garden the following spring. However, it is a cold-tender perennial, becoming a graceful victim with the frost. Its seedheads turn a beautiful bronze hue as the stems redden in preparation for dying back.

Planting and Care—Once started, epazote is a tenacious herb. Begin by sowing seeds in fall. Germination usually takes 3 to 4 weeks. Stems can be rooted in water but it's a slow process. No more than one to two plants per garden are recommended. It is important to pinch established plants back, particularly the center branches. This discourages sproutings that can take over as well as straggly upright growth, keeping plants bushier and more attractive. We recommend that epazote be planted in a neglected area such as a semishaded spot along a fence so that it will not claim precious garden space.

Plants can regrow from roots after frost kills tops. After time, epazote can become woody. Clip often to keep foliage fresh and growing.

Harvesting and Use—This wild green is indispensible in Mexico for cooking black beans, certain quesadillas and a large number of Veracruz and Yucatan dishes. To retain flavor of the fresh herb, shred, chop or mince leaves and add early to dishes that require long cooking. Sprinkle a chopped teaspoonful over roasting meat and in simmering beans, peas or soups to enjoy its pungency. Do not use as a garnish; its taste is camphor-bitter. Use fresh when possible; its flavor does not translate when leaves are dried. Substitute fresh oregano if fresh epazote is unavailable.

A decoction can be made from the leaves to calm upset stomachs, especially useful after a rich meal.

Fennel
Foeniculum vulgare

Tender herbaceous perennial
Culinary, Ornamental
3 to 5 feet high, 3 to 4 feet wide
Full sun
Well-drained soil high in organic matter

Fennel is a member of the parsley family and native to the coastal region of the Mediterranean. Its scientific name is derived from *foenum,* the Latin word for hay, which refers to fennel's fresh haylike scent. It was used by the resourceful Romans and Greeks for medicinal and culinary purposes. Roots, stems, leaves and seeds were eaten raw in salads, cooked as a vegetable and baked in breads and cakes.

Throughout history, fennel has been prized for its curative effect on the eyes, including its ability to strengthen sight. It is claimed by some to increase one's resolve not to overeat. The seeds, when chewed or taken as a tea, curtail hunger.

Fennel is an herbaceous perennial. It grows from its roots year after year. Plant tissues are soft, not woody or covered with bark. It looks much like dill, growing 3 to 5 feet high. Leaves are green and feathery, stems are blue-green, smooth and glossy, flattened at the base. Small yellow flowers bloom in late summer and early fall, forming clusters that look like upturned, flat-topped umbrellas.

Bronze fennel, or smoky fennel, *Foeniculum vulgare* 'Rubrum', is a spectacular perennial cultivar of herb fennel. Its feathery leaves are coppery brown. This fennel does not grow as easily or as sturdily as its green cousins, but as an accent plant in the garden or in fresh bouquets it has no peer. In cooking, use the fronds and seeds the same as other fennels. We especially love to include its bronze leaves in herb vinegar. As the vinegar ages it turns a beautiful blush color and takes on a wonderful anise flavor. In the garden bronze fennel is striking planted behind white shasta daisies, white chrysanthemums, cosmos or zinnias. The dark, delicate foliage framing the large white flowers is extraordinary.

Another popular culinary variety,

F. v. var. *azoricum*, is commonly known as Florence fennel, finocchio, sweet anise or vegetable fennel. Florence fennel is an annual that grows to 2 feet high. It has blue-green, fernlike leaves and clasping, succulent leaf bases that swell to form a bulb. This is in contrast to the thickened celerylike *stalk* of the herb fennel. Its bulb can be used like celery and the leaves harvested for seasoning as well. If allowed to *bolt*—go to seed— Florence fennel will grow to about 3 feet high and produce flowers similar to those of herb fennel. Florence fennel grows best, and forms bulbs of maximum size, only with the onset of cooler weather, much like cauliflower.

Planting and Care—Start from seed sown in place in spring or late summer. Thin seedlings 10 to 12 inches apart. Plant in well-drained soil improved with organic matter in a sunny, sheltered location. Because of its tall stature, plant at the back of the herb bed or use as a high border.

Harvesting and Use—Fennel's tender leaves and stems are suited for relishes, salads and garnishes. Italian bakers place leaves under loaves of bread in the oven to impart a strong anise flavor. Leaves have qualities similar to French tarragon, helping remove fishy odors when cooking seafood. They complement fish sauces and flavor soups and stews. Ripe fennel seeds add a special taste to puddings, spiced beets, sauerkraut, spaghetti, breads, cakes, candy and alcoholic beverages.

Feverfew
Tanacetum parthenium
(Chrysanthemum parthenium)

Cold-hardy herbaceous perennial
Craft, Dye, Household, Medicinal,
Ornamental
2 to 4 feet high, 1 to 1-1/2 feet wide
Full sun to partial shade
Rich loam to average, well-drained soil

Feverfew once had a reputation for treating fevers. Indeed, the common name for the plant is derived from the Latin word *febrifuge,* a term still used by doctors to mean "fever reducer." Plants were believed to be good for many other ailments, including nervousness, hysteria, insomnia and low spirits. The leaves are quite bitter and a concentrated tincture could only be worse. Perhaps this is where the phrase "bitter medicine" originated.

Native to southeastern Europe, feverfew has spread to many parts of the world where it has naturalized. You'll often see it in meadows and along roadsides. It is an upright, short-lived perennial with bold, somewhat coarse foliage. Leaves are slightly downy and divided, similar to those of chrysanthemum.

Feverfew is grown for its profuse, daisylike flowers that appear midsummer and into fall, adding charming splashes of white and yellow. Flowers, which are thought to be pollinated by beetles, appear to repel honeybees but may attract wasps.

Selected cultivars offer additional color and size choices. The double-flowered form has more finely divided leaves and fuller flowers, which make delightful, long-lasting bouquets. 'Aureum', also known as golden feverfew, has striking, golden green leaves and reaches to only 12 inches high. It is an attractive edging plant.

Planting and Care—Easy to grow from seed and self-seeds profusely. Left unchecked it can become invasive, so site plants carefully. Sow in fall or spring. Thin or transplant to 12 inches apart. You can also start seed indoors and transplant after the last frost. Like many members of the sunflower family, feverfew does best in full sun. Although tolerant of partial shade, plants may become leggy. Prefers rich loam, but does fine in average, well-drained soil. For profuse flowers, water plants regularly throughout the season. Accepts some dry periods.

Harvesting and Use—Flowers preserve well and add color to potpourri and dried flower arrangements. Fresh leaves and stems may be used to produce a greenish yellow dye. Place dried leaves in sachets to deter moths. Do not use feverfew flowers in sachets. They may contain the cigarette beetle, the larvae of which eat woolens and other clothing.

"There are many miracles in the world to be celebrated and, for me, garlic is the most deserving."
—Leo Buscaglia

Garlic-Baked Eggplant

Slice several peeled cloves of garlic and roll in a mixture of 1 part salt to 2 parts minced fresh basil. With the tip of a knife, make slits all over the surface of an eggplant and push a seasoned garlic slice into each cut. Drizzle with olive oil and bake at 350F until the eggplant is soft, about 30 to 45 minutes.

Above: Epazote's wild nature allows it to reach a height of up to 5 feet, supported by erect, woody stems. Alternate and coarsely toothed, lanced-shaped leaves appear to mimic goose feet.

Above right: When selecting garlic bulbs for planting, pick only large, well-formed cloves having the firmness of an apple.

Right: Feverfew is grown for its profuse, daisylike flowers that appear midsummer and into fall, adding charming splashes of white and yellow.

Below: Young feverfew plant in a container.

Left: Bronze fennel (foreground) is a spectacular perennial cultivar of fennel. Its feathery leaves are coppery brown. It does not grow as easily or as sturdily as its green cousins, but makes an exceptional accent plant in the garden or in fresh bouquets. Common fennel (background) looks much like dill, growing 3 to 5 feet high. Leaves are green and feathery, stems are blue-green, smooth and glossy, flattened at the base.

Below: Small yellow flowers of fennel bloom in late summer and early fall, forming clusters that look like upturned, flat-topped umbrellas. Birds love to eat the seeds that follow.

Garlic-Grilled Tomatoes

2 tablespoons melted butter

1 clove garlic, minced

1 teaspoon fresh summer savory, minced

1 teaspoon fresh thyme

6 large ripe tomatoes

1-1/2 cups fresh Parmesan cheese, grated

1 small yellow squash, sliced and sautéed

Parsley sprig

Preheat broiler. Mix melted butter with garlic and herbs. Cut tomatoes in half vertically and arrange on baking sheet. Spoon butter mixture onto cut surfaces. Sprinkle thickly with cheese. Place under broiler and cook until cheese is melted and golden brown, about 10 to 12 minutes. Serve garnished with sautéed slices of yellow squash and parsley springs. Serves 6.

Garlic
Allium sativum

Herbaceous perennial
Craft, Culinary, Medicinal, Ornamental
Grows 1 to 3 feet high, 2 feet wide
Full sun to partial shade
Plant in average, moist, well-drained soil

This pungent bulb has been used for so many years in so many ways that books have been devoted to its wonders. Garlic is an indispensable herb not only in the kitchen but also in the garden, and, according to folklore, in the medicine chest.

Legend has it that garlic will clear an acne-plagued complexion. For minor skin infections, garlic juice applied externally works wonders. Since the earliest of times it has been chewed, chomped and crushed as an aphrodisiac. In some countries, Jewish grooms wore a clove in their wedding attire to symbolize a happy and fertile marriage. Roman charioteers ate garlic for its supply of strength.

Garlic has long been used as a disinfectant, a cold remedy, an antidote for poison and even a safeguard against vampires. Today it retains its reputation for conferring long life and protection from evil.

Garlic grows as a hardy, perennial herb with strap-shaped stems 2 to 3 feet high. Plants often develop a somewhat floppy growth habit. From spring to summer, fuzzy, round, pompon flowers appear on stalks that thrust upward from the plant's center. These white to pink blossoms are edible and are attractive when used fresh or dried in floral arrangements.

Consider growing other varieties such as elephant garlic, *Allium scorodoprasum,* or Mexican red or purple garlic, *A. roseum.* They are as easy to grow as common white garlic and require the same growing conditions. Elephant garlic is about twice as large as common white garlic with a milder flavor. It usually has four to eight cloves. Mexican red garlic, also called purple garlic, has a reddish purple outer skin and a pungent, peppery flavor. Much smaller than common garlic, it's the first garlic to mature at the beginning of the season.

Society garlic, *Tulbaghia violacea,* is an ornamental variety. For informa-tion on this plant, see page 110.

Planting and Care—Plant garlic bulbs in early spring or fall in a sunny location in well-drained soil. When selecting bulbs for planting, pick only large, well-formed cloves having the firmness of an apple. Discard rotten, mushy cloves or those showing mold. Separate and plant individual cloves about 2 inches deep and 6 to 8 inches apart with the pointed end facing up. Do not overwater.

Garlic and roses benefit each other. Garlic will inhibit the growth of peas, beans and other legumes. A spray made from freshly crushed garlic cloves and soap can be an effective pest-control method. See page 150.

Harvesting and Use—Dig up bulbs after leaves are completely dry. Shake off excess soil and lay bulbs on a screen, or hang in a well-ventilated place to thoroughly dry the outer skins. After drying, which typically takes two to three days, store in a cool location away from direct light. Do not store whole garlic in refrigerator.

Few dishes are not improved by garlic. It imparts its own unique aroma, heightening the taste of a dish. It has the additional benefit of aiding digestion, especially with rich foods.

Garlic's strong odor and the infamous garlic breath are overwhelming to some. For more delicate garlic flavor, rub a cut clove across the saucepan, casserole dish or wooden spoon you'll be using for cooking, rather than using the whole clove.

Baking garlic with lamb, pork, veal, beef, tomatoes, eggplant or zucchini also subdues the flavor. For the addict who can never have enough, the ideal breathmint to neutralize garlic breath is fresh parsley. To remove garlic's odor from your hands, sprinkle them with salt and rinse with cold water.

Scented Geranium
Pelargonium species

Tender herbaceous perennial
Cosmetic, Culinary, Ornamental
2 to 4 feet high, to 6 feet wide
Full sun to partial shade
Almost any well-drained soil

Scented geraniums are among the most pleasant herbs to grow. They come in an extraordinary variety of intense fragrances and diverse, soft-leaved patterns. These include the old-fashioned rose geraniums; lemon, lime and other fruity scents; the spicy scents of ginger, nutmeg and peppermint; as well as pungent oakleaf and eucalyptus fragrances.

The fragrance of scented geraniums vary from person to person, but seldom do they disappoint. Leaf forms may be lacy, fan shaped or divided like a pheasant's foot, a crow's foot, an oak leaf, a maple leaf, a ruffle, a grape leaf or a spreading umbrella. Textures may be velvety or sticky. In fact, there are more than 250 varieties. Of these, 50 to 75 are commonly cultivated. Not surprisingly, the primary appeal of scented geraniums is in perfumery. Their essential oils add an uplifting note to soaps, lotions and colognes.

On their own, the spreading scented geraniums make wonderfully fragrant hanging container plants. The fruit-scented types continue to grow through the winter; large-flowered varieties typically go dormant.

Of scented geraniums, the old-fashioned sweet rose, *Pelargonium graveolens*, is the all-time favorite. These have woody stems, rounded, lobed, fragrant leaves and rose-pink flowers. Leaves of rose geranium yield an essential oil similar to that of the rare and valuable *attar of roses*. In France, leaves are harvested on a large scale for distillation. One pound of leaves, when distilled, will yield one gram of oil. This is one of the principal oils used in soap, potpourri and perfume.

A Selection of Scented Geraniums

P. crispum. A lemon-scented geranium with small ruffled, flute-cut leaves. Growing on stiff upright stems, its pyramidal evergreen shape is most flattered by a tub planting.

P. crispum 'Prince of Orange'. A worthwhile compact variety for garden or home. Small crenate leaves offer a royal citrus odor and sport delicately pale orchid blooms.

'Prince Rupert'. An upright evergreen, this little prince grows quickly to a showy shrub size. Its lemon scent graces the best of pot gardens.

P. X fragrans 'Nutmeg'. Nice and spicy, this variety does well where its small, gray-green leaves can trail over pots or border geranium beds.

P. glutinosum. Has deep cut, marked, brown leaves that look less like foliage and more like birds' feet. Need a fast-growing, good-looking background for a bed or box? This tough, adaptable plant fills the bill.

P. graveolens. A gentle giant that's great in tea and jellies. Large, deep-cut, gray-green leaves and lavender blooms produce a whisper of rose.

P. graveolens 'Camphor Rose'. Leaves are velvety soft to the touch and camphorous-rose to smell.

P. g. 'Rober's Lemon Rose'. Sweetest of the rose scents, this plant produces long thick leaves for potpourri or tea.

P. X limoneum. With small, toothed, fan-shaped leaves, the lemon geranium is a must for lemon lovers.

P. X nervosum. The lime geranium is a compact plant that packs a tropical punch. Small leaves and lavender flowers carry a lime flavor and scent.

P. quercifolium 'Beauty Oak'. Although its large oak-shaped leaves are marked by a rough, brown texture, it is one of the most eye-catching trailing plants. Tiny rose flowers are touched with purple and have a minty perfume.

P. tomentosum. Shrubby with large, velvety soft, grapelike leaves scented with sweet peppermint. Sure to please children, and children at heart. Tolerant of shade.

Planting and Care—Plant from containers in spring or fall in mild-winter regions. In such climates scented geraniums are perennial plants and can grow 2 to 4 feet high and up to 6 feet wide. Propagate by cuttings placed in ordinary garden soil. They will root over winter and be ready for planting outdoors in spring.

In cold-winter climates, scented geraniums are best grown in containers and brought indoors to avoid killing freezes. With plenty of sun, well-drained soil and regular irrigation (avoiding overwatering), they make wonderful, long-lived houseplants. Pinch tips throughout the growing season to promote bushiness.

Harvesting and Use—Flowers are small and for most varieties are not very significant. The fragrant leaves are valued for potpourris and to flavor cakes and puddings. Their fragrance is most intense on warm days

Rose Geranium Tea

In a tea pot, brew your favorite pekoe tea as usual. Add one fresh rose geranium leaf per cup of water. A slice of orange instead of the usual lemon makes a nice final touch.

Right: Scented geraniums come in an extraordinary variety of leaf shapes and scents.

Below right: *Pelargonium tomentosum* is shrubby with large grapelike leaves. Plants tolerate shade.

Below: Geraniums are well adapted to grow in containers. This velvety-leaved variety is peppermint geranium.

Left: Prostrate germander works well as a low-growing ground cover, reaching not much more than 6 inches high.

Below: During summer, germander is often covered with spikes of attractive, hairy, 3/4-inch, red, purple or occasionally white flowers.

Fresh Ginger Baklava

Nut Filling
1 pound shelled pecans
1/2 cup sugar
1 tablespoon orange
flower water
1 tablespoon finely grated
fresh ginger root
In a food processor, finely
chop filling ingredients.

1 pound phyllo dough
1 pound unsalted butter,
melted

Brush the bottom and sides
of a 9x13-inch glass pan
with butter. Cut phyllo
sheets in half to fit pan.
Stack half of sheets and
cover with plastic wrap.
With second half of phyllo,
lay out one sheet on bottom
of pan and brush with butter. Continue layering and
brushing each sheet lightly
with butter before laying the
next on top in pan. Spread
nut filling mix evenly over
phyllo. Continue layering
with stack of phyllo that has
been covered with plastic.
Before baking, use a sharp
knife to cut pastry into
squares, triangles or
diamond shapes. Bake in
preheated 350F oven for 1
hour or until golden brown.

Syrup
1-1/2 cups sugar
1 cup water
1 tablespoon orange
flower water
1 tablespoon fresh lemon
juice
1 teaspoon vanilla extract

While the baklava bakes,
mix sugar and water
together in a saucepan. Boil
until liquid reaches 240F
(soft-ball candy stage).
Remove from heat and add
orange flower water, lemon
juice and vanilla. When
baklava comes out of oven,
pour syrup evenly over the
top. Cool before serving.
Makes about 24 pieces.

and when leaves are brushed or
lightly bruised.

Leaves of rose geranium provide
the flavor of rose water to powdered
sugar used in baking. Place one or two
fresh young leaves in a food processor
with sugar and process until finely
minced. Use the sugar on fruit and in
cookies, frostings, jellies and teas.
Note: Other geraniums are available
that resemble sweet rose geraniums at
certain stages but they are not suited
for culinary use. Be sure to use only
rose geranium for cooking.

For a special winter-warming
beverage, try the recipe for Rose
Geranium Tea, page 67.

Germander
Teucrium chamaedrys

Hardy perennial shrub
Craft, Culinary, Medicinal, Ornamental
1 to 2 feet high, 3 feet wide
Full sun
Average well-drained soil

Germander is a reliable small shrub in
all climate zones. Plants normally
grow 1 to 2 feet high. Germander
excels as a decorative edging for
perennials, on slopes or included
among rocks and boulders. Its low
growth is well suited to earth berms
or as a colorful carpet at the base of
accent plants. During summer, spikes
of hairy, 3/4-inch, red, purple or occasionally white flowers cover plants.
These flowers attract bees.

'Prostratum' reaches just 6 inches
high, spreading to 3 feet. It can even
be used as a lawn substitute in small
areas.

Planting & Care—Plant from containers almost any time, but the best
period is early spring. Can also be
planted in fall in mild-winter areas.
Space plants 2 feet apart and at least 3
feet away from companion plants.
Tolerant of high heat, prefers full sun
and well-drained soils. Accepts low-
water applications after establishing.
Trim back branches in late winter to
encourage new growth.

Harvesting and Use—Maintaining a
germander hedge or topiary shape
has traditionally required trimming in
spring and again in midsummer.
However, as a 16th-century medicinal
favorite for fevers, indigestion and

gout, germander's branches were
more frequently pinched, dried and
steeped as a teatime remedy. This
tonic reputedly strengthened the
brain and relieved achy arms and
legs. It was also prescribed as a
diuretic and stimulant for coughs and
asthma. Troubled by gout, Emperor
Charles V himself became its most
famous advocate when completely
cured after taking a decoction of
germander for 60 successive days.

Households of the late medieval to
early Renaissance period also prized
germander's mild garlic-spice aroma.
It was habitually hacked and strewn
on top of the rushes that covered the
floor, creating, literally, a breathtaking
wall-to-wall carpet. Its branch tips
still make a good moth and flea repellent for stored woolens.

Today, germander is a popular and
inexpensive landscape plant for ornamental knot-garden designs. Tolerant
of repeated clippings and pinchings, it
is one of the toughest and tidiest
herbs as an evergreen low hedge for
the perennial border, herb garden or
herbal ground cover.

Ginger
Zingiber officinale

Tender herbaceous perennial
Culinary, Medicinal, Ornamental
2 to 4 feet high, to 2 feet wide
Partial shade
Rich, warm, moist, well-drained soil

Ginger is native to the moist tropical
forests of southeast Asia and is now
grown in tropical climates throughout
the world. The portion used is the fat,
knobby *rhizome*, a type of underground stem. It is generally called
ginger *root*, which is technically a
misnomer.

Ginger is a striking perennial plant,
similar to bamboo. A green stem supports a number of long, narrow,
blade-shaped leaves. An inhabitant of
the understory of the moist lowland
forests of the Asian tropics, it grows
outdoors only in similar warm and
wet habitats. In climates where temperatures drop below 50F, plants can
be grown in a container and brought
indoors in winter. We've provided a
guide on page 146.

The exotic flavor of ginger was

prized by Greek bakers and later introduced to northern Europe by the Romans. It became one of the most popular spices of the Middle Ages, used in marinades (to disguise the taste of less-than-fresh meats and fish), sweet dishes, cakes and biscuits. Its warming, rich, pungent flavor was believed to stimulate the gastric juices and helpful in thwarting colds. Ginger is also an old-time remedy for queasy stomachs. Early Greek sailors used gingerbread "cookies" to treat seasickness on ocean voyages. It potential as a nausea remedy was even tested by shuttle astronauts.

Planting and Care—Purchase fresh, organic ginger rhizomes (sold as "roots") at a food market in late winter. Choose those that are plump and have many buds. Place in warm water and soak overnight. Plant whole or break into pieces. Set 2 inches deep in a soil high in organic matter. Soil temperatures of 75F to 85F are essential before the dormant rhizomes sprout. Water lightly at first, then increase moisture as growth begins. Place plants in partial shade, never in direct sun. Only light fertilization will be needed if the soil is rich in nutrients. Water regularly so soil remains moist but do not allow it to become wet. Ginger may go into dormancy during short winter days. Let the soil remain dry during this period. Ginger rarely blooms in cultivation, although it sometimes flowers if grown in a greenhouse. Yellowish green flowers bloom in a cluster on top of a stalk 3 feet high. Green bracts surround flowers with a mauve or deep purple lip.

Harvesting and Use—If you grow ginger in ideal conditions, plants may be dug up and harvested every year or two. Rinse harvested rhizomes gently to remove soil. Avoid abrading the skin before use. Dry well to avoid mold during storage.

The pungent rhizome is an essential ingredient in many Asian dishes. It is sold fresh, dried, canned, candied, ground or preserved in brine, vinegar or sugar syrup. Curries, spiced meat, fish, rice and vegetable dishes are enhanced with the flavor of ginger. It spices up fruit salads, pickles, preserves, fish and many orange vegetables such as pumpkin, squash, carrots, sweet potatoes and yams.

Remove the outer skin of the rhizome before using. Dried powered rhizome is sold as the spice ginger and is popular in baking, especially in its namesake gingerbread and other spicy desserts. Rhizomes and stems can be brewed to make a stimulating tea. Ginger also sweetens the breath.

Ginseng (North American)
Panax quinquefolius

Hardy herbaceous perennial
Medicinal
6 to 18 inches high, 12 to 36 inches wide
Full shade
Rich loam high in organic matter

The North American ginseng, *Panax quinquefolius*, is a sister species to the Oriental ginseng, *Panax ginseng*. Oriental ginseng has been used medicinally for more than five thousand years, primarily as a stimulating body tonic and a supplement for longevity. The power lies in the roots, which often have a shape that resembles the human body. The name *ginseng* derives from the Chinese word meaning *root of man*.

Plants grow 6 to 18 inches high and are crowned with an umbrellalike whorl of leaves that may reach 2 feet wide. They grow best in cool, moist forests on north or northwestern slopes, preferring cool air but warm soils. If you find ginseng in the wild, it's best to leave it alone. It is illegal to harvest wild ginseng in many states.

Planting and Care—Start from seed that has been refrigerated for four months. Seedlings can be grown in a greenhouse and transplanted to their garden location when two years old. Seedings require shady, moist conditions with good drainage. Prefers rich loam soil, high in organic matter, with a pH of 5.0 to 6.5. Water regularly but do not waterlog plants; roots rot easily. Reduce but don't eliminate water in fall. Excessively wet soils will kill the roots, as will overly dry soils. Mulch plants well in winter. Ginseng can be grown in containers. If left outdoors in winter, mulch plants to protect from cold or move to a frost-free location. Small green flowers bloom after plants are four years old, generally during summer. Fruits are bright red, containing two to three white

"Had I but a penny in the world, thou should'st have it for gingerbread."
—Shakespeare

"I will reveal to you a love potion, without medicine, without herbs, without any witch's magic; if you want to be loved, then love."
—Hecaton of Rhodes

Ginseng Hunters

North American ginseng was first brought to China in 1718, and sold for the phenomenal sum of $5 per pound. Many people, notably Daniel Boone, earned a good living collecting wild ginseng. Even Thomas Jefferson recognized ginseng as an important natural resource. Today, most North American ginseng is cultivated in Marathon County, Wisconsin, and in scattered pockets in New York and Vermont.

seeds. Roots can be harvested after five to seven years, but their value and utility increase with maturity.

Harvesting and Use—Many claims have been made about the powers of ginseng. Unfortunately, studies proving its usefulness are controversial. Ginseng does appear to help bodily functions return to normal more quickly, so recovery from stress, illness or endurance events such as marathons is believed to be shortened by ginseng. It is also reputed to be an effective aphrodisiac.

But buyer beware: Recent tests by independent agencies determined that "...twenty-five percent of [ginseng] products sampled contain no ginseng at all." If the product is not manufactured in the United States, it need not comply with U.S. labeling laws.

Hoja Santa, Hierba Santa
Piper sanctum (Piper auritum)

Tender perennial
Ornamental
7 feet or more high and as wide
Partial shade
Rich, well-drained soil

Hoja santa is a distinctive herb that will command your attention with its large, heart-shaped leaves. *Hierba* means "herb," *hoja*, "leaf" and *santa*, "sacred." Author Lucinda Hutson lists it as *Piper auritum*. Herbalist Madalene Hill classifies it as *Piper sanctum*.

Classification differences aside, this plant adds an ornamental playfulness to any garden during spring and summer. Its semiwoodsy growth with continuously emerging new shoots quickly forms a clubhouse-sized clump of individual plants. (Children seem to instinctively calculate its great play-fort potential.) Each multiple branch spreads with ever larger heart-shaped leaves, 8 by 10 inches or more. Throughout summer it launches spikes of rough, white flowers. The fruits that follow are hard and inedible.

Planting and Care—Tolerates sunny locations if watered frequently, but prefers a shady afternoon site with rich, well-drained soil. A slight freeze will cause leaves to droop, darken and die back, but plants rebound rapidly when warm spring weather returns. A hard freeze will kill plants, so locate in a warm, protected microclimate if possible.

Harvesting and Use—For generations, Mexican cooks have wrapped foods in folded hoja santa leaf packets and placed them over a hot fire to cook. Wrapping food in leaves protects and flavors dishes, keeping them moist and savory. When heated, leaves produce a sweet, musky anise steam.

Caution: Some recent studies have shown that eating hoja santa may cause cancer. Until additional studies provide more detailed information, it would be wise not to use it as a culinary herb.

Hops
Humulus lupulus

Hardy deciduous perennial vine
Cosmetic, Craft, Culinary, Medicinal, Ornamental
Vine to 25 feet or more
Full sun to light shade
Fertile, deeply worked soil

The first recorded uses of hops were as a spring vegetable similar to asparagus and as a shade-producing vine. Hops were not added to beer until about 800 years later, when it was discovered they extended preservation. Imparting a zesty, bitter taste, the conelike fruits called *strobili* are popular in brewing today.

Hops are native to North America. Native Americans and Europeans independently discovered their medicinal properties. Both considered the flowers a sedative and both partook of hop flower tea to induce sleep.

It grows as a hardy perennial vine to 25 feet in a single season, although 40 feet has been recorded. It tolerates a wide range of climates and may be found throughout temperate areas of North America from New Brunswick to New Mexico.

Humulus lupulus var. 'Aureus' is a yellow-leaved variety. Excellent in containers. *H. japonicus* 'Variegatus', variegated Japanese hops, is grown not for making beer but for its ornamental qualities.

Planting and Care—A new main stalk forms each year on established plants. The old wood gradually dies each fall. Energy for the winter is stored in the

Left: Hoja santa is a distinctive herb that will command your attention. Its stature and large, heart-shaped leaves add a playfulness to the garden during spring and summer.

Below left: Hops grows as a hardy perennial vine to 25 feet in a single season. It tolerates a wide range of climates.

Below: Ginger is a striking plant, similar in appearance to bamboo. A green stem supports a number of long, narrow, blade-shaped leaves. In climates where temperatures drop below 50F, plants can be grown in containers and brought indoors in winter.

Hops

It was John Gerard, the 16th-century surgeon and apothecary to England's King James I, who insisted that beer made from hops was more of a medicine than a refreshment. Enjoy, then, the benefits of hops by infusing three fresh or dried heads in a cupful of hot water for 10 minutes. Sweeten to taste and drink while hot. Even better, follow this tisane by taking a warm bath to which a strong hop infusion has been added, and slip into bed with a sleep pillow filled with dried hops. Sweet dreams.

roots. Hops have separate male and female plants. Because the female fruits are most commonly used, gardeners usually prefer to grow hops from cuttings or root divisions. Plants grown from seed will not flower for three or more years. Divisions flower often in the first year, another reason for this method of propagation.

Locate plants in full sun in deep, fertile soil high in organic matter. Water evenly through the growing season. Hops grow well in a large (3-foot diameter) container outdoors. Provide a trellis or plant near a fence or wall to support growth.

Harvesting and Use—Flowers can be infused, strained and added to bath water. Do not add the flowers themselves because they can irritate the skin. Vines are wonderful for making wreaths and baskets. Wear gloves to protect from the barbs on the stems, which can irritate the hands. Fresh leaves can be infused to make a brown dye. Sip a tea infused from fresh or freshly dried flowers for a nighttime sedative. Dried flowers lose their potency rapidly. Spent hops from a brewery make a rich mulch or organic matter for the compost pile.

Horehound
Marrubium vulgare

Semihardy herbaceous perennial
Craft, Medicinal, Ornamental
2 to 3 feet high, to 1 foot wide
Full sun
Moderate to sandy soils

This bushy member of the mint family has been used medicinally for more than four thousand years. It grows wild in the dry climates of western Asia, southern Europe and North Africa, where it receives as little as 12 inches of rainfall per year.

The scientific name, *Marrubium*, comes from the Hebrew *marrob*, meaning bitter. Despite its bitter flavor, horehound has long been valued as a cough and cold remedy. (It might take a tablespoon of honey to help this bitter medicine go down easily.) It is fortuitous that horehound flowers are loved by bees; the honey produced from horehound is dark and flavorful.

In the language of flowers, horehound offers wishes for good health. In the past it has been used to remove magic spells, treat dog bites, settle upset stomachs, relieve heartburn and treat malaria. These treatments have largely fallen from favor in the last century. But remaining popular are horehound cough remedies and candies, common in many forms in drug stores and supermarkets.

Horehound is a musky, aromatic perennial. Downy white stems and crinkled oval leaves have a whitish woolly covering. Plants may reach 3 feet high, although 2 feet is more common. In the first year plants typically grow to 1 foot wide, then spread further in the following years as stems take root. Left to itself, horehound could become invasive, but regular fall or spring cleanup and thinning curtails this problem.

Plants flower in the second year. White burrlike flowers appear in dense whorls around the square stems, and attract bees. Flowers may bloom all summer if plants are given sufficient moisture.

Silver horehound, *Marrubium incanum,* is an ornamental species with soft, downy, silvery leaves and stems; hardy to -30F. It makes an attractive silver accent plant and an excellent background for colorful flowers in containers.

Planting and Care—Propagate by division, because its seeds need cold stratification. Stratified seed is available for purchase; start indoors and transplant seedlings outside after danger of frost has passed.

Like many members of the mint family, horehound requires full sun. Leggy, unsightly plants typically develop in light shade.

Horehound does best in sandy, well-drained soils. It is naturalized in North America, and can be found along railroad tracks or in vacant lots. Accepts slightly acidic to alkaline soils. Tolerates low water applications, but for handsome, healthy plants and flowers, provide regular water. Horehound does well in a container outdoors, as long as potting soil is well drained.

Harvesting and Use—The dense whorls of flowers are charming in dried flower arrangements. Horehound is added to cough drops, cough syrup and throat lozenges. Tea infused from dried or fresh horehound leaves and mixed with honey has a high concentration of mucilage, soothing to a sore throat. Dried leaves may be infused as a spray on cankerworm in trees. Dried leaves can be infused in milk and set in a shallow dish as a fly killer.

Black horehound or stinking horehound, *Ballota nigra*, is a strong-smelling weed and is not to be confused with white horehound. Black horehound can be toxic if ingested in large quantities.

Hyssop
Hyssopus officinalis

Hardy evergreen shrub
Cosmetic, Culinary, Medicinal, Ornamental, Wildlife
2 to 3 feet high, 1 to 2 feet wide
Full sun to part shade
Light, well-drained soil

This esteemed Mediterranean herb has a long history of use. Bundles of aromatic herbs were once tied together and burned. The smoke was believed to cleanse and purify altars, temples, homes and people.

The Romans made a wine called *hyssopites* from this plant, and also used the tender young leaves as a potherb. In about the 10th century Benedictine monks brought hyssop into Europe to flavor their liqueurs. In the Middle Ages, hyssop was a popular strewing herb. It was also a remedy for jaundice and curses imposed by witches. It was later brought to the New World by colonists for tea, pipe tobacco and as an antiseptic.

Hyssop is native to the Mediterranean region, where it is evergreen and grows wild on rocky outcrops and dry banks. A subshrub, it does not become very tall or woody. Plants sometimes sprawl, rooting from stems that touch the ground. However, hyssop is much less aggressive or invasive than many other members of the mint family.

Flowering occurs through summer with dense whorls of bluish violet flowers. Pink and white forms occasionally appear in plants grown from seed and are sometimes available at nurseries. 'Rosea' has pink flowers; 'Alba' white flowers. Flower color holds true in cuttings or divisions.

Rock hyssop, *Hyssopus officinalis* var. *aristatus*, is a shorter, more compact plant that does well in knot gardens or as a hedging plant. Flowers are blue-purple, the leaves are narrower. 'Netherfield' has variegated leaves and white flowers. It is more compact and useful as an edging.

Planting and Care—Grow from seed, cuttings or divisions. Seed can be sown indoors. Harden seedlings and transplant into the garden after danger of frost has past. Space seedlings one foot apart. In warmer regions, sow seed and lightly rake into the soil in March or April. Divide plants or take softwood cuttings from lush new growth or nonflowering stems in spring or fall.

Hyssop prefers full sun but tolerates light shade. Plant in any light, well-drained soil; the pH can range between 6.7 to near 7.9. Hyssop also grows well in limestone soils. Like many Mediterranean plants, it can survive on little water. For robust, healthy plants, water evenly but allow soil to dry between waterings.

Plants do best over time if pruned back in early fall or spring. Protect plants with a thick layer of mulch if temperatures drop below 20F. Hyssop does well in containers and can even be brought inside for the winter if placed in a sunny location.

Harvesting and Use—Leaves and flowers of hyssop brighten potpourri. Hyssop oil may be added to perfumes and soaps. Hyssop makes a relaxing bath. Add in thyme, mint and rosemary to enhance the experience. A steaming hyssop facial cleanses the skin. Medicinally, a leaf poultice can treat bruises and wounds. An infusion makes a sedative expectorant for flu or bronchitis.

Fresh, tender leaf tips, used sparingly, add a tang to soups and salads and go well with strongly flavored fish or meat dishes. Dried or fresh leaves reduce the grease in sausage. Instead of cilantro, try a hyssop leaf in your salsa. It also flavors liqueurs such as Benedictine and chartreuse.

In the garden, hyssop may distract cabbage moths, also called cabbage-white butterflies, from cabbages. Bees, butterflies and hummingbirds enjoy

Horehound as a Cash Crop

The Shakers are said to have been the first Americans to grow medicinal plants for profit. Early in the 19th century this became an important industry for their communities at Harvard, Massachusetts, and Mount Lebanon, New York. The principal herb crops were black nightshade, dandelion root, aconite, poppy, lettuce, sage, summer savory, marjoram, dock, burdock, valerian and horehound.

Above: The pinkish red flowers of Joe Pye weed bloom in mid- to late summer.

Above right: Lady's mantle is one of the hardiest and least troublesome perennials, ideal for situations that call for medium-sized plants in sun or partial shade.

Right and below: Horehound is an aromatic perennial with downy white stems and crinkled oval leaves. It grows to 2 feet high, occasionally up to 3 feet.

its nectar-rich flowers. Beekeepers sometimes rub their hive boxes with hyssop to encourage the hive to stay or to attract a swarm into a new box. *Caution:* All information sources warn that hyssop should not be used by women who are pregnant.

Joe Pye Weed, Sweet Joe Pye Weed
Eupatorium purpureum

Hardy herbaceous perennial
Medicinal, Ornamental, Wildlife
6 to 10 feet high, to 2 to 3 feet wide
Full sun to partial shade
Prefers rich, humusy soil

Joe Pye weed is a member of the *Eupatorium* genus, which is part of the sunflower family. Several *Eupatorium* species flower in late summer and are bewilderingly similar in appearance. All reach 6 feet or more with large, fluffy, dome-shaped clusters of soft, purplish pink flowers. Native Americans used the roots of this genus medicinally and passed their knowledge on to New World colonists. In fact, Joe Pye weed is named for an indian who cured a grateful New Englander of typhus using the roots of the plant.

Grows as a hardy herbaceous perennial. Lance-shaped leaves extend up to 1 foot long and are arranged in whorls around the stems. They are coarse to the touch and emit a faint scent of apple peel when bruised. Pinkish red flowers appear in mid- to late summer, when many garden annuals are done flowering, providing a color accent at one of the hottest times of the year.

Planting and Care—Propagate from seed or divisions. Collect fresh seed and sow in early fall where you want plants to grow. Rake the seed in and keep the area moist until the plants are established. Mulch around the plants for winter. Take divisions in spring or fall. Accepts full sun to part shade. A clump may spread 2 to 3 feet wide in the first year, but in subsequent years growth slows and is not overly aggressive. As a native of the marshes and wet areas of eastern North America, Joe Pye weed requires a marshlike area for best growth.

Does best in rich, humusy soil but tolerates wet clay and acid to moderately alkaline soils.

A great plant to attract wildlife. Butterflies dance around the flowering heads in summer, and goldfinches flit around the seedheads in fall.

Harvesting and Use—Flowering tops and leaves were once dried and infused for a tonic against biliousness and constipation. Joe Pye weed tonics are now believed to be too strong and may border on being toxic.

Roots are dried and used in small doses as a tincture or infusion to induce perspiration, relieve gout and rheumatism, and aid in the elimination of stones from the bladder, hence the nickname "gravel root."

Admired as a long-lasting cut flower, it makes a nice arrangement with goldenrod, which blooms about the same time. Crush seedheads and boil for a pink-red dye.

Lady's Mantle
Alchemilla vulgaris

Hardy perennial
Cosmetic, Craft, Medicinal
1-1/2 feet high, 1 to 2 feet wide
Full sun to partial shade
Well-drained fertile loam

Many legendary uses of lady's mantle are connected with women's complaints. The medieval Christians dedicated this herb to the Virgin Mary because the leaves were thought to resemble her cloak. One belief held that if the leaf were placed under a pillow, the herb would promote quiet sleep. The drops of dewlike water that collect in the center and on tips of its leaves were once called "water from heaven" and considered a vital aid to women's beauty.

In the garden, lady's mantle is outstanding as a hardy, low-maintenance perennial. It is ideal for planting situations that call for medium-sized plants in sun or partial shade.

Broad leaves and stems are softly hairy and evenly scalloped into 7 to 11 slightly rounded, toothed lobes.

Before the plant opens into full bloom, leaves are stylishly pleated in soft folds. When open, the plant's clump symmetry contrasts handsomely with the distinctive foliage of

Lady's Mantle Lotion

A lotion using a strong infusion of lady's mantle can be used night and morning to help cleanse and refine your skin.
To make, pour a cupful of boiling water on 4 teaspoons of dried lady's mantle leaves. Allow to infuse for 10 minutes. When tea is cool, strain. Dip cotton balls in the lotion and wipe your face. Leave on the skin to dry. Make up a fresh infusion each day between morning and evening and keep it in the refrigerator. Lady's mantle lotion can also be added to the bath water to soothe, and helps heal minor cuts and abrasions.

Four Thieves Herb Vinegar

This is a delicious robust vinegar. Use it to enhance a salad, soup, meat, chicken or fish dish—just splash on!

1 heaping cup (loosely packed) mixed fresh herb leaves: mint, rosemary, bay, sage or lavender

1/4 cup whole garlic cloves, peeled

1 teaspoon each whole cloves, whole nutmeg and black peppercorns

1 3-inch cinnamon stick

2 cups red wine vinegar

Place herbs and spices in a clean, sterilized jar. Pour the vinegar over, and use a wooden spoon to lightly bruise herbs and spices. Allow the herb-vinegar mixture to steep. Store in a dark place at room temperature, shaking the jar every couple of days. Taste the vinegar after one week. If the flavor is not strong enough, let it stand for another one to three weeks, checking the flavor weekly. When the flavor reaches the right strength, strain the vinegar, pour into sterilized bottles, garnish with fresh herbs and spices and cap or cork tightly.

other herbs. Dense clusters of small, mustard yellow blooms make long-lasting cut flowers that also dry beautifully.

Planting and Care—Easy to grow indoors and out. Accepts full sun to partial shade. Flowering begins the second year after seeding and lasts up to two months in dry weather. Neither leaves nor flowers are scented. Once established, plants reseed freely. It is a common plant in the far north and requires no special winter protection.

Harvesting and Use—Traditionally, lady's mantle was used for healing wounds and curing women's ailments. It is mildly astringent, diuretic and anti-inflammatory. Herbalists have prescribed it as a tea for digestive disorders. Externally it is used in bath preparations for wounds, bruises and skin disorders. An ancient beauty treatment promised that a woman "who washes her face in this precious water [made from the leaves of lady's mantle] removes all blemishes."

Lamb's Ears
Stachys byzantina
(Stachys lanata)

Hardy perennial
Craft, Ornamental
1 to 1-1/2 feet high, 3 feet wide
Full sun to partial shade
Fertile, well-drained soil

This is one of the most delightful of all herbs. Lamb's ears, also called wooly betony, is pure enchantment for those of us who like to touch and smell plants. Its long, oval leaves are covered by whitish downy hairs that look similar to the furry ears of a lamb. They feel like velvet when touched. Downy stalks and flower stems invite touching as well. When pressed between heavy books for drying, both the stems and leaves emit a fresh, apple scent—a lovely reminder during winter of brighter summer days.

This furry herb was once collected for brewing a popular tea to cure headaches and calm the nerves. In medieval Europe it was called "woundwort" and leaves were used as bandages on cuts to stop bleeding and to provide absorbent dressing.

Lamb's ears is often used as an

edging, providing a low-growing, contrasting border. Plants form rosettes of gray-green leaves close to the ground, multiplying themselves easily by offshoots. Late in summer, tall stalks emerge out of the leaves, the tips covered with whorls of tiny, delicate, purple blooms. *S. byzantina* 'Silver Carpet' is a useful, nonflowering cultivar.

Several other *Stachys* species have similar appearance, cultivation requirements, and healing properties. Betony, *S. officinalis*, is a hardy perennial, native to Europe. It reaches up to 2 feet high, with hairy, long, oval leaves and spikes of purple-red flowers from mid- to late summer. A legendary medicinal herb, betony, too, was taken as a tea for many ailments, from asthma and bronchitis to nervousness and heartburn, worms and varicose veins.

S. officinalis 'Grandiflora' has showier flowers.

Planting and Care—Can be grown from seed. Select a sunny site with moist, well-drained soil. Or propagate by separating and replanting side shoots from established plants in spring or fall. Well adapted to containers and especially attractive in a clay or wooden planter for small patios or balconies.

Harvesting and Use—Leaves, stems and bloom stalks can be collected near the end of the season for use either fresh or dried in flower arrangements and herbal bouquets. Pick leaves in clusters, while they are soft, and dried face down on screens. They will hold their color and texture, while the magenta flowers fade.

Lavender
Lavandula species

Hardy semiwoody perennial
Cosmetic, Craft, Medicinal, Ornamental
3 to 4 feet high and as wide
Full sun
Plant in well-drained soil

Best known for its fragrance, lavender is a favorite herb of many gardeners. Greeks and Romans bathed in lavender-scented water, and it was from the Latin word *lavare* (to wash) that this herb took its name. Washerwomen in England were known as *lavenders*.

Lavender was highly esteemed by royalty. Queen Victoria kept her castle filled with lavender to enjoy its fresh scent. Napoleon is said to have used up to 60 bottles of lavender water each month, pouring it on himself whenever he washed.

Lavender is a shrubby perennial with gray-green, sharp-scented leaves. Spikes of fragrant white, pink or pale to deep purple blooms form at the ends of branches. Narrow leaves make a striking evergreen hedge.

Select from a range of varieties. *Lavandula angustifolia*, English lavender, is easiest to grow, most fragrant and most shrublike, with compact growth to 3 to 4 feet high and as wide. It flowers from July through August, with 1-1/2- to 2-foot spikes that produce a rich fragrance. 'Munstead' is a dwarf form that grows to 1-1/2 feet high and as wide. Makes a neat, controlled foreground plant in the perennial border or in rock gardens. Flowers are deep blue-lavender and bloom late spring into summer. Other hardy varieties include 'Hidcote', which produces deep purple flowers.

Species suited for warmer climates include Spanish lavender, *L. stoechas*, and French lavender, *L. dentata*.

French lavender is distinguished by its narrow, 1-1/2-inch, gray-green, square-toothed leaves. In addition, it has short, lavender-purple flower spikes and petal-like bracts. Flowers bloom over a long period, especially in mild-winter gardens. Plants grow to 3 feet high. Hardy to 15F.

Spanish lavender is smaller and has a more compact growth habit, reaching 1-1/2 to 3 feet high. Flowers are typically a darker purple than other lavenders and appear in short spikes early in the season.

Worth the search is *L. angustifolia* 'Alba', or white lavender. This robust plant has broad, silver-gray leaves and spikes of large, snow white flowers that have a rich, clean fragrance. Plants grow as rounded 3-foot mounds. They are less hardy to cold than other species.

Planting and Care—Plant from containers in well-drained soil in a sunny, sheltered location. Expect only a few blossoms to appear on one-year-old plants; maximum flower production typically develops by the third year.

Cut back flower stems after bloom period has passed. Rejuvenate old plants that have become ragged or woody by cutting back branches. Don't shear but prune branches selectively to retain the natural form. Deer usually find lavender distasteful, while butterflies adore it.

Harvesting and Use—Gather flowering stems just as flowers open. Pick leaves anytime. Dry flowering stems by laying them on open trays or hang in small bundles. Dried lavender retains its scent longer than any herb.

Lavender is the basis for numerous products—perfumes, soaps, sachets and potpourris. It is even included in tobacco mixtures. Herbalists ascribe medicinal benefits ranging from relief of fatigue, aches, sprains and rheumatism to stimulation of the appetite.

Lavender pillows may help promote restful sleep. We use the dried stems as incense, and the fresh stems as barbecue skewers. (See photos, page 161.) Bags or bundles of dried flowers chase away moths as well as counteract the odor of mildew, especially in old chests lined with cloth. Its essential oil is helpful in massage, bathing and scenting rooms for those who have difficulty sleeping.

Lemon Balm
Melissa officinalis

Hardy perennial
Crafting, Culinary, Medicinal, Ornamental
Grows 1-1/2 to 3 feet high, to 6 feet wide
Full sun to partial shade
Moist, fertile, well-drained soil

From the earliest of times, lemon balm has been celebrated by poets and herbalists for its "uplifting" qualities. At one time, the whole dried plant—root, leaves and seed—was sown into a piece of linen and worn under ladies' dresses to promote "an agreeable disposition."

Lemon balm is native to the Mediterranean. The genus name, *Melissa*, is derived from the Greek word meaning "honeybee." This herb's lemony fragrance attracts bees. Hives were rubbed with its leaves to bring in swarms. Housekeepers once used handfuls of fresh balm leaves to polish and scent their furniture.

The Lemon Herbs

Lemon herb tea, either from lemon balm or lemon verbena, is refreshing and cooling. Lemon balm tea is similar to a sweet mint tea with a touch of added lemon. Lemon balm is sometimes called "the scholar's herb." It is reputed to increase the memory and clear the head. Lemon verbena is stronger and sweeter in fragrance and has a mild sedative effect.

Triple Lemon-Aid

It's late summer in the garden, and it's too hot to do anything but enjoy a glass of icy lemonade in the shade, preferably in a hammock.

1 generous bunch of each, all with long stems:
Lemon balm
Lemon verbena
Mint
1 large can frozen concentrate lemonade, reconstituted
Juice of two large lemons
1 lemon, cut into thin slices
3 cups water

Rinse and pat-dry herbs. Place herbs in a large glass pitcher and cover with the juices. Gently stir and bruise leaves with a large wooden spoon. Add water and lemon slices. Chill overnight, stirring occasionally, pressing down on the herbs with the wooden spoon. Pour into tall, iced glasses. Garnish with a sprig of lemon verbena and a borage blossom.
Serves 8 thirsty gardeners.

Top: The light gray leaves of lamb's ears contrast nicely with a dark green backdrop.

Above: Lamb's ears is also a terrific herb for close-up viewing; the woolly leaves beg to be touched.

Right: Flowering giant lavender adds color and fragrance to a benchside planting.

Above left: *Lavandula dentata,* rear, and *L. multifida,* foreground. Note differences in flower colors and textures.

Above: English lavender is the easiest lavender to grow and is the most fragrant. It grows in a shrublike form 3 to 4 feet high and as wide.

Left: Spanish lavender is recommended for warmer climates. It has a compact growth habit, reaching 1-1/2 to 3 feet high. Flowers are usually darker purple than other lavenders and appear on short spikes early in the season.

Lemony Lamb Chops

1/4 cup canola oil
1 tablespoon fresh
 lemon juice
2 cloves garlic, minced
1/2 teaspoon salt
Dash of white pepper
1 teaspoon curry powder
4 5-inch-long blades of
 lemongrass
4 lamb chops, 1 inch thick

In small saucepan, warm
oil, lemon juice, garlic, salt,
pepper and curry powder.
Place lamb chops on large
sheet of foil on broiler pan.
Pour oil/lemon mix over
chops. Place a blade of
lemongrass across each
chop. Seal foil. Bake at 375F
for one hour or until well
done. Remove lemongrass
before serving.
Makes four servings.

Lemon balm thrives in cooler climates. It develops into a bushy plant with substantial roots and a stalk reaching 1-1/2 to 3 feet high. Leaves are smooth, heart-shaped and smell strongly of lemon. Yellow buds open into tiny white flowers by the end of summer.

Planting and Care—Easy to grow although seeds are slow to germinate. Start from cuttings, root division or plant from containers. Plant as soon as the ground can be worked in spring. Accepts partial shade to full sun exposure. Prefers moist fertile soil with good drainage.

Once established, plants endure in the garden unless a determined effort is made to eliminate them. They reseed easily and spread wide, so provide plenty of space. In small gardens, try growing in containers to control plants. The leaves die down to the ground with the first frost. In cold-winter regions place a thick layer of mulch over the crown to protect plant; each spring it will regrow from its roots.

Harvesting and Use—One of the sweetest scented of all herbs, which makes it a delightful ingredient for sachets and potpourris. Fresh-cut stems retain their fragrance well and lend a casual flair to floral arrangements. In the kitchen, lemon balm adds a light, lemony flavor to soups and stews, fish and lamb. Use freshly chopped but sparingly with fruit or salads. It's a flavorful replacement for salt and an inexpensive lemon zest substitute.

Always add lemon balm near the end of cooking because its volatile oils are dissipated by heat. Its flavor keeps well in baked goods because it is captured by the surrounding medium. Use as a fresh garnish in hot tea and lemonade or brew as a tea. A leaf or two improves a glass of white wine. Along with hyssop (see page 75), it is an important ingredient in the liqueur chartreuse.

Lemon balm is recognized as an aid to digestion and circulation. It is reported to help relieve feverish colds, headaches and tension. Its oil is believed to be beneficial in dressing wounds, especially insect bites.

Lemongrass, Melissa Grass
Cymbopogon citratus

Tender perennial grass
Aromatic, Cosmetic, Culinary, Medicinal, Ornamental
4 to 6 feet high, spreading to 3 feet
Light shade
Well-drained, slightly acid sandy loam

Long before Marco Polo wandered over to the Orient, people had been growing and using lemongrass to flavor food and as a medicinal tea. Plants were often located at the edges of fields; occasionally they were used to stabilize soils. Leaves were woven to make crude temporary baskets.

Plants grow up to 6 feet high in a dense clump that spreads to 3 feet across. They develop from a slightly bulbous base and are tufted with long, thin, pointed, blue-green leaves defined by prominent, pale midveins. Leaves are fragrant when bruised, releasing a sharp, lemony scent. Rarely, greenish flowers tinged red bloom in clusters in summer.

A native of India, Ceylon and the tropical areas of southeast Asia, lemongrass is cultivated around clearings and meadows with the hope that it helps keep tigers away.

Cymbopogon nardus, citronella grass, is a sister species from which Ceylon citronella oil is extracted for perfumes and as mosquito repellent.

C. martinii, gingergrass, yields an oil said to aid skin-cell renewal. It has a gingery, floral scent.

C. flexuosus, Indian lemongrass, is another source of lemongrass oil.

Planting and Care—For large, robust plants, propagate from divisions. Seed is often difficult to grow, although growers in warm, moist, sunny climates are often successful when starting with seed. Use divisions from a nursery or order from catalogs.

Plant in full sun to light shade. Soil should be well-drained, slightly acid sandy loam. Provide regular water but allow soil to dry slightly between irrigations. Grows well in a container, outside or indoors, as long as it's grown in a sunny area.

Lemongrass does not survive temperatures below freezing. If plants are healthy, they can survive a light freeze if protected with a layer of mulch.

Harvesting and Use—Lemongrass oil is used in perfumes, soaps and cosmetics; it cleans and tones oily skin. The oil is added to bath water as a relaxant.

Popular in Thai cuisine for fish and chicken dishes. It can be purchased fresh or dried in some supermarkets. In Asian shops it's usually called *sereh;* in Spanish it's called *limoncillo.*

Fresh leaves are peeled, sliced or chopped. Dried leaves are tied in a bunch or placed in a small muslin sack and removed after cooking, like bay leaves. Powdered leaves are very strong, so use sparingly. Chop tender stalks into salads, where their concentric rings add a nice visual effect. Or add crumbled dried leaves to salad dressings. Lemongrass tea is used to treat diarrhea, stomachache, headache, fever and flu. The tea is also considered an antiseptic.

Lemon Verbena
Aloysia triphylla

Tender deciduous perennial or shrub
Cosmetic, Culinary, Medicinal, Ornamental
6 feet high or more, to 5 feet wide
Full sun to partial shade
Almost any well-drained soil

Pleasing and versatile, lemon verbena attracts bees and butterflies in the landscape. Leaves are delightful in iced beverages and, when dried, in potpourri. Plant outdoors in frost-free areas where the lemony leaves and the fragrant, white to pale purple flowers can be touched and enjoyed. In regions where temperatures drop well below freezing (lower than 15F), grow as a container plant and move inside in winter. See page 146.
Planting and Care—Natural legginess and rampant growth (see photo, page 84) require the tall stems be pruned in late spring and summer. If growth looks ragged after late frosts, reduce height by one-third to stimulate new growth and to keep plants more compact. Plant in well-drained soil.
Harvesting and Use—The most lemony of all herbs, lemon verbena has the intense citrus taste of lemon zest without being bitter. It brings out the sweetness of fruit, so you don't have to add as much sugar to fresh

fruit salads, cooked sauces, pies or cobblers. Prolonged heat does destroy its zippy flavor. Try adding one or two teaspoons of the dried herb to a rice pilaf (four servings), or to a two-layer carrot cake. To dry, lay branches on a screen and place in a cool, dry place for a week. Store dried leaves in a tightly covered glass jar away from sun and heat. To use, rub dried leaves together to release their aroma before adding to recipes.

Lemon verbena was, and still is, an ingredient in perfumes and liquors. It's one of our favorites at the farm, and we harvest it in abundance, drying the leaves for our sweet-smelling potpourris and sachets. Fresh sprigs can brighten tussie-mussies, finger bowls or simple wreaths. For aromatic relief, add an infusion of fresh or dried leaves to bath water.

Lovage
Levisticum officinale
(Ligusticum levisticum)

Hardy herbaceous perennial
Cosmetic, Craft, Culinary, Medicinal, Ornamental
6 to 7 feet high, 1-1/2 to 2 feet wide
Full sun to partial shade
Rich, well-drained loam, but tolerates most soils, including alkaline

Native to the Mediterranean mountains of France, Italy, Greece and the Balkans, lovage has long been popular for its intense, celerylike flavor. Its leaves were once placed inside shoes to revive weary travelers, and at inns those same travelers could quench their thirst with a lovage cordial. Leaves were combined with yarrow and sugar, then steeped in brandy to make a love potion.

Because the leaves look like oversized parsley, lovage was often called *love parsley.* Lovage tea was said to calm an upset stomach, relieve rheumatism and reduce water retention.

Children loved it too. The hollow stems served as drinking straws and were even used in early classrooms to shoot peas or spitwads.

Lovage was brought to England by Roman soldiers. Over the years, it escaped cultivation and naturalized. European settlers brought lovage to

Lemon Verbena Sugar Cookies

Lemon verbena is considered the queen of aromatic herbs. No one knows this better than the cooks who lovingly add it to baked sweets, hot teas and iced drinks.

1/2 cup sugar
1/2 cup powdered sugar
1 6-inch sprig fresh lemon verbena, about 16 leaves
1 cup unsalted butter, softened
1 large egg
2 cups plus 2 tablespoons unbleached all-purpose flour
1/2 teaspoon baking soda
1/2 teaspoon cream of tartar
1/4 teaspoon salt
Sugar for garnish

Preheat oven to 375F. In a mini-food processor, combine the sugars and lemon verbena leaves. In a medium bowl, cream together butter with the lemon verbena-sugar mix. Add egg. Thoroughly blend flour, baking soda, cream of tartar and salt into butter mix. Shape dough into 6 to 12 large balls. Place 3 to 4 inches apart on lightly greased cookie sheets. Using a small, flat-bottomed glass, flatten each ball to about 1/4-inch thick, dipping glass in sugar each time. Bake about 18 to 20 minutes or until edges are lightly browned. Transfer cookies to racks to cool.

Right: Lovage leaves are shiny on the upper surface and grayish green beneath. They resemble those of celery, but are larger and more tropical in appearance.

Far right: Plant lemon verbena outdoors in frost-free areas where the lemony leaves and the fragrant flowers can be touched and enjoyed.

Center: Lemongrass leaves are fragrant when bruised, releasing a sharp, lemony scent.

Below right: Lemon balm thrives in cooler climates, developing into a bushy plant reaching 1-1/2 to 3 feet high. Smooth, heart-shaped leaves have a strong, lemony scent.

Below: Leaves of Mexican mint marigold are narrow, deep glossy green above, pale green beneath. On undersides of leaves are tiny glands filled with oil that smells like anise. Small, daisylike, yellow-orange flowers appear in fall.

North America, where it has naturalized in open areas.

A hardy perennial, lovage reaches 6 to 8 feet high within a few years, so locate it carefully, giving it plenty of room in the garden. Plants have sturdy hollow stems and large leaves divided into broad, oval, toothed leaflets. Leaves are shiny on the upper surface and grayish green beneath, resembling those of celery but larger and more tropical in appearance. Plants die back to the ground in winter, but regrow from the roots in spring. Rounded umbels up to 4 inches across appear mid- to late summer, the greenish yellow flowers glistening with nectar. The root is thick with tender, edible, white flesh. With age, roots become woody.

Planting and Care—Propagate from seed or divisions. Collect fresh seed and sow in early fall where you want plants to grow. Rake seed into soil and keep area moist until plants are well established. Mulch around plants in winter. Divide plants in spring or fall. Make sure each division contains some new buds.

Tolerates most soils, including alkaline. Does best in a rich, well-drained loam with a pH of 6.5. Lovage survives dry soil, but for plentiful, tender, young growth, preferred for cooking, keep soil evenly moist.

Harvesting and Use—Harvest young tender leaves to flavor green salads, clear soups, stews, cheeses, vegetables, poultry, red meat and sauces. Also use in place of celery in a stuffing for poultry. Seeds are spicy sprinkled over meat, on cheese and in salad dressings, candy, bread or cookies. Also useful as a salt substitute.

An infusion of leaves, roots or stems is believed to reduce water retention. It is also thought to help cleanse and detoxify the body. Lovage has a diuretic effect, so do not use if you are pregnant or nursing or have kidney ailments. An infusion of the roots is a purported remedy for coughs, bronchitis, ulcers, cystitis and menstrual pain. Used in the bath to cleanse, refresh and deodorize.

Leaves and stems make a long-lasting backdrop for cut flowers. Consider lovage for a child's garden for its fast growth and stature.

Mexican Mint Marigold
Tagetes lucida

Semihardy herbaceous perennial
Aromatic, Cosmetic, Culinary, Medicinal, Ornamental
1-1/2 to 2 feet high, 1 to 1-1/2 feet wide
Full sun
Moist acid to alkaline soil

(Also called Winter Tarragon, Texas Tarragon, False Tarragon)
Tagetes, the marigold genus, originated in the cool mountains of Mexico. Natives began cultivating many of the marigolds over five thousand years ago. Mexican mint marigold was valued for its medicinal properties. It was used to kill intestinal parasites, sooth upset stomachs, relieve diarrhea and ease menstrual cramps, and as a general tonic.

Mexican mint marigold has many common names in Mexico and Central America, including *hierba de anis, hierba de San Juan, flor de Santa Maria* and *pericon*. The flavor is sweet, somewhat like anise.

Many slender stems rise unbranched from the base of this semihardy perennial. Narrow leaves are deep glossy green above, pale green below. Underneath are tiny glands filled with oil that smells like anise. Small, daisylike, yellow-orange flowers appear in fall and can be showy in the garden.

Planting and Care—Sow seed after danger of frost has passed. Cover seed lightly with soil and keep evenly moist. Dividing plants is the easiest method; do this in spring or fall. Arch a stem to the ground, cover the center with soil, and the stem will often root at the nodes.

Even in the mildest climates these plants are winter dormant. As plants set seed, let them begin to dry out. If the weather remains too moist when plants are dormant they will rot. Allow three to four months of dormancy before watering again. Locate plants in full sun to moderate afternoon shade; without enough sun they may not flower. Tolerates any soil, including clay or loam, alkaline or acidic, even limestone soils.

Mexican mint marigold does well in containers as long as the soil does not dry out. In northern climates

Mexican Mint Marigold Vinaigrette

2/3 cup virgin olive oil
1/3 cup light sesame oil
1 tablespoon white wine vinegar
2 tablespoons Mexican mint marigold leaves and flower petals, finely chopped
4 tablespoons chopped parsley
1 teaspoon Dijon mustard
1 teaspoon honey
Salt and pepper to taste

Combine all ingredients in a blender and mix well. Drizzle over tossed salad greens and serve.

Making Mint Mind . . . Without Losing Yours

1. Partner it with annuals.
When you rework and replant your garden's annuals each spring, it's prime time and little trouble to dig and divide the previous year's mints. Provide each mint with at least one square foot of space. Curly mint, pineapple mint and grapefruit mint are diminutive enough to use as borders. Apple and silver mint are tall enough to blend with basils, peppers and zinnias. Peppermints and spearmints are good companion plants among most vegetables.

2. Pot it up.
Curly spearmint and variegated pineapple mint are pretty in patio pots. 'Eau de Cologne' hangs gracefully from a basket. Peppermint, spearmint and apple mint are best in large pots. Half barrels are roomy enough for several plants. Water, fertilize and prune container-grown mints regularly. Any pot used for growing plants must have well-draining soil—potting soils work well. Containers must have drainage holes.

3. Confine it.
To keep mint behaved and within bounds alongside perennials or other plants, you must prevent the roots from spreading. Bottomless pots, flue tiles, boards laid on edge, landscape timbers, and plastic or steel landscape edging are common barricades. To do their job, they must reach 6 to 8 inches down into the soil and project a few inches above the soil surface.

allow plants to go dormant and store them in a cool area for the winter. Move them to a sunny spot and begin watering in late winter to bring them out of dormancy.

Harvesting and Use—Dried leaves are mildly aromatic in potpourri. A warm decoction works well to tone skin, help cleanse pores and treat acne.

When cooking, the sweetish, anise-like flavor of leaves and stems can be substituted for tarragon. Fresh leaves and flowers complement chicken, fish, veal and mutton. Stuffed peppers, squash, tomatoes and traditional turkey stuffing are enhanced by the subtle flavor. Do not overcook; add near the end of preparation.

Sprinkle fresh leaves and flowers in green and fruit salads. Wonderful in herb vinegar; the flavor is strongest with white wine vinegar as a base. When harvesting leaves use sharp shears to cut rather than crush the stems. This helps prevent the flavorful oils from escaping. Chop as you add to dishes when cooking.

The golden orange flowers make a spicy tea and can be blended with black tea for flavor.

Mints
Mentha species

Vigorous perennial
Cosmetic, Culinary, Medicinal, Ornamental
4 inches up to 3 feet high with rapid, invasive, wide-spreading growth
Partial to full shade
Rich, moist soil

Almost everyone enjoys the cool, penetrating, sometimes fruity kiss of mint. Mints are attractive and boast a variety of handsome leaves—shiny, fuzzy, smooth, wrinkled, green or variegated. They also sport spiked or clustered heads of tiny lavender or pink to soft white flowers.

The genus *Mentha* includes 18 pure species. However, mints are promiscuous cross-pollinators and commonly produce hybrid seedlings that bear little resemblance to their parents. In fact, there are more than two thousand *named* variations of mint, but few are significantly different.

Some of our favorite mints are 'Eau de Cologne', 'Orange Bergamot', 'Orange Mint' and water mint, *M. aquatica*, which spreads like wildfire! Their pungent perfume lingers long after you've touched their leaves.

Peppermint, *M. X piperita*, is a hybrid of spearmint, *M. spicata*, and *M. aquatica*. Its cool-scented, icy white flowers cluster in little rounded heads at the top of trailing stems. We love to use peppermint's pointed oval leaves to lace sweets. Chocolate mint, 'Mitcham,' 'Blackstem' and 'Candymint' are cocoa sweet-smelling and sweet-tasting cultivars of peppermint. Shiny, dark green leaves spread daintily over brownish purple stems. Plants may reach up to 2 feet high.

Grapefruit mint, *M. X piperita* var. *citrata,* has rounded, more substantial foliage than most mints. It puts on a show of lavender-pink flowers in summer.

Pennyroyal, *M. pulegium*, is a low-growing, plain-looking, pungent green, respected for its ability to repel insects. This mint is not suited for culinary use. See page 98.

Corsican mint, *M. requienni*, has shiny, delicate stems that cling close to the soil. Say "mmmm" to this herb's crème-de-menthe sweetness. Lavender flowers are small but packed with flavor.

Spearmint, *M. spicata*, blooms with fuzzy white flowers that resemble mini-bottle brushes. Spearmint spreads a firm mattress of vigorous upright stems with slightly crinkled leaves. 'Crispata' ('Curly') has rounder, shorter, more ruffled stems.

Silver mint, *M. spicata* var., dresses in a suit of woolly gray leaves topped with a floral lavender spike. Upright to 30 inches high, this mint gets noticed. We value the shimmery contrast it provides to brighter plants.

Apple mint, *M. suaveolens*, adds a mild, appealing flavor zing to iced tea, wine coolers and fruit plates.

Pineapple mint, *M. suaveolens* 'Variegata', has diminutive features with dainty, dappled, bright green and white leaves. This mint is one of the prettiest to own. It congregates in dense clumps, growing to about 12 to 15 inches high.

Woolly mint, *M. X villosa* var. *alopecuroides,* decorates the garden with fuzzy, oval, pale green leaves and upright stems. It grows up to 20 inches, even 30 inches high.

Planting and Care—As wonderful as mints can be, almost everyone becomes exasperated by their invasive habits. Depending on the variety and growing conditions, a single plant from a 3-inch pot can spread to fill a square foot in its first garden season. It may smother a square yard by its second year. As mint spreads, its runners stitch the roots of neighboring plants into a dense, snarled mat; new shoots of mint pop up where they don't belong. The challenge is to find suitable strategies and spots for growing them. See "Making Mint Mind . . . Without Losing Yours."

Propagate mint by cutting or division. Choose a spot with rich, moist soil in full sun to partial shade. Set new plants 2 feet apart; they will quickly fill in. Separate different varieties to maintain their scent, flavor and appearance integrity. Most mints are hardy throughout the U.S.

Harvesting and Use—Mint leaves are best when fresh, but may be used dried in teas, potpourri and bath bags. Freeze small, individual sprigs in ice cube trays for beverages. Harvest anytime—the more you clip the better mint will be. Hang bunches to dry, or spread leaves on screens.

Peppermint and spearmint are used commercially in everything from chocolates and colognes to toothpaste. In your kitchen, brew mint into refreshing teas (good for indigestion, headaches and hangovers); sprinkle its zesty flavor over potatoes, salads and steamed vegetables. Blend it minced into yogurt, butter or cream cheese. Leaves are a great garnish for iced drinks and jellies and are an inseparable companion to lamb.

Mugwort
Artemisia vulgaris

Hardy shrubby evergreen perennial
Aromatic, Cosmetic, Craft, Medicinal, Ornamental
4 to 6 feet high, to 1-1/2 feet wide
Full sun
Average to poor soil if well drained

Mugwort, also called St. John's plant, moxa herb, felon herb and sailor's tobacco, is considered a noxious weed in portions of North America, Europe and Asia. It is native to southern Europe and western Asia, where it is often found on disturbed soils. Spread by sheep and goats, it is surrounded by a number of superstitions. In England, leaves were used to flavor and preserve ale, hence the name mugwort. Flowering tops were a traditional ingredient in goose stuffing.

A sturdy, shrubby perennial, mugwort grows to a height of 4 to 6 feet. Plants are heavily branched with reddish stems. Divided leaves are deep green on top, silvery underneath. Plants spread vigorously by underground rhizomes and self-seed prolifically. Spikes of small, greenish yellow or red flowers appear in oval clusters in midsummer.

Other Artemisias
Selected *Artemisia* species deserve mention, including southernwood and wormwood. French tarragon, a culinary herb, is described on page 115.

With cloudlike, gray-green foliage and beady flower spikes, silver king artemisia, *A. ludoviciana* var. *albula,* makes one of the best bases for fresh or dried herb wreaths. See photos page 36 and 92. A similar plant, silver queen, distinguishes itself with finer leaves, fuller foliage and smaller spikes. Both can easily reach 4 feet high and rapidly spread as wide. Curtail their takeover habit by pulling or digging up *Artemisia* shoots that extend over boundaries, which is usually light work.

A. ludoviciana, cudweed or white sage, has a broader leaf than silver king but smaller, 2-foot stature. It works well in a silver-gray border.

Silver mound artemisia, *A. schmidtiana* 'Nana,' is elegant and hardy, growing to 1 foot high.

The sagebrush of the West, *A. tridentata,* reaches up to 12 feet high.

A. lactiflora is known as sweet mugwort or white mugwort. It has green leaves and produces fragrant white flowers. Plants grow up to 5 feet high.

Planting and Care—Be prepared to control mugwort; it can be invasive. Propagate by seed, root division or cuttings. Start seeds indoors if spring comes late in your area and transplant seedlings to a sunny site after last

A Carpet of Mint

Roll out the green carpet. Both Corsican mint and pennyroyal make a fragrant green mortar for paths and as ground cover under trees, roses and shrubs. Although pennyroyal is the least picky, we recommend planting any mint only if your soil is well drained and you can commit to frequent watering. Alternatively, plant a mint necklace around the base of trees in your lawn; most mints survive on the same amount of water it takes to keep grass green. Regular mowing keeps the mint from spreading into your lawn, and the mint buffers the tree's trunk from the mower. The bases of fences, walls, or vacant lots are other good carpeting spots.

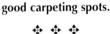

Above: A selection of mints, from left: curly mint, chocolate mint, blue balsam tea mint, spearmint and peppermint.

Right: Iced tea flavored and garnished with peppermint is the perfect refreshment after a "workout" in the garden.

Left: Apple mint as a mass planting. It's wise to plant mint within a well-defined border to contain it.

Below left: Bill Varney examines a mint bed. Mint can be highly invasive so keep an eye on plantings, even those within bordered areas.

Below: Sylvia Varney samples the fragrance of mint flowers.

frost. Sow seed where you want plants to grow in spring or fall.

Growing mugwort in a container is one way to keep it from taking over your garden. To avoid rampant reseeding, cut spent flower stalks and discard them before seeds ripen. In spite of its weedy disposition, mugwort provides a useful, carefree filler in a mixed border or similar planting.

Some nurseries carry variegated and golden-leaved forms. They make an attractive backdrop for smaller-stature flowers or rich green mints.

Harvesting and Use—Leaves have a scent that is similar to sage or basil and can be stitched into sachets. The fragrance is said to induce vivid dreams as well as to repel moths. An herbal bath "tea bag" (see page 172) combining mugwort, agrimony and chamomile relieves muscle aches. The slender, feathery-leaved stalks dry well, adding a nice texture to informal arrangements.

Caution: As with all *Artemisia* species, use mugwort with moderation. Pregnant women should not use it at all.

Mullein
Verbascum thapsus

Hardy biennial
Craft, Culinary, Medicinal, Ornamental
2 to 4 feet high, flower spikes to 7 feet high, to 2 feet wide
Full sun in sheltered location
Almost any well-drained soil

This herb has many common names. Some call it candlewick plant, torches, velvet dock, flannel plant, feltwort, Aaron's rod, shepherd's staff or cow lungwort. There are many others but we call it mullein.

The colonists introduced mullein into North America, and the natives adopted it for relief from chronic coughs, bronchitis and asthma. They smoked its dried leaves for treatment, and even used the acrid leaf smoke to revive the unconscious.

There's no mistaking mullein in the garden. Thick, velvety, spiral-leaved and weedy, this plant is covered in silvery white down supported by a rod-like stem. In summer, usually the second year after planting (mulleins are biennials), it produces a spike up to 6

feet high covered with yellow flowers. It is a literal exclamation point in an herb or perennial garden.

Planting and Care—To grow mullein in the garden, sow seed in spring or fall in well-drained, ordinary soil receiving full sun and protection from the wind. It is a prolific self-sower. To keep under control, remove flower-heads before seeds ripen and disperse. Plants may need protection from slugs, which have a particular liking for this fuzzy plant.

Harvesting and Use—Like other herbs used in magic, mullein has a long history as a healer and a helper. When dried, mullein makes superb tinder, useful for lighting fires. Before the introduction of cotton, the ancients used its leaves and stems as candle wicks. Dried stems and flowers can be dipped in suet or (better yet) tallow, to extend the burning time. Due to mullein's flammability, it was carried as a torch in religious processions and considered a protector from witchcraft, evil spirits and *scrofula*, chronically swollen lymph glands, which was later recognized as a symptom of tuberculosis. Today, an infusion is recommended by herbalists to help soothe coughs and sore throats and treat diarrhea. Mullein has a bitter taste but is tolerable when sweetened.

Outdoors, the lanky, imposing mullein offers pollen and nectar to attract winged wildlife to your garden. In the kitchen its dried flowers exude a honeylike scent, lovely for flavoring liqueurs. Dried flowers also add natural color to potpourris.

Mustard
Brassica species

Hardy annual
Cosmetic, Culinary, Medicinal
3 to 6 feet high, to 1-1/2 feet wide
Full sun to partial shade
Almost any well-drained soil

Mustards are greens that keep on giving: They offer a leafy vegetable for dinner, yellow flower spikes for garden and garnish and an abundance of seeds for spice. Mustards belong to the *Brassicaceae* family. The tangy flavor comes from essential oils found throughout plants.

The species used for greens is different from that used for spices. *Brassica nigra* is the epicurean hot black mustard seed; *B. hirta* is the milder white or yellow mustard seed; *B. juncea,* brown mustard seed, is the common Russian variety.

Mustards have many uses. The Chinese serve a condiment of mustard, and praise its medicinal qualities. Europeans valued black, brown and white mustards as a condiment and medicine. Native Americans used all members of the mustard family for food and medicine.

Mustard's rapid growth and weedy appearance require pinching and regular water to maintain plant appearance. *B. nigra* reaches 6 feet high, *B. hirta* 4 feet high, and *B. juncea* 3 feet high. All species spread 1 to 1-1/2 feet wide. Small, bright yellow flower clusters appear about 60 days after seedlings emerge.

Planting and Care—Plant mustard from seed in spring. Or plant in fall in mild-winter regions. It self-sows readily. Locate in full sun and almost any well-drained soil. Accepts some drying, but regular irrigation ensures best flower and seed production. Pinch or trim young plants to encourage branching and flowering stalks. Most mustards prefer cool soils. In the South and Southwest, mustards can be grown in a winter garden.

Harvesting and Use—Whole mustard seed is used in pickling, chutney, stews, white sauces, Cajun crayfish and shrimp. Grind seeds with mortar and pestle just prior to use.

For a pungent crunch, add young leaves to salads, but keep in mind they are strong in flavor. Brown mustard is best for greens. Add clusters of the tiny yellow flowers for color and flavor in green salads and cold appetizers. A mass of mustard flowers is attractive in herbal vinegars and pickled vegetables. Sprout seeds of black mustard and use in salads as you would alfalfa sprouts.

The stimulating properties, particularly of black mustard, are reported to ward off the effects of lethargy, colds and flu. Mustard footbaths and poultices are renowned folk remedies for aching feet. To use as a hand deodorizer, rub pulverized seed onto hands for a few minutes, then rinse well.

Nasturtium
Tropaeolum majus

**Hardy annual; perennial in mild-winter areas
Culinary, Ornamental
1-1/2 feet high (6 feet with support), to 6 feet wide
Full sun to partial shade
Moist, well-drained soil**

Nasturtiums are frequently cultivated for the color they bring to herb and flower gardens. What a delightful surprise to discover the light peppery flavor their leaves and flowers lend to a salad or sandwich.

Nasturtiums originated in the New World where they were occasionally called "Indian cress" due to the tartness of the leaves. Sailors ate the pickled seeds as a remedy against scurvy. Today they are valued as a source of vitamin C, iron and sulfur.

Plants are annuals or tender perennials in mild-winter regions. Open, trumpet-shaped flowers bloom in brilliant colors of gold, orange, scarlet, rose and a range of hues in between. Five-petaled flowers are carried well above the compact, bright-green, pancake-shaped leaves by thin hollow stems. They bloom all summer and into the first cool days of fall.

There are several types of nasturtiums. Sprawling and climbing vine types grow with support up to 6 feet. These are ideal for a cool greenhouse or protected sunporch where the soil will not freeze. The more common dwarf and bushy types, 'Tom Thumb' or 'Whirlybird', rarely reach more than 1-1/2 feet high. They make colorful edgings for garden beds or in window boxes and planters.

Planting and Care—The big wrinkled seeds are easy to press into the soil, a perfect opportunity to get children involved in the garden. Or buy container plants at nurseries or propagate from root cuttings started in water.

For winter gardens in mild climates, start seeds in pots in August or September. Plant in early fall when the warm soil encourages rapid germination. For spring gardens, plant in full sun to partial shade in ordinary moist soil with good drainage.

Harvesting and Use—Chop fresh leaves to add a tangy taste to a salad

Nasturtium Hors d'Oeuvres

For hors d'oeuvres that are a real conversation piece, stuff large nasturtium leaves with tuna, shrimp, crab or chicken salad.

Use about a teaspoon per leaf. Roll up, secure with toothpicks and cover with French dressing. Marinate before serving.

Right: Nasturtiums are hardy annuals or tender perennials in mild-winter regions. Here they combine with bougainvillea in a southern California garden.

Below: The cloudlike, gray-green leaves and beady flower spikes of silver king artemisia make one of the best bases for fresh or dried herb wreaths.

Bottom: Nasturtium leaves make an interesting planting pattern.

or use whole like its cousin, watercress, in rolled tea sandwiches. President Eisenhower added finely chopped nasturtium flowers, leaves and stems to his vegetable soup. Likewise, use them in green salads for color and flavor. Mince flowers and leaves into whipped sweet butter for savory dinner rolls. Blossoms serve as unusual, colorful containers for dips and sandwich fillers.

Nigella, Love-in-a-Mist
Nigella damascena

Tender annual
Craft, Culinary, Ornamental
1 to 2-1/2 feet high, 6 inches wide
Full sun to partial shade
Light-textured, well-drained soil

(Also called Black Cumin, Fennel Flower, Nutmeg Flower, Roman Coriander)
Although one of its common names is black cumin, this member of the buttercup family is no relation to cumin, which is in the parsley family. Even more confusing, it is sometimes called Roman coriander or fennel flower. The velvety black seeds smell like nutmeg, thus the common name nutmeg flower. Originally from southwestern Asia, nigella was carried into North Africa and parts of Europe. It has been used for centuries as a substitute for pepper.

Nigella grows to 1-1/2 feet high, with finely divided, lacelike green leaves. The blue-purple or sometimes white flowers look much like bachelor's buttons and bloom midsummer through early fall.

Love-in-a-mist is the common name for *Nigella damascena*. The seed is not used as a spice but its lacy foliage and charming flowers make it an attractive and worthy ornamental.
Planting and Care—Sow seed in place in spring or fall in full sun. Plant in a light-textured, well-drained soil. Generally withstands light frosts and prefers cool soils, so direct seeding works well. Nigella grows well outdoors in a container or window box but does not do well indoors.
Harvesting and Use—Interesting brown seed pods are attractive in dried flower arrangements. Seed can be used as pepper substitute. Harvest the brown pods before they open, and place them in a large paper bag. The pods will curve open as they dry, releasing the black, velvety seeds into the bag. Grind seeds and use as a topping on salads and in breads and cakes for an unusual taste. Also excellent in curries and pickled vegetables. *Caution:* Many members of the buttercup family are toxic. Do not eat flowers or leaves of nigella. Eat only the seeds.

Oregano
Origanum species

Hardy evergreen perennial
Culinary, Ornamental
1 to 2 feet high, to 1-1/2 feet wide
Full sun
Ordinary well-drained soil

Oregano, also known as wild oregano, wild marjoram or sweet marjoram, was named by the Greeks: *oros* means mountains, *ganos* means joy, beauty or brightness.

Oregano's sweet, spicy scent was said to have been created by Aphrodite as a symbol of happiness. Bridal couples were crowned with garlands of its leaves. Plants were placed on tombs to give peace to departed spirits.

Herbalists claim medicinal benefits ranging from relieving toothaches to curing opium addiction. Native Americans have used oregano as a medicinal tea and flavoring for meats.

Popularly known as the pizza herb, oregano developed its spicy reputation in American kitchens with the return of U.S. soldiers from Italy and Greece after World War II. Varieties are abundant in England, Greece, Spain, Mexico and Sicily. The spice available at the grocery is often a blend of these. Flowers may be white, pink or purple.

Oregano is a hardy perennial reaching to 2 feet high. Square hairy stems are often tinged purple. Small, oval, downy leaves grow in pairs along stems.
Planting and Care—Start from seed sown in spring or fall. Plant from containers in spring. Propagate from cuttings or root division. Plant in well-drained soil, in full sun in an area free of weeds. Provide room for its widespreading lateral roots. Fertilize

Love-in-a-Mist

Love-in-a-mist, a pretty plant with a romantic name, receives its botanical identity from two sources. Nigella, a diminutive of niger, or "black," refers to the color of its seeds. Damascena refers to Damascus, Syria, one of the places this herb calls home.

Oregano or Marjoram?

Confusion abounds with respect to the difference between oregano and marjoram, a controversy not easily resolved. They are sister species of a single genus. The confusion is recorded as far back as the writings of two Greek scholars and physicians, Theophrastus and Dioscorides, more than two thousand years ago.

Origanum vulgare sub-species vulgare is known as common oregano, marjoram or wild marjoram.

Origanum vulgare sub-species hirtum is known as Greek oregano or Turkish oregano.

Origanum onites may be sold as French oregano or pot oregano.

Origanum libonaticum and Origanum rotundifolium are considered ornamental oreganos. A number of cultivars of each species are available.

Origanum marjorana is called sweet marjoram or knotted marjoram.

Origanum marjorana 'Variegata' is a lovely variegated sweet marjoram, with yellow borders on its green leaves.

Origanum marjorana 'Aureum' is a sweet marjoram with yellow-green leaves. It may be sold as golden marjoram.

Origanum heracleoticum, a native of Greece, is still used there as a folk remedy for earache. It is occasionally sold as Greek marjoram or winter marjoram.

lightly once a month.

Lightly trim oregano during summer and use as needed. This keeps plants neat and compact. In fall cut plants back by one-half before they die back in winter. Roots survive to -20F if protected with a thick mulch. plants in pots can be brought indoors during winter and grown in a sunny window.

Harvesting and Use—This herb is best known for the warm spice it gives to tomato-based dishes such as lasagna, spaghetti, chili con carne and meatloaf. For a taste of sunny Spain, add a few chopped fresh leaves to scrambled eggs or omelettes.

Harvested branches dry quickly and leaves are easy to remove for storage. Allow a few plants to go unharvested until they reach flowering stage. The fragrant blossoms, fresh or dried, are beautiful in tussie-mussies, floral arrangements and in potpourri.

Orris, Orris Root

Iris X germanica var. *florentina*
(*Iris germanica, I. florentina, I. X germanica, I. germanica* var. *florentina*)

Hardy perennial
Aromatic, Cosmetics, Crafts, Ornamental
2 to 2-1/2 feet high, to 1 foot wide
Full sun to part shade
Rich, well-drained soil

Iris is the sacred flower of the Greek goddess of the rainbow, Iris, who took messages of love from the eye of heaven to earth using the rainbow as a bridge. *Iris* plant species come in a rainbow of colors, with the exception of clear red. The most common species has large white flowers tinged with lavender and adorned with yellow beards. Although it is commonly called orris *root,* it is the *rhizome,* the thick, underground stem, that is used.

Orris, also called Florentine iris, is native to Persia. It is likely that the ancient Babylonians first discovered the potent, violetlike fragrance of the dried rhizomes. They passed this knowledge to the Egyptians. Cosmetics with orris root have been discovered in Egyptian tombs.

The tall, swordlike leaves are striking. The showy flowers appear in early summer. Both flowers and

rhizomes have a violetlike scent.

Planting and Care—Propagate by dividing rhizomes in midsummer or late fall. Plant rhizomes just below the surface and space 12 to 15 inches apart. Rhizomes are stout, and may grow only a few inches in a season. Fall chores include cutting back the plant to within 4 inches of the rhizome and removing dead or shriveled leaves. Otherwise, allow plants to grow undisturbed for a few years for greater rhizome growth. Rhizomes divided in early spring may not yield flowers in that year. Plant in full sun to partial shade, in a rich, well-drained soil. Keep plants evenly moist. Feed with an all-purpose fertilizer to enhance production of rhizomes and flowers.

Harvesting and Use—Other than as a garden ornamental, the primary use of orris root is in cosmetics. In home crafts, it is a *fixative* for potpourri. See page 170. Harvest rhizomes for fixative in late fall. Scrub clean and dry in a cool, dark place until rock hard. Grind the dried rhizomes into powder or chop into small pieces. For potpourri, use about one tablespoon for each quart of dried flowers.

Caution: In the Middle Ages, dried orris root was used medicinally as a cathartic and diuretic. Dosages were chancy and people died from uncontrollable vomiting and diarrhea. Because of this potency, wash your hands well after handling roots. Do not ingest any part of the plant.

Parsley

Petroselinum species

Hardy biennial or short-lived perennial
Cosmetic, Culinary, Medicinal, Ornamental
12 to 14 inches high, 12 to 16 inches wide
Full sun to partial shade
Moist, fertile soil

Parsley is one of the oldest and most-versatile herbs. It is certainly at home in the kitchen, but it is also valued for its medicinal, cosmetic and domestic properties.

Parsley was one of the first plants used in wreath making. Chaplets of it were worn at Roman and Greek banquets to absorb the fumes of wine and thereby protect the diners from drunkenness so they could prolong their drinking enjoyment. They also used parsley as a breath-freshener.

Parsley contains significant amounts of vitamins A, B and C, plus iron, calcium, magnesium and chlorophyll. Leaves and seeds are used to relieve cramps, alleviate flatulence and act as a diuretic.

Curly parsley, *Petroselinum crispum,* is a hardy biennial usually cultivated as an annual. Its bright green, tightly curled leaves make an excellent border and potherb in a culinary garden.

P. var. *neapolitanum,* Italian parsley, also is a hardy biennial cultivated as an annual. Large, smooth leaves are similar to those of a fern. It may be cut in quantity for salad greens or cooked as a vegetable.

Planting and Care—If soil temperatures are cool, parsley is one of the slowest herbs to germinate. Start from container plants, available at nurseries. If you do start from seed, soak them in water one day before planting to improve germination. Plant in deep, moist, fertile soil in full sun to partial shade. Thin seedlings to 12 inches apart. If growing parsley in containers, plant in at least a 6-inch pot to provide enough root space.

Harvesting and Use—Parsley tea works well as a skin toner, reducing oiliness and enhancing complexions. It is also said to prevent thread veins and remove freckles. Apply the tea with a cottonball where desired. For an effective facial mask, extract parsley's elements with boiling water, cool, thicken with egg white or egg yolk and apply to skin. Leave for 10 minutes, then rinse thoroughly.

Parsley is considered by some herbalists to be a desirable companion plant to roses, increasing vigor and flower fragrance.

In cooking, parsley is the party girl of the herb family—it brings dishes to the table in fancy dress. Use this mild-flavored herb fresh as often as possible as an ingredient in and garnish for sauces, salads, vegetables, potatoes, egg dishes, soups and casseroles. To increase parsley's potency in dishes, use it generously and include the stems—they are more strongly flavored. Add charm to your next dish with Green Bouquet Garni, at right.

Patchouli
Pogostemon cablin

Tender perennial
Aromatic, Medicinal, Ornamental
3 to 4 feet high, 1-1/2 to 2 feet wide
Full sun to afternoon shade
Rich, well-drained loam

Native to the tropical East Indies, this member of the mint family is grown for its essential oil, which has a deep, rich, spicy, slightly musky aroma.

There is a long tradition of using patchouli leaves to protect the painstakingly hand-woven Persian carpets from insects. It was also used in Chinese red ink paste and in the original India ink.

In southeast Asia the whole plant is used medicinally: as a stimulant, anti-depressant, antiseptic and treatment for poisonous snake and insect bites. In aromatherapy, patchouli oil is a treatment for acne, eczema and athlete's foot.

Shrublike plants grow 3 to 4 feet high and to 2 feet wide with medium green, furry leaves having broad, unevenly toothed edges. Like all members of the mint family, patchouli has square stems and leaves borne in pairs opposite each other.

Small white flowers tinged with purple appear mid- to late summer and attract bees. Beekeepers should pinch off the flower spikes because honey made from the flowers has a bitter aftertaste.

Pogostemon heyneanus, Java patchouli, is similar to *P. cablin* in use and appearance, but its oil is considered inferior. It is also more difficult to grow and tends to die quickly if plants are allowed to dry out.

Planting and Care—Does not tolerate frost, so grow in a container and bring indoors during winter. Or pot up garden-grown plants in late summer. The plant then has time to adjust before going indoors (often stressful for plants) for winter.

Patchouli prefers full sun. In hot-summer areas, however, plants do better with afternoon shade.

Propagate any time from nonflowering cuttings rooted in moist sand. When purchasing plants, look for well-branched specimens.

Harvesting and Use—Harvest leaves

Iris

Iris means "eye of heaven." It is the name given to the goddess, the orris root's flower and the center of your own eyes, signifying that each of us carries a bit of heaven wherever we go.

This plant symbolizes communication and messages. Greek men would often plant iris on the graves of their beloved women as a tribute to the goddess Iris, whose duty it was to take the souls of women to the Elysian fields.

Green Bouquet Garni

Make a sandwich of two 2-inch lengths of celery stalk, a bay leaf, 3 sprigs fresh parsley (preferably Italian), and 1 sprig fresh thyme. Tie with kitchen string. Immerse in soups and stews while they cook. Discard bouquet when ready to serve.

Above: In addition to being a garden ornamental, orris root, *Iris* X *germanica* var. *florentina,* is primarily used in cosmetics. In home crafts it is a fixative for potpourri.

Right: In hot-summer regions, pennyroyal calls for a moist, semishaded location. In cooler areas plant in full sun and protect from freezing temperatures.

Far right: Patchouli does not tolerate frost. In all but the mildest winter regions, grow in a container and bring indoors during winter.

Right: Oregano is a hardy perennial growing to 2 feet high. Square hairy stems often have a purple tint.

Opposite page
Curly parsley is a hardy biennial that is usually cultivated as an annual. Its bright green, tightly curled leaves make an excellent border plant and potherb for the culinary garden.

Patchouli Oil

Patchouli oil is useful as an antiseptic, particularly as an anti-inflammatory first aid remedy for minor burns. Add several drops to a warm bath along with several teaspoonfuls of almond oil to soothe dry or irritated skin. Patchouli oil is also believed to calm irritated nerves and anxiety. Its strong, sensual, musky aroma is said to have aphrodisiac powers.

Mexican Black-Eyed Peas

1/2 cup minced white onion

3 tablespoons olive oil

1-1/2 cups Italian tomatoes with liquid

2 tablespoons hot sauce

3 cups cooked black-eyed peas

2 tablespoons minced fresh Mexican oregano

2 tablespoons minced Italian parsley

Fresh Parmesan cheese, grated for topping

Salt and pepper to taste

In a large skillet, heat olive oil and sauté onions until translucent. Add tomatoes and simmer over low heat for 15 minutes. Stir in hot sauce and black-eyed peas. Season to taste with salt and pepper and continue to simmer another 5 to 10 minutes. Add oregano and parsley. Transfer to heated dish and serve with cheese.

two or three times a year. Dry leaves and put them in a muslin bag prior to placing among clothes or linens. Dried leaves can be used in potpourri.

Some cats like patchouli and respond to it almost as if it were catnip. Other cats react as though an invader has entered their territory. Test the reaction of your cat before leaving patchouli within reach. Do not allow your cat to eat the leaves; they can cause constipation.

Pennyroyal
Mentha pulegium

Perennial
Household, Ornamental,
5 to 16 inches high, 12 to 18 inches wide
Full sun to partial shade
Cool, moist, well-drained soil

In medieval Europe, pennyroyal and other mints, as well as thyme and rosemary, were scattered atop the rushes that covered the stone floors of castles and earthen floors of cottages. The herbs helped freshen the air with each step.

Pennyroyal has strong associations with the holiday season and is said to bloom on Christmas Day. It forms a mat over the ground to 16 inches high. Heavily branching, deep reddish stems support small, oval, glossy, dark green leaves that are are slightly serrated. Long spikes hold tiny purple-red flowers.

Planting and Care—In hot-summer regions, pennyroyal calls for a moist, semishaded garden. In cooler areas, locate in full sun and protect from cold temperatures. Plant rooted pieces of pennyroyal 6 inches apart in spring or fall. They quickly grow together to become an aromatic carpet. Pennyroyal may also adorn barren crevices and tumble over unsightly paving if watered regularly during dry periods. To maintain health of plantings, they may need to be replaced every three or four years. Pennyroyal is a good herb for window boxes and in containers. It can be easily controlled yet enjoyed—without taking up prime garden space.

Harvesting and Use—Its best known use is warding off insects, particularly fleas. One if its former names was "flea-away." Oil of pennyroyal,

spread in pantries, keeps out ants and other pests. A strong infusion of pennyroyal leaves makes an effective insect spray. Some people regard the smell of pennyroyal as "peppermint-like," while others associate it with citronella.

Caution: Avoid all contact with pennyroyal if you are pregnant.

Poliomintha, Mexican Oregano
Poliomintha longiflora

Tender shrub or perennial
Culinary, Medicinal, Ornamental
Grows 3 to 4 feet high, to 2 feet wide
Full sun, tolerates afternoon shade
Well-drained, moderately sandy soil

Poliomintha came into the North American nursery trade as a heat-tolerant ornamental for mild-winter regions. It is in the same family as Greek or Turkish oregano, *Origanum vulgare* subspecies *hirtum,* with similar flavor and uses.

Poliomintha grows as an attractive shrub with small, elliptical, glossy green leaves, and smooth, slightly reddish bark. Plants are easy to grow in containers. If you live in an area that freezes, use a container that is not too big to move indoors. Plants are more likely to survive low light conditions indoors if you taper off watering as fall approaches. This allows plants to enter a less-active growth phase.

The best feature of this semievergreen is the abundant, long, tubular, pinkish to lavender flowers that bloom throughout the spring and early fall. They come in whorls at the ends of branches and attract hummingbirds. New flowers often appear daily for weeks, especially if plants receive adequate moisture. Flowers are more profuse if not given fertilizer near or during bloom.

Planting and Care—Most easily propagated by nonflowering stem cuttings. Take any time during the growing season and root in moist sand or well-drained potting mix. If you live in an area that receives frost, take stem cuttings in August and overwinter them indoors.

Locate plants in full sun for more flowers and flavor, but supply some afternoon shade in hottest regions. Accepts any moderate, well-drained soil, even rocky soil. Provide with regular water.

Harvesting and Use—Unlike most herbs, the best time to harvest Mexican oregano is after flowering. Fresh, dried or frozen leaves can be used like oregano. Don't cook too long. The fresh leaves begin to lose their lovely, complex taste as soon as they are heated.

Flowers have a faint tang of oregano and make a colorful addition to green salads. Also use as an edible garnish on cooked greens, omelets, casseroles or meat platters. Medicinally, poliomintha has been used as a decoction to treat coughs and colds, especially those involving upper respiratory infections.

Rose
Rosa species

Hardy perennial shrub, climber, ground cover
Aromatic, Craft, Culinary, Medicinal, Ornamental
Size varies according to form and variety
Full sun
Fertile, well-drained soil

Unlike the assertive aromas of many flowers, the fragrance of roses is mysteriously haunting. The Romans believed that red roses are the flowers of love, growing from the blood of Venus when she was wounded by Cupid's dart. A Roman symbol of success and valor, roses are also believed to protect against the ills of overindulgence. They were strewn on the floors of banquet halls and woven into wreaths to crown the heads of guests. Perhaps because of this hedonistic history, and because they adorned the sensual statues of Cupid, Venus and Bacchus, roses were banned from the early Christian church.

Roses have played a perfumy part in Middle Eastern and European cuisine and medicine for centuries. They originated in Persia, where an extensive rose-water trade began as long ago as the 8th century. Roses, especially red roses, gained importance among the other herbs of the apothecary's garden. They were cultivated as an ingredient in syrups and conserves for the relief of many illnesses.

Fragrant roses worthy of your herb garden include:

Rosa gallica officinalis, the apothecary's rose, an achingly sweet, light crimson, semidouble flower dusted with golden stamens. Shrub form 3 to 4 feet high with similar spread.

R. centifolia, the cabbage or Provence rose, a predominantly pink bloomer with numerous petals composing each blossom—like a cabbage. It usually reaches 4 to 6 feet high.

R. damascena, usually a rich pink but occasionally a white-flowering species. Traditionally considered the rose for making *attar*, the fragrant rose oil. Attractive, often with sprawling growth, it grows 3 to 8 feet high, depending on variety.

R. X alba, produces sweet-scented, white or blush pink flowers supported by beautiful, gray-blue leaves. Ideally suited for border plantings in small gardens.

R. rugosa, which means rough or wrinkled leaves, is an attractive plant with thick, leathery, deeply veined leaves. Thick, prickly stems support pretty, large-petaled flowers that produce a clovelike fragrance. Naturally salt tolerant and cold hardy. Most plants grow 6 to 8 feet high.

R. eglanteria, sweetbrier rose, a strong apple-scented leaf shrub. This literary favorite from Chaucer to Shakespeare is hardy and fragrant, even when not in full bloom. Large, (10 to 12 feet) rambling and thorny, it bears pink flowers with five petals.

R. chinensis 'Old Blush', also known as 'Parson's Pink China' is a popular China rose. Plants are long-lived and produces profuse, fragrant, double pink flowers.

Planting and Care—Roses have a long list of cultural requirements. The basics include a minimum of six hours of sun daily. Afternoon shade rather than morning shade is preferred. Fertile, friable soil having good drainage, occasional insect and disease control, mulch and good air circulation aid healthy growth. If the summer is dry, provide regular, deep water. If winters are cold, plants need protection. Color and bloom time of these perennial shrubs vary according to variety. They range from 1-foot miniatures to climbers that reach up

Pennyroyal as Pest Control

Hanging baskets of pennyroyal on the porch will help keep insects away. Fresh leaves rubbed on picnic guests' arms and legs ward off mosquitoes, bees, flies, wasps and even chiggers.

Pennyroyal leaves applied to the hair of humans or the fur of pets will repel insect pests such as mosquitoes. It should not be used near the eyes or tender facial areas.

Below: Poliomintha, also known as Mexican oregano, is an attractive shrub with small, glossy green leaves and smooth, slightly reddish bark. Plants are easy to grow in containers.

Right: 'Old Blush', also known as 'Parson's Pink China', in combination with larkspur.

Below left: Rose hips (foreground) are the fruit of the rose.

Below right: Rose hips as they appear on a rose plant. This is 'Frau Dagmar Hartopp', a *Rosa rugosa* hybrid.

Left: Rue (background) is an attractive perennial shrub, growing 2 to 3 feet high, with chalky green, woody stems covered with flat, patterned, blue-green leaves. Flowers are bright yellow with scooped-end petals.

Below left: Rosemary flowers come in shades of blue to white, blooming in the axils of clustered leaves on older stems. They cover the aromatic foliage from late winter to early spring and are highly attractive to bees.

Below: In mild-winter regions, rosemary is a workhorse landscape plant. Prostrate rosemary covers and protects this steep slope.

Growing Roses Without Chemicals

A mild liquid soap solution helps control aphids. Add 2 tablespoons household dishwashing soap to 1 gallon of water and mix well. Spray, wait about one hour, then use a garden hose to wash away all traces of the soap. Do not use this treatment if temperatures are 90F or above or plant leaves may be damaged.

We also plant garlic and chives around our roses. From an ornamental viewpoint the effect is marvellous, but the efficiency of garlic and chives as bug deterrents is controversial.

to 20 feet. The diversity of their perfume ranges from no aroma to overwhelming. Older rose varieties usually have more fragrance than newer hybrids and the best cold tolerance.

Harvesting and Use—Step back in time and use your rose petals to perfume your life and flavor your food. First, smell and taste each type of rose before using. Some are bland and others are bitter. Strongly scented ones usually taste like their fragrance. In general, more fragrance usually equals more flavor.

Before preparing flowers for kitchen use, be certain they have not been sprayed with chemicals. Hothouse roses have likely been sprayed and aren't suitable for culinary use. Rinse organically grown blossoms in a bath of one tablespoon of vinegar to one cup of cold water to remove most insects. Shake flowers well. Grasp the open flower in one hand so that the stem is pointing upward. With a sharp pair of scissors, snip right below the stem. The petals will fall freely so you can inspect them for brown wilt and stray bugs. Trim off the white part at the base of each petal; it is bitter.

Rose petals can be added to jelly, butter, vinegar, syrup, tea cakes and desserts. They are ideal for crystallizing, are good macerated with wine and fruit, and make excellent garnishes for desserts and salads.

To prepare roses for crafts, pick flowers just as the blooms begin to open, but before they reach their full glory. Strip off thorns from the base of stems but do not remove leaves; these make a nice dark green filler. Keep bunches small to protect petals, and hang up to dry as soon as possible in warm air away from direct sunlight. Once dry, they will be brittle and easily damaged, so handle carefully and add roses last to projects or displays. Rose petals or rosebuds are classic ingredients in potpourri, too.

Medicinally and cosmetically, rose oil is appreciated for its feminine, sensual fragrance. Include this antidepressant in your massage, personal skin care, baths and vaporizer to treat sadness or long-term stress. Rose oil is often included in skin creams for its mild, antibacterial, astringent treatment of sensitive skin.

For a complete discussion of roses, refer to the Ironwood Press book, *The Natural Rose Gardener.*

Rosemary
Rosmarinus officinalis

Semihardy, woody perennial, low shrub
Craft, Culinary, Medicinal, Ornamental
2 to 6 feet high, to 6 feet wide
Full sun to partial shade
Almost any well-drained soil

Brush a sprig of rosemary through your fingers. The fragrance it releases is reminiscent of a seacoast with pines.

Rosemary is an herb of strong, diverse symbols. It has been considered the emblem of loyalty, friendship and remembrance. Where basil symbolized the quickening of love, rosemary was a token of its long-lasting qualities. Bridesmaids wove rosemary into the bridal wreath they presented to the bridegroom on the wedding day. It was also placed under nuptial mattresses to encourage faithfulness and discourage insects and mildew.

According to custom, rosemary twined in your hair stimulated the memory or helped prevent baldness, depending upon your need. Also connoting friendship, no more cherished party favor could be offered than a gilded rosemary twig.

Rosemary flourished through medieval and Renaissance periods. Every garden seemed to have a single bush or several, often pruned in fanciful or symmetrical shapes. The essential oil or the leaves and flowers were used as a bath freshener and mouthwash, in liniments and as a moth repellent.

Rosemary has been grown in gardens for so long that natural hybrids have occurred, resulting in forms suitable for many landscape situations. *Rosmarinus officinalis* has an upright, shrublike growth habit, reaching 3 to 6 feet high and as wide. Plants blend well with many gray-foliaged plants found in the herb garden.

R. officinalis 'Prostratus' is the ground-hugging form, more commonly grown in mild-winter regions of the West. It performs well as a cascading ground cover draped over a wall, on slopes or in the foreground of a flowerbed. The gray-green leaves create a dense, 2-foot-high plant that can spread 4 to 6 feet in diameter.

Leaves of all forms are needlelike with decurved edges and whitish undersides. Flowers come in shades of blue to white. They nestle in the axils of clustered leaves on younger stems and cover the aromatic foliage from late winter to early spring. They are highly attractive to bees.

Planting and Care—Plant from containers in early spring or in fall in mild-winter areas. Accepts almost any well-drained soil. Plant in full sun to partial shade. Water needs are low to moderate once established. Overwatering and too much fertilizer cause growth to become rank. To maintain a low, flowing form, cut back to hard wood, reducing foliage buildup in center of plant. Prune to maintain natural plant form every year or two in late winter, prior to the strong surge of early spring growth.

In cold-winter regions, rosemary cannot survive as a landscape plant, but it can be grown using the indoors-to-outdoors method described on page 146. Use a mix of perlite or large-grained, sterile sand, humus and potting soil for good drainage and aeration.

Grow outdoors in a sunny location. Accepts low water but performs best with regular irrigation. Reduced sunlight and lower daytime temperatures indoors lessen the need for water.

Harvesting and Use—Rosemary's components of tannin and camphor give it a moderate bitterness and pepperiness, especially good with foods high in fat like lamb roasts and pork or with bland foods such as potatoes or legumes. Dried rosemary generally can be substituted for fresh. Whole needles must be dried to preserve its oils. Tie in a cheesecloth bag or mince well before adding to foods so you won't chew on the tough needles. The flavor strength of the dried herb varies greatly, but usually one part dried equals about four parts fresh.

To sample the clean aroma and piney tang of rosemary, try the recipe for Mixed Herb Rice, shown at right.

Rue
Ruta graveolens

Perennial evergreen subshrub
Crafting, Ornamental
2 to 3 feet high, to 6 feet wide
Full sun to partial shade
Almost any well-drained soil

Priests in the early Christian church used rue branches to sprinkle holy water, giving it the name "herb o'grace." Rue has been a symbol of inner vision, sharpened eyesight and protection against evil and witchcraft. It is one of the classic herbs of Shakespeare and romance.

In Lithuania, rue is still used to announce engagements. In Britain, the floors of courtrooms were strewn with rue to prevent judges from catching "jail fever" and other diseases. During the plague, rue's pungent branches were sold in city markets to repel insects and ward off disease. The Chinese use rue tea today as an antidote for poison and malaria.

The plant is an attractive, small perennial shrub, growing 2 to 3 feet high, with chalky green, woody stems. It stands upright and is covered with flat, patterned, blue-green leaves. Its terminal leaflets are club-shaped, which give it a delicate, lace-like appearance. The flowers are bright yellow with scooped-end petals. Rue's musky scent is believed to repel garden pests such as the Japanese beetle.

Planting and Care—Plant seeds, container plants or cuttings in full sun to partial shade in average to poor soil. Locate rue as a low ornamental hedge toward the back of the border where it is less likely to come in contact with people, but where the foliage, flowers and seedheads can be enjoyed.

Harvesting and Use—Rue stays green well into winter, so it can be picked during cooler holiday months for fresh and dried arrangements. Press leaves rather than hanging them to dry. Rue's beautiful, beadlike seed pods with an open cross on top make unusual decorations and can be included in potpourri.

Caution: Do not take internally. Large amounts are toxic. Rue is especially dangerous to pregnant women. In warm weather, if your bare skin

"Young men and maids do ready stand With sweet Rosemary in their hands A perfect token of your virgin's life."
—Traditional ballad

Mixed Herb Rice

Cook long-grain white rice as usual except use chicken broth for liquid. Add 2 teaspoons each of fresh minced thyme, basil and rosemary, plus 1 tablespoon minced parsley to rice while cooking.

Above: Tricolor sage (left) and garden sage, also called common sage.

Above right: Tricolor sage shows off its attractive, multicolor foliage.

Right: From summer through fall, violet-blue flowers of garden sage appear in whorls. The flowers attract bees, hummingbirds and potpourri enthusiasts.

Bottom: *Salvia officinalis* 'Icterina', sometimes called 'Variegata', is known by the common name gold sage.

brushes against rue leaves, releasing plant oils, and is then exposed to sunlight, it can cause a rash or dermatitis.

Sage
Salvia species

Hardy to tender perennials or subshrubs
Cosmetic, Culinary, Ornamental
2 to 3 feet high, to 3 feet wide
Full sun
Almost any well-drained soil

In the Middle Ages, sage was prescribed as a cure-all and used much as aspirin is today. Its name from Latin *salvus*, means "safe" or "healthy." It was honored by the Chinese as a symbol of immortality.

Sage's culinary use in rich dishes developed from its reputation as a digestive aid. The Greeks and Romans used sage as a calmative for stomach and nerves. Regular use of sage tea was said to bring an even disposition to excitable natures and healthy old age to everyone. Sage was particularly recommended to older persons to help them restore failing memories and lift depression.

The Native Americans chewed fresh sage leaves to strengthen their gums and whiten their teeth. Sage tea has been used as a rinse to darken gray hair and relieve sunburn.

Among 800 or so known varieties of *Salvia*, *S. officinalis*, common or garden sage, is a cornerstone of the herb garden. After its first year as a tender-leafed plant, it becomes a sturdy, woody shrub 2 to 3 feet high. Its broad, long, gray-green leaves are slightly pebbly to the touch due to tiny hairs on its veined surfaces. The whole plant is aromatic, with the taste and smell of rosemary, pine and mint.

From summer through fall, violet-blue flowers appear in whorls on long spikes. They attract bees, hummingbirds and potpourri enthusiasts.

S. elegans, pineapple sage, has pineapple-flavored and scented leaves and flowers. Tubular scarlet flowers are most profuse in fall. Bright green leaves are more pointed and longer than those of common sage. It is less cold hardy (to 30F) so give it a protected location or plant in containers. Provide plenty of space and water to reach its full 4-foot height and spread, although plants seldom reach this size.

S. officinalis 'Icterina', sometimes called 'Variegata', known as gold sage, has bright gold and green primrose-marbled leaves. 'Tricolor' has green, cream and purple-red leaves. 'Purpurascens' has velvety gray-green leaves suffused with purple and violet-blue flowers in summer.

All are cold tender so grow in containers in all but the mildest climates.

Planting and Care—Germination from seed is tricky at best. Purchasing small transplants or making root cuttings in sand is usually more successful. If growing sage from seed, sow in early spring in slightly limey or sandy soil. Or propagate in early fall or spring by dividing established plants.

Plant in a well-drained, slightly elevated, sunny spot. As plants become established, water only when soil is dry. When sages become woody with age, remove all dead twigs and branches. Trim plants frequently to encourage healthy new growth and more profuse flowers.

Harvesting and Use—Sage helps balance the richness of certain foods. Use alone or in combination with thyme, marjoram or savory with pork, goose, duck, veal and fatty fish. A pinch of fresh or dried sage significantly improves the flavor of soups; onion, eggplant or tomato dishes; egg or cheese recipes; and cream sauces and gravies.

In addition to its traditional use as seasoning for Thanksgiving turkey and dressing, sausage, game and liver, sage adds its rich, lemony flavor to vegetables, breads and even sweets.

Common sage is favored by most cooks. It keeps its aroma and flavor well through extended cooking and drying periods. Others, such as pineapple sage, lavender sage and mint-leafed sage, are best when included in cold dishes or dried for potpourris and ornamental bouquets. To experience sage's versatile flavor, mince a small amount and add to your favorite cheese spread, whole-wheat muffin recipe or fresh apple cake before baking.

Sage is said to encourage the growth of rosemary, lavender and thyme; to repel the cabbage butterfly;

Sage and Cheese Torta

This recipe is our idea of the perfect pair—cheese and herbs—ancient essences with romantic bite. Layered with nuts and molded into an appealing shape, these earthy ingredients form a rich, tangy appetizer.

1/2 pound cream cheese, softened

3 tablespoons chopped fresh sage leaves, plus a few whole leaves or flower spikes for garnish

1/2 pound extra-sharp yellow cheddar cheese, shredded

1 cup pecans, toasted and chopped

Place cream cheese in food processor with chopped sage and blend well. Line a 2-cup mold with a thick cheesecloth. Arrange whole leaves or spikes in a decorative pattern on the cheese-clothed-lined mold. In layers, spread on half the cream cheese, then cheddar. Smooth out the layer and press gently. Top with pecans, press again, then smooth remaining cream cheese over pecans.

Fold ends of cheesecloth over top of mold and press lightly. Refrigerate torta overnight. To unmold, fold back the top of the cheesecloth. Invert a serving plate on top of the torta and flip them over together. Lift off the mold and carefully remove the cheesecloth. Serve torta with crackers.

and to improve the flavor and digestibility of cabbage if grown nearby.

Sage may still be found in hair preparations to prevent graying and in cleansing lotions for oily skin. It is also an ingredient in deodorants, perfumes and soaps.

St. John's Wort, Hypericum
Hypericum perforatum

Hardy, semiwoody, herbaceous perennial
Medicinal, Ornamental
1 to 3 feet high, to 1-1/2 feet wide
Full sun to partial shade
Accepts average to poor, acid to alkaline, even limestone soils

In the European Dark and Middle Ages, *Hypericum* was believed to have many magical and medicinal properties. It was known as "Heart of Jesus Oil" and "Grace of God." In England it treated mania, in Russia it protected from rabies, in Brazil it cured serpent bite, and in France the crushed leaves and flowers warded off evil spells.

With the rise of Christianity, hypericum became known as St. John's wort because it was often in flower on St. John's Day, June 24th. (*Wyrt* is Old English for *plant*.)

A medicine was made by placing flowers and leaves in oil or wine and allowing the mixture to sit for up to two years. It was viewed as miraculous that golden flowers, green leaves and pale liquid would produce a bright red pigment. The mixture was rubbed on joints or muscles to heal sprains and other injuries.

Plants reach 1 to 3 feet high. The smooth elliptical leaves are arranged opposite one another. Each leaf has numerous translucent oil glands that resemble tiny sunlike holes, hence the species name *perforatum*. The bright yellow lemon-scented flowers have five petals with a center sunburst of delicate stamens. The thin, dark green leaves provide a nice backdrop and create an informal garden border.
Planting and Care—Grow from seed, divisions or cuttings. The tiny, shiny black seeds are best planted in the fall; spring sowings generally result in poor germination. Take nonflowering stem cuttings in early summer and root in moist sand. Divide established plants in the fall or early spring.

Locate in full sun, although some shade is acceptable. Plants naturally occur in waste places, so virtually any soil will do, even limestone soil. Fertilization is not necessary.
Harvesting and Use—To capture the most intense essence, plants should be cut as flowering begins. For craft weavers and spinners who prefer subtle and variable shades, the flowers of St. John's wort yield a yellow dye with alum, or a violet-red silk dye with alcohol. Seasonal wreaths and bouquets are enhanced by fresh or dried sprigs. Although these may seem purely ornamental, St. John's wort's decorative traditions are poignant. Because its bright flower symbolized the sun, which casts out darkness, St. John's wort was once tied in bunches at the windows and doors of homes and churches to protect newborn children, ward off lightning and fire and banish evil spirits. To evoke illumination, eager young girls would hang the herb nearby or sleep with it under their pillows on St. John's Night (Midsummer's Day) to enable them to foresee who would become their husbands.

The leaves and flowers of St. John's wort are not perfect nor instant cures for calming the mind. They do offer some promise for healing the body. AIDS patients given St. John's wort tincture reported gains against the virus, including improved immune function, reduced fever, reduced swelling of lymph nodes, improved appetite, and heightened energy and mood. Bruises, wounds, varicose veins and burns treated with an ointment infused with St. John's wort may heal faster and with less scarring than with conventional treatments.

Antidepressant drugs inhibit the chemical activity of monoamine oxidase (MAO) in the body; hypericin (a component of the herb's red oil) appears to be a member of this important drug class. Doctors in Germany claim that after taking St. John's wort tincture or tea for at least two to three months, many patients with mild to moderate depression show improvements in appetite, feelings of self-worth and sleep patterns.
Caution: St. John's wort may be harm-

ful if too much is consumed, or if consumed for too long a period. High doses of the herb may also cause sensitivity to the sun. It is sold over the counter in capsule form. Read and follow all label directions.

Santolina, Lavender Cotton
Santolina species

Hardy perennial
Craft, Ornamental
1-1/2 to 2 feet high, to 4 feet wide
Full sun
Almost any well-drained soil

Two species, *Santolina chamaecyparissus* and *S. virens,* are commonly grown as ornamental plants, often in combination with each other. *S. chamaecyparissus* has buttonlike, bright yellow flowers that bloom in summer on unclipped plants. Where hardy, its aromatic, silvery growth serves as a ground cover, border, accent or foreground. Leaves are also aromatic. For a clean and compact look, clip off spent flowers.

S. virens is a vivid green cousin with rough, threadlike, textured leaves, and smaller yellow flowers. It establishes faster than *S. chamaecyparissus* and tolerates more moisture.
Planting and Care—Plants are generally available in containers at nurseries. Also readily propagated from cuttings. Early spring or fall plantings in mild-winter areas are preferred. These tough small shrubs thrive in hot, sunny conditions in well-drained soil. For a solid ground cover, space at 3-foot centers; for border or low, informal hedge, plant at 2-foot centers. Shape plants after bloom into a flowing pattern or as a formal hedge.
Harvesting and Use—Prune santolina throughout its growing season. To dry, spread foliage on screens. Leaves and twigs make effective moth fumigants for winter wardrobes. Santolina's rough foliage (it reminds one of sea coral) adds texture and pungent aroma to wreaths, potpourri and tussie-mussies. See page 167. To make an entrance more bug-resistant, place fresh-cut santolina stems beneath the welcome mat. Plants are also effective deer deterrents.

Soapwort, Bouncing Bet
Saponaria officinalis

Hardy herbaceous perennial
Aromatic, Cosmetic, Medicinal,
 Ornamental
1 to 3 feet high, to 2 feet wide
Full sun to light shade
Fertile to poor well-drained soil

(Also known as Latherwort, Sheepwort, Bruisewort, Wild Sweet William, Fuller's Herb)
Before people knew how to make soap, plants that produced lathering substances, known as saponins, were highly valued. Soapwort was, and is, the quintessential soap plant. Cleansing saponins can be found in the leaves, stems, roots and even in flowers. This middle-eastern native proved so popular that it was soon carried around the world. Soapwort was used medicinally for skin problems, but it is a strong purgative and is not recommended for internal consumption.

In optimal growing conditions, plants can reach 3 feet high, forming spreading clumps. Whorls of oval, pale green leaves surround the upright, sturdy stems. Pink to whitish flowers bloom mid- to late summer. Some gardeners grow soapwort just for the faintly sweet, raspberry-scented flowers. *Saponaria officinalis* 'Rubra Plena' and 'Flora Plena' are garden-worthy cultivars with double flowers.
Planting and Care—Plant seeds indoors in late winter. Seedlings can be set out after danger of frost is past. Sow seed directly in place during spring or fall, but plants may not reach flowering stage the first year. Soapwort is easy to propagate by dividing creeping rootstocks in early fall.

Plants form dense clumps in full sun but tolerate light shade. Any soil is acceptable, but prefers moist, rich, well-drained soil. They are enthusiastically invasive, spreading by roots and seeds. Avoid by cutting off spent flowers before they can set seed.
Harvesting and Use—Fresh bouquets impart a light, fruitlike scent with a hint of clove. The fragrance may remind you of carnation, a member of the same family. Flowers can also be

Bouncing Bet

Why the name "Bouncing Bet?" This herb's soap-lathering branches are said to have been used by bar-maids to clean beer bottles. These spunky maids of early England were often referred to as "Bet" or "Betsy."

Right: Soapwort can reach 3 feet high and forms spreading clumps. Whorls of oval, pale green leaves surround the upright, sturdy stems.

Far right: Pink to whitish flowers of soapwort bloom mid- to late summer.

Center: A comparison of foliage of silvery *Santolina chamaecyparissus* and bright green *Santolina virens*.

Below: *Santolina chamaecyparis-sus* has buttonlike, bright yellow flowers that bloom in summer on unclipped plants. Where hardy, its aromatic, silvery growth serves as a ground cover, border, accent or foreground in shrub beds.

Far left: Sweet woodruff grows as a shade-loving ground cover with rough hairy stems and whorls of dark green, pointed leaves. A profusion of tiny, white, star-shaped flowers appear in early summer.

Left: St. John's wort produces bright yellow, lemon-scented flowers that have five petals with a center sunburst of delicate stamens.

Below left: Southernwood's gray-green leaves are finely divided, creating a light, feathery texture.

Below: The role of society garlic, *Tulbaghia violacea,* is primarily an ornamental one. It is a popular herb garden border and companion in flower and vegetable beds.

New Potatoes with Society Garlic Blossoms

2 pounds new potatoes
1/3 cup sour cream
1/4 cup society garlic
　　blossoms, minced
Salt and pepper to taste
2 tablespoons society
　　garlic blossoms (garnish)

Cover unpeeled potatoes with water in a saucepan and simmer for 20 minutes or until tender; drain. Cut potatoes into quarters. In a bowl, combine sour cream, 1/4 cup blossoms and salt and pepper. Add potatoes and toss gently. Sprinkle blossoms on top for garnish. Serves 6.

Sorrel Cheese Spread

6 ounces Armenian
　　string cheese
1 pound ricotta cheese
1/2 cup young sorrel
　　leaves, coarsely chopped
1 garlic clove, minced
Cayenne pepper to taste
Salt and pepper to taste

Shred string cheese into fine strands. Mix with other ingredients. Let stand at least one hour at cool room temperature to blend flavors. Serve spread with unsalted crackers.

Yields about 2-1/2 cups.

dried and used in potpourri, although they lose some of their scent. Leaf, stems or roots can be boiled in soft water and used to shampoo hair or wash delicate tapestry fabrics. In the garden, soapwort proves to be a low-care but attractive, dense ground cover.

Caution: For external use only. Soapwort has been proven toxic when ingested by livestock. Roots are very high in saponins, which can kill aquatic life, including fish, frogs and salamanders. Do not plant near ponds or ditches or where runoff occurs.

Society Garlic
Tulbaghia violacea

Tender perennial
Culinary, Ornamental
1 to 1-1/2 feet high, to 1 foot wide;
flower stems to 2 feet high
Full sun to partial shade
Light, sandy soil

This plant looks and smells as though it belongs in the *Allium* genus, but society garlic, *Tulbaghia violacea,* is related only by common name. Belonging to the lily family (as do onions and garlic), its origins are South African. Society garlic's role is primarily an ornamental one; it is a popular herb garden border and creative companion in flower and vegetable beds. Its lovely starburst flowers are often praised for their long-blooming service from early summer through fall. The grayish green leaves, flat and reedlike, grow in a neat, round clump. The leafless, straw-thin stalks, with a cluster of 7 to 20 flowers, shoot up taller.

‘Silver Lace’ has green leaves edged with white. ‘Tricolor’ has delicately variegated leaves in shades of green, white and pink.

Planting and Care—Society garlic grows profusely in mild-winter regions. It will not survive where temperatures drop below 20F. Plants do best in full sun and light, sandy soil. Divide individual bulblets from the mother plant in the fall or early spring. Set 8 to 12 inches apart, just below the surface of the soil. When they become crowded, dig them up (perhaps every four or five years) and

reset. You may start from seed but growth is slow. Northern gardeners will need to move potted clumps outdoors in summer and bring inside when cold weather returns. Alternatively, transplant pots into the ground during summer and repot in the fall. A low-maintenance herb; we suggest cutting spent blooms, keeping soil moderately moist when flowers are in bloom and keeping soil dry when plants are dormant.

Harvesting and Use—This herb thrives when it is pinched and nibbled—clip leaves and flowers anytime. Savor a garlicky onion-scented leaf. It's tasty when chopped like chives. The dainty blossoms lack the oniony odor but certainly deserve an opportunity to garnish your dinner salad. Also add to stir-fries, salads, soups, egg dishes and steamed vegetables whenever a hint of garlic is desired.

Sorrel, Miner's Lettuce
Rumex acetosa

Hardy herbaceous perennial
Culinary, Ornamental
1-1/2 to 4 feet high, 1-1/2 feet wide
Full sun
Rich, moist, well-drained soil

Sorrel is one of the first greens to show up after winter. It is most enjoyed in spring and early summer.

Two common varieties are available: French sorrel, *Rumex scutatus,* and English or garden sorrel, *R. acetosa.* French sorrel has small, rounded, spear-shaped, bright green leaves. Growth is low and spreading. The English variety has long, broad, dull green leaves and stems.

Sorrel had the reputation for preventing scurvy, and to "cool any inflammation and heat of the blood— a cordial to the heart." Juice from the leaves was supposed to remove stains from hands. Today sorrel is valued for its high content of vitamins A and C.

Inconspicuous, brownish red flowers borne in slender, loose spikes appear early to midsummer. They are followed by tiny hard fruits. Flower spikes can be dried and used in arrangements and potpourri. However, to encourage leaf production and prevent leaves from becoming tough, cut back flowering stems.

Planting and Care—A hardy perennial that is resistant to frost. Easy to grow from seed sown outdoors in midspring, or transplant from containers. Prefers full sun and rich, well-drained soil. Does moderately well in partial shade. Hot weather can cause leaves to taste bitter. Adding a 3- to 4-inch layer of mulch will cool roots and retain moisture.

Harvesting and Use—In the kitchen, sorrel is known for two classic French dishes—sorrel soup and sorrel sauce. Its flavor is slightly sour with a hint of lemon zest. Leaves are used like spinach to brighten egg and vegetable dishes, and in sauces for beef, chicken or fish. Cooked foods need less salt when sorrel is used. Add a fresh leaf to any cream soup during the last few minutes of cooking. Use young leaves (less than 6 inches long) sparingly to perk up a simple salad. This herb, like parsley, freshens the breath. Relish its clear, cooling accent in the recipe for Sorrel Cheese Spread, page 110.

Southernwood
Artemisia abrotanum

Hardy woody perennial shrub
Craft, Ornamental
3 to 4 feet high, to 2 feet wide
Full sun
Almost any well-drained soil

Southernwood is an herb traditionally included in a bride's wedding plans. It is the lover's plant, known as *lad's love* or *maiden's ruin*. Believed to be an aphrodisiac and love charm, sprays of southernwood were included in bouquets country boys offered to their lady loves.

This woody perennial forms a multistemmed clump 3 to 4 feet high. Soft fragrance from its lacy leaves fills the air, and can be lemon, camphor or tangerine, depending on the variety. Gray-green leaves are finely divided, creating a light, feathery texture. Tiny yellowish white flowers occasionally bloom mid- to late summer. With periodic trimming it is used as a shrubby border or small hedge.

Planting and Care—Plant in spring from root divisions, stem cuttings or containers. Allow about 2 feet between plants for the aggressive, spreading root system. Grows in almost any soil if it has sunlight and regular water. If grown in containers and brought indoors, it has a dormant period when the small, needlelike leaves drop but new leaves will replace them.

Harvesting and Use—New Englanders in the 18th and 19th centuries appreciated the plant's stimulating odor and carried branches to church to prevent drowsiness during long sermons. Before there were commercial insecticides, housekeepers would place branches of the camphor- and lemon-scented varieties in food closets and wardrobes to repel moths, fleas and ants. Southernwood is said to deter a variety of garden pests, the tomato hornworm in particular.

The strong, sweet, aromatic leaves are wonderful additions to sachets and potpourris. Herb baskets and wreaths can be made from the pliable, sturdy branches. Branches also produce a yellow dye.

Sweet Annie
Artemisia annua

Annual
Craft, Medicinal, Ornamental
6 to 10 feet high, to 2 feet wide
Full sun
Average to poor soil if well drained

(Also known as Sweet Wormwood, Sweet Mugwort)
An attractive annual that can reach 10 feet in a season, sweet Annie is adorned with lacy, bright yellowish green leaves that have a sweet, basil and honeylike fragrance. The entire plant turns a beautiful red with cool crisp weather in fall. Spikes of small, yellowish green flowers on typically reddish stems appear in midsummer.

Native to southern Europe and western Asia, sweet Annie often grows as a weed in disturbed soils. At some point plants were carried to China, perhaps as seeds stuck to Mongol saddle cloths. The Chinese were quick to incorporate sweet Annie into their pharmacopoeia. They used it to treat jaundice and malaria, as well as to stop bleeding of wounds.

Planting and Care—Sow seed in place in fall or start seed indoors in

Sweet Annie Caution

If you are sensitive to pollen, you may have an allergic reaction (sneezing, coughing, eyes watering) when working with sweet Annie. Try harvesting it just before it blooms, or mist harvested plants with water or hair spray to prevent pollen from dispersing.

Southernwood Coat Hanger Insect Repellent
This is an effective moth repellent for winter suits and coats when they are in storage during the summer months.

1 heaping tablespoon dried southernwood
1 teaspoon crushed cinnamon stick
Muslin bag, triangular, each side 2 inches long

Crumble the dried southernwood and mix with the crushed cinnamon. Add this mixture to the muslin bag. Attach the bag to the coat hanger with a ribbon.

Southernwood Fragrant Floor Cleaner

Boil a large bunch of lavender, southernwood or wormwood and tansy in 2 to 3 gallons of water for 10 to 15 minutes. Add 1/4 cup vinegar, then cool. Strain the mixture and pour into a bucket. Mop floors for a cleansing, pleasing fragrance.

Above right: Tansy grows as an upright, short-lived perennial with rich, green, featherlike foliage.

Above: Tansy produces numerous, golden yellow, buttonlike flowers midsummer through fall.

Right: In the garden, French tarragon is a tidy perennial with erect stems draped by slender, smooth, dark green leaves.

Below: Sweet Annie is adorned with lacy, bright yellowish green leaves that have a sweet, basil and honey fragrance.

early spring, but seedlings typically do not transplant well. Overplant, then thin survivors to 1-1/2 to 2 feet apart. Locate in full sun in any well-drained soil. Survives with little water but performs best with regular irrigation. Plants self-seed prolifically.

Harvesting and Use—Leaves can be picked before flowering or whole plant can be cut when flowering peaks. Leaves have a sweet fragrance and are wonderful in potpourri. An herbal bath with sweet Annie and chamomile helps relieve muscle aches. The slender, feathery-leaved stalks dry well and add a nice texture to informal arrangements. See photos, page 169. Keep a wreath of sweet Annie in the bathroom; the steam will cause it to release its wonderful, herbal fragrance.

Caution: Pregnant women should not use sweet Annie.

Sweet Marjoram
Origanum marjorana

Tender perennial grown as annual
Cosmetic, Culinary, Medicinal,
Ornamental
2 feet high, to 2 feet wide
Full sun
Rich, light, well-drained soil

Native to the Mediterranean and the Orient, sweet marjoram has been grown as a culinary and medicinal herb since ancient times. It came to convey the sentiment of a blush, happiness and consolation.

The ancient Greeks and Romans included sweet marjoram in their food, perfumes and medicines. They crowned young lovers with it, and the dead were considered blessed if it grew on their graves. Marjoram was introduced to Britain during the Middle Ages and was used as a strewing herb.

A tender perennial, it is usually grown as an annual unless planted in a frost-free location. It grows as an upright shrub to 2 feet high with reddish stems and small, fuzzy, greyish oval leaves. Small white or purplish two-lipped flowers bloom in midsummer, arranged in roundish clusters or knots in the leaf's axils. All parts of the plant are aromatic.

Planting and Care—Sow seed out-doors in spring in somewhat rich, light, well-drained soil. Also propagate by cuttings or root division. Seeds germinate well but seedlings are slow growing. Providing seedlings with some shade often improves growth. Do not overwater. After plants are established encourage new, bushy growth by removing flower-buds before they open.

Harvesting and Use—Marjoram is cultivated commercially in many countries, including the United States. Its essential oil with a spicy fragrance is considered beneficial for gastrointestinal disorders and digestion. It is an ingredient in ointments and preparations for alleviating rheumatism.

Sweet marjoram is primarily grown as a culinary herb, adding an unexpected bitter bite backed up by a minty-camphorous sensation. Use it to enhance soups, sauces and meat dishes. Leaves can be picked from the garden as needed. Potency is best just before flower clusters begin to appear, but unlike many herbs, marjoram retains much of its flavor months after drying. To savor marjoram, try our recipe for Marjoram Cornbread, provided at right.

Sweet Woodruff
Galium odoratum

Hardy herbaceous perennial
Aromatic, Culinary, Ornamental
6 to 12 inches high, to 12 inches wide,
rooting at nodes
Full shade
Moist, humusy, well-drained soil

(Also called Woodruff, Waldmeister, Musc de Bois)
Sweet woodruff is a European herb long valued for its sweet scent reminiscent of new-mown hay, honey and vanilla. It was strewn on floors, protected linen and scented potpourri. Like many members of the genus *Galium,* it was stuffed in mattresses and was preferred over straw because of its sweet fragrance and ability to repel bedbugs.

Sweet woodruff is probably best known as an ingredient of German May wine, a wine used to celebrate the end of winter. It is made by macerating woodruff in early white wine. This is one way to make a thin, harsh-

Sweet Marjoram Cornbread

3/4 cup cornmeal, preferably stone ground
2-1/4 cups all-purpose flour
3/4 cup sugar
1 teaspoon baking powder
2 teaspoons baking soda
Pinch of salt
2 tablespoons minced fresh marjoram leaves, or 1-1/2 teaspoons dried leaves
1 cup buttermilk
2 eggs
1/4 cup vegetable oil or melted butter
3/4 teaspoon lemon extract

Preheat oven to 375F. Mix cornmeal, flour, sugar, baking powder, baking soda and salt in a large bowl. Add marjoram.
In a small bowl, combine liquid ingredients and whisk for one minute. Add liquid ingredients to the dry and blend well.
Pour batter into greased extra-large muffin tin (six muffins) and bake for 30 minutes, or until a cake tester inserted in the center comes out clean.
Let bread cool for 10 minutes before serving.
Serves 6.

tasting wine palatable.

This herb grows as a shade-loving ground cover, with rough hairy stems and whorls of dark green, pointed leaves. A profusion of tiny, white, star-shaped flowers appear in early summer.

Galium verum, lady's bedstraw, is similar to sweet woodruff, producing yellow flowers. It grows in the same mat-forming manner as sweet woodruff. It is used for dye and as a curdling agent for cheese.

Planting and Care—Plants root readily at the nodes. The best way to propagate is by division or rooted cuttings. Both can be done at almost any time. When planting, place starts with roots close to soil surface, spacing about 1 foot apart. Seed is slow to germinate. Requires moist, humusy, well-drained soil. Responds well to regular applications of nitrogen fertilizer.

One of the few herbs to require deep to partial shade. Strong direct sunlight will burn plants; excessive heat will kill them. In warm, dry-summer regions, plants may die back above ground, but roots often survive beneath the soil surface. They sometimes recover with cooler weather if the soil is kept moist.

Harvesting and Use—The long stems make an excellent backing or central core for herbal wreaths. Weave the core while stems and leaves are fresh and allow to dry. Leaves and stems can be used in potpourri and perfumes or sewn in muslin bags to scent closets, linens or dresser drawers.

For a type of May wine, add fresh sprigs of sweet woodruff to sherry and steep overnight. Serve this concoction chilled or pour over fresh fruit such as melon or strawberries.

Caution: In general, internal use of sweet woodruff is not recommended. Immoderate consumption of infusions and decoctions has induced symptoms of poisoning, including dizziness, vomiting and internal bleeding. The United States Food and Drug Administration considers sweet woodruff safe for use only in alcoholic beverages.

Tansy, Featherfoil
Tanacetum vulgare

Hardy herbaceous perennial
Craft, Ornamental
3 to 4 feet high, 2 to 3 feet wide
Full sun to afternoon shade
Average soil high in organic matter

The name tansy is derived from the Greek word *athanasia*, meaning *immortality*. In ancient times, tansy was used in burial preparations. It has also been used as a strewing herb, insecticide and disinfectant. Horses were rubbed down with tansy leaves to repel stinging flies and to make their coats shine. Bundles were hung near meat to help keep flies away, and plants were located beside doors for the same purpose.

Native to Europe, tansy has become naturalized in North America. It grows as an upright, short-lived perennial with rich, green, featherlike foliage. Leaves are highly divided, similar to marigold leaves, only a bolder green. Numerous golden yellow, buttonlike flowers appear midsummer and last through fall, adding a charming splash of golden yellow color to the herb or perennial garden. Flowers appear to repel honeybees but do not seem to affect wasps. Be aware of this if you grow tansy near other bee-pollinated plants, especially if you plan to collect seed for replanting. (It is thought tansy flowers are pollinated by beetles.) Tansy is reputed to be a deer-proof ornamental.

Tanacetum vulgare var. *crispum*, curled tansy, is similar except it grows to 2 feet high. Fragrant leaves are crinkly, curly and darker green. It seldom flowers.

T. capitulatum, an alpine plant native to the American West, forms a dense, low cushion with characteristic feathery leaves.

T. nuttallii, named for the botanical explorer Nuttall, is an alpine tansy that does well in rock gardens.

Planting and Care—Sow fresh seed or divide plants in fall or spring. Spreads prolifically from underground stems and can become invasive. Site plants carefully and consider curtailing spread with an underground edging.

A member of the sunflower family,

tansy prefers full sun. Accepts partial shade, although the plants may become leggy. Pinch lanky stems to correct. Planting along a wall or fence supplies extra support. Pinch long branches to encourage shorter, fuller plants. Grows well in rich loam as well as in average soils. For best bloom, water plants evenly throughout the season, but soil must be well drained. Accepts some drying.

Harvesting and Use—Flowers are considered "everlasting." They dry well, retaining bright color and are nice additions to potpourri and flower arrangements.

Tansy boasts a strong, gingerlike scent. Place dried leaves only in sachets to deter moths. Do not use the flowers because they may contain cigarette beetle larvae, which eat woolens and other clothing.

One unusual use for tansy is as a compost pile ingredient. It appears to be efficient at taking potassium out of the soil. Bolster your compost's potassium content by adding tansy, minus its seed heads.

Caution: Like other members of the genus *Tanacetum* (which includes costmary and feverfew), do not take tansy internally. It has caused violent physical reactions and even death when consumed as a medicinal tea. Expectant mothers should not use the plant at all.

French Tarragon
Artemisia dracunculus var. *sativa*

Hardy perennial
Culinary, Ornamental
2 feet high, 1-1/2 feet wide
Full sun to partial shade
Rich, light or sandy well-drained soil

(Also called Dragon's Mugwort, Tarragon)
French tarragon has become an herb not for the cook, but for the chef. Americans who have come to appreciate tarragon's licoricelike flavor and aroma can thank European gourmets who introduced this herb to our cuisine.

The word *tarragon* probably comes from the Arabic *tarkhun*. Its similarity to the Greek word *drakoneion*, little dragon, has given rise to its reputation as "the dragon herb." Nibbling the fresh herb does cause the tongue

to feel slightly numb. Others point to its coiled, serpentlike roots as the source of this herb's beastly identity.

French tarragon is often confused with its Russian cousin, *A. dracunculus* sub. *dracunculoides*. The true French green offers the sensory satisfaction of anise and vanilla. In the garden, it appears as a tidy perennial, with erect stems draped by slender, smooth, dark green leaves. Russian tarragon, by contrast, has little flavor, its leaves are larger and its growth is more coarse.

Planting and Care—French tarragon can be tricky to grow. It rarely blooms and never sets seed. If you see seed for "tarragon," it is probably the weedy, tasteless Russian version, which will attempt to take over your garden. The culinary tarragon is propagated entirely from root or stem cuttings. Treat a new plant as you would an asparagus crown, planting it in fairly rich, well-worked soil. Tarragon tolerates partial shade but prefers full sun. If you live in a hot, humid climate, try growing tarragon in a sphagnum-lined basket that can be moved to a cooler spot in summer heat or at midday. If that doesn't work, consider growing Mexican mint marigold, *Tagetes lucida*, as a flavorful substitute. See page 85.

As tarragon matures, the roots of tarragon grow inward, twisting tighter and tighter, strangling the plant, and its quality consequently deteriorates. It is best to dig the "little dragon" up every third spring, divide the roots and reset them. This will ensure a garden of healthy, abundant and more flavorful tarragon.

Winter warning: In areas where the temperature dips well below freezing and there is no insulating snow cover, provide tarragon plants with a blanket of winter mulch (hay, loose straw, or pine boughs). This protects its shallow root system from repeated freezing and thawing.

Harvesting and Use—Harvest sparingly the first year, but after plants are established leaves may be used fresh anytime. The plant can be completely cut back if needed twice during the season. Wrap fresh sprigs in paper towels, seal in a plastic bag and refrigerate up to one week. Fresh is best, but when you must use the dried leaf,

Tarragon

Charlemagne, a French king in the eighth century, liked the flavor of tarragon so much that he ordered it planted on all his estates. Later it became popular in England and was listed as a garden plant in Dutch settlements in North America in 1650. Thomas Jefferson grew tarragon and shared his plants with friends.

Absolut Tarragon

A libation sure to please the tarragon lover.

1 quart Absolut vodka
1 large bunch of fresh tarragon sprigs, rinsed and patted dry
1 tablespoon mixed whole peppercorns
1 tablespoon sugar

Mix all ingredients, re-bottle and allow flavors to infuse for at least one week before consuming. Store in a cool, dark cupboard.

Above: A selection of thymes. From left: Common thyme, lemon thyme, English thyme, silver thyme and woolly thyme.

Right: *Thymus citriodorus* 'Aureus' makes a touchable, fragrant mat.

Below right: Silver thyme, *Thymus vulgaris* 'Argenteus'.

Below: English thyme (left) with 'Lemon Mist' thyme (right).

substitute one-third the amount. Tarragon marries successfully with sweet basil, oregano, thyme, garlic and parsley, chervil and chives—the classic French blend, *fines herbes.*

On its own, tarragon's pronounced flavor dresses up chicken, veal and seafood, as well as cheese and egg dishes. It does not go especially well with strongly flavored vegetables such as broccoli, brussels sprouts, or cauliflower, nor does it add much to baking, sweets, pastas or tea. Better choices are spinach, salad greens, tomatoes, carrots, mushrooms or zucchini. Because of tarragon's high essential oil content, use it sparingly. Add it at the last moment of cooking. Otherwise, its potency tends to cook out or it becomes bitter.

Tarragon is delicious preserved in white wine vinegar or extra virgin olive oil. It makes a memorable mustard and one of the best herb butters. Excellent as a salt substitute.

Thyme
Thymus species

Hardy evergreen perennial
Cosmetic, Crafts, Culinary, Medicinal, Ornamental
1 to 2 feet high, 1 to 2 feet wide
Full sun to partial shade
Light, well-drained soil

Thyme has long been a symbol of bravery, and valued for its antiseptic qualities. Dating back to the classical age, the powerful *Thymus capitatus,* which flourishes throughout Greece, was commonly harvested by people of the region. Its tiny leaves were used in baths, strewn in temples and burned as incense to purify the air. In the 17th century, England's Culpeper recommended thyme for coughs, melancholy, even hangovers: "an infusion of the leaves removes the headache occasioned by inebriation."

There are about 350 species of this classic, aromatic herb. The most common include:

Common thyme (garden thyme), *Thymus vulgaris,* has long been appreciated as a versatile culinary seasoning. Growth is upright with woody stems. It is a perennial evergreen and seldom reaches over 1 foot high. Leaves are narrow, dark green to gray-green, and profusely aromatic. Bees find plants irresistible.

Creeping thyme, *T. praecox* sub. *arcticus,* has tiny spreading leaves that hug the ground, making it an attractive and useful ground cover.

Mother-of-thyme, *T. praecox arcticus (T. serpyllum),* is ideal for that most trying of conditions—spaces between flagstone or other paving—as well as on banks and in rock gardens. Although it is not useful in the kitchen, its red-purple flowers provide an appealing carpet. The soft, floppy branches spread quickly, forming a dense cover.

Woolly thyme, *T. pseudolanuginosus,* grows scarcely 1/2 inch high, producing touchable, woolly gray foliage. It, too, is well-suited to growing between stepping stones.

T. X citriodorus, lemon thyme, is low growing and a delicious culinary herb. Lemon-scented, oval, dark green leaves are wonderful for cooking and crafts. Pale lilac flowers bloom in summer.

T. X citriodorus 'Aureus', golden lemon thyme, produces colorful, gold-splashed, lemony leaves. Plants require winter protection.

T. vulgaris 'Argenteus', silver thyme, grows as a shrub in an irregular shimmery mound. Leaves are olive-green bordered with a narrow, yellowish white band.

T. vulgaris 'Broadleaf English' grows upright, similar to 'Narrowleaf French' but with greener broad leaves that have hearty flavor.

T. vulgaris 'Narrowleaf French' produces stiff upright growth with narrow, gray-green leaves and a sweet, pepper-pine flavor.

T. herba-barona, caraway thyme, is a wiry, creeping, slow-growing sub-shrub. Minute, dark green leaves smell irresistibly of nutty spice. Bears clusters of pink to mauve flowers.

Planting and Care—Easy to grow from seed. Sow the tiny, round seeds on moist soil and cover with a fine layer of sifted soil. Water well and keep the soil evenly moist. In one to two weeks, if soil temperatures are near 70F, seedlings should emerge.

In the garden, thymes thrive and are most flavorful when given lots of sun—an absolute minimum of four hours each day. They also need well-

Walnut, Thyme and Gorgonzola Crostini

1/2 cup butter at room temperature
18 1/4-inch-thick baguette bread slices, cut diagonally
6 tablespoons chopped toasted walnuts
3 ounces Gorgonzola cheese, crumbled
3 tablespoons fresh thyme, leaves only
Fresh thyme sprigs for garnish

Preheat oven to 400F. Spread butter over one side of each baguette slice. Arrange baguette slices on baking sheet, butter-side up. Bake baguette slices until golden, about 12 minutes. Cool. Reduce oven temperature to 350F. Mix walnuts, Gorgonzola and thyme in medium bowl.

Spoon nut mixture evenly on top of baguette toasts, pressing to adhere. Bake toasts until cheese melts, about 6 minutes. Cool crostini slightly. Arrange on platter and garnish with thyme sprigs.

Serves 6.

Violet Salad

Tear the leaves of violets,
butter lettuce, salad burnet
and endive and place in a
large bowl. Add a dressing
of olive oil and masala wine.
Toss, garnish with violet
blossoms and serve.

Sloe Gin and Valerian

Sloe gin originally contained
pennyroyal and valerian
extracts to calm the fraught
housewife, which gave it the
name "mother's ruin."

drained soil; sandy loam is ideal. Thymes are content to grow in containers outdoors or indoors.

Because thyme is so hardy, a plant may thrive for years. If grown for culinary use, replace plants every two to three years, or prune severely each spring. This will ensure fresh, more flavorful growth on young stems.

Harvesting and Use—Thymes belong to the mint family, and, like their relatives, plants are rich in volatile oils. The primary oil *thymol* is a powerful antiseptic, beneficial in healing lotions and salves. It is claimed to relieve respiratory and intestinal ailments. Used as a gargle and mouthwash, as a wash for cuts and an appetite stimulant.

Thyme can serve as a deodorant and its astringent, healing qualities benefit skin. In the home it can be an air purifier. Its oil can be used to scent candles. Pamper yourself and your family by sprinkling dried thyme among household linens. Thyme can be an ingredient in soaps and perfumes as well as in potpourri and herb pillows.

Thyme is a versatile and strong seasoning herb, so avoid using it with a heavy hand. Strip stems and add leaves to soups, salads, stuffings, pork or lamb, marinades and herb vinegars, oils and teas.

Valerian
Valeriana officinalis

**Hardy herbaceous perennial
Cosmetic, Medicinal, Ornamental
3 to 5 feet high, spreading to 3 feet wide
Full sun to light shade
Rich, moist, well-drained soil**

(Also called Garden Heliotrope, True Valerian, European Valerian, German Valerian, Great Wild Valerian, Vandalroot, Allheal)

This is an ancient medicinal herb grown for its fleshy root. In the past, it has been used as a sedative to treat epilepsy, hysteria, nervous afflictions, emotional distress, insomnia, convulsions and intestinal spasms. It is still used in Europe as a nonprescription sedative. The USDA and FDA have not approved valerian for drug use in the U.S.

Oil of valerian root is used to add a mossy note to perfumes. Cats and rats are attracted to the scent of the roots,

especially when the roots are dried. The Pied Piper, who lured the rats from Hamelin, may have carried valerian root.

Plants reach 3 to 5 feet high and spread to 4 feet wide in one season. Leaves are blue-green and finely divided into seven to nine segments. Dense clusters of tiny white to pinkish flowers bloom early in spring. They stand stiff and have a musty, vanilla fragrance. If you plan to harvest the plant's storage root, remove flower buds so that all energy goes into developing the root.

Centranthus ruber, red valerian, is a hardy perennial. It has similar uses as true valerian but different cultivation requirements. Red valerian is more colorful in the garden with brilliant red flowers that attract butterflies. (See photo, page 27.) It prefers dry locations. True valerian produces white flowers and requires moist soil conditions.

Planting and Care—Propagate from divisions taken in spring or fall or plant seed in spring. Cats love the smell of valerian. Protect tiny seedlings or cats will roll in them.

Thin seedlings to 2 feet apart. Plants set seed well and can become invasive. To prevent, harvest seedheads before they mature. Grows in full sun to partial shade; in deep shade plants become leggy. Pinch to encourage smaller, bushier plants. Prefers rich, moist loam soil but tolerates limestone and even alkaline soils. Water regularly and mulch plants to keep roots cool and moist.

Leaves are rich in minerals and can be added to compost and mulch. In addition to its appeal to cats and rats, valerian is said to attract earthworms.

Harvesting and Use—The large, radishlike roots are the plant parts harvested for use. They form beneath the central growth area of the plant, and are typically the size and shape of a peanut in its shell or larger. Harvest them about every other year. Sliced thin and dried, the root adds a musky fragrance to potpourri. Some cats love this scent, but do not allow them to eat valerian due to its sedative properties.

An infusion of the roots is used as a mild sedative tea or for a facial wash to treat acne and skin rashes.

Violet
Viola odorata

Hardy herbaceous perennial
Craft, Cosmetic, Culinary, Medicinal,
Ornamental
2 to 12 inches high, to 12 inches wide
Partial shade; full sun in cool climates
Rich, moist, well-drained soil

The sweet, delicate fragrance and simple beauty of violet have long been admired, not only by herbalists, but also by poets, artists and lovers.

Historically, violets have been used to treat health problems ranging from epilepsy to depression. A tea made from the leaves was prescribed for quelling anger and inducing sleep. The bacchanal Romans wore wreaths of violets in the hope of preventing drunkenness and hangovers. The flower, fresh or candied, was a favorite edible decoration at medieval banquets.

Violets are low-growing, hardy perennials that are practically synonymous with spring. No sooner does winter slip away before violets begin appearing from under hedges and trees. They are excellent choices for a colorful edging, as a small-scale ground cover or in containers. They spread by branching stems above ground and grow 2 to 12 inches high, depending upon the variety. Leaves are dark green and heart-shaped. Long-stemmed, fragrant flowers come in shades of deep violet, white and (rarely) bluish pink.

Planting and Care—Easy to grow from seed, by division or from containers. Partial shade is ideal, but violets tolerate full sun in cooler climates. Prefer rich, moist soil with good drainage.

Harvesting and Use—Violet is valued as a hardy ornamental. For cooks, flowers and leaves flavor and color salads, butters, jams, jellies and syrups, dessert decorations, herbal vinegars and even wine. Flowers and leaves are excellent sources of vitamins A and C. A half-cup serving of violet leaves contains as much vitamin C as four oranges.

Violets are commercially cultivated in France and England, largely for their oil. Essence of violets, beautiful and elusive, is treasured by perfumers. It is used in colognes, soaps, powders and all manner of body potions. The antiseptic properties of violet are useful in aromatherapy. Its essence relieves bronchial complaints, exhaustion and skin ailments.

Flowers can be dried and pressed for decorative floral arrangements and as colorful additions to potpourri.

Winter Savory
Satureja montana

Hardy woody perennial
Culinary, Ornamental
4 to 16 inches high, 3 to 8 inches wide
Full sun
Rich, moist well-drained soil

Winter savory grows slowly, reaching no more than 12 inches high. Mature, glossy, deep green leaves are pointed and narrow, developing from short woody stems.

This is an especially decorative, low-growing and densely spreading shrub. White or lavender-blue flowers bloom on short spikes in late summer. A good border plant for an herb or a vegetable garden. Winter savory also excels in a rock garden, where its evergreen branches can trail gracefully over the edges of stones.

Savory was well-known to the classical Greeks and Romans. Its genus name *Satureja* may derive from *satyrus,* or *satyr,* referring to its aphrodisiac effects. Hippocrates ascribed medicinal properties to it.

Winter savory was well known in early England, as well. Culpeper recommended it for ringing ears and in poultices for easing the pain from bee and wasp stings. This last remedy of rubbing a bruised sprig on a bee sting remains valid today. Early American settlers treated colds and fevers with savory tea.

Summer Savory
Satureja hortensis, summer savory, is equally valuable in the kitchen and medicine chest. It is a cold-tender annual with narrow, dark green leaves on stout stems that become branched and treelike in late summer. Summer savory has a different aroma and flavor than winter savory. Although both have a definite, peppery bite, reminiscent of thyme and

In the seventeenth century, vinegar-soaked sponges were sniffed to combat illness, applied to an aching brow or squeezed to refresh feverish hands. Victorian ladies wore bottles of aromatic vinegars on chains around their necks. If the ladies were to faint, the vinaigrette's sharp scent served to revive them.

Above: Winter savory is an especially decorative, low-growing and densely spreading shrub. White or lavender-blue flowers on short spikes dot the tops of leaves in late summer.

Above right: Summer savory is a cold-tender annual with narrow, dark green leaves on stout stems that become branched and treelike in late summer.

Right and below: A sturdy, shrubby perennial, wormwood grows to 4 feet high. Plants are usually heavily branched with downy stems and aromatic, divided leaves, silvery green on top, deep silver underneath. Spikes of yellow flowers appear in midsummer.

Above left: Yarrows are tough, persistent, dependable plants. Most bloom late spring and well into summer.

Above: Flowers of yarrow vary from yellow and white to red and pinkish red.

Left: Sweet violet has dark green, heart-shaped leaves. Fragrant flowers on long stems come in shades of deep violet, white and (rarely) bluish pink.

Below: Sweet violet in combination with colorful ornamental kale.

Baked Beans with Winter Savory

1-1/2 pounds dry
cannelli beans or
small white beans
1 bay leaf
1 large onion, chopped
1 14-ounce can plum
tomatoes
1/3 cup molasses
1/4 cup olive oil
4 garlic cloves, minced
2 teaspoons fresh winter
savory, minced, or 1
teaspoon dried
1 teaspoon ground
mustard seed
1 teaspoon salt
1/8 teaspoon cayenne
pepper
Several grinds of black
pepper

Soak beans overnight in two quarts cold water. Drain and rinse beans, removing those that are excessively soft or discolored. Place in a pot with the bay leaf and cover with one inch of water. Boil, reduce heat, cover and simmer for 30 to 45 minutes. Drain beans and reserve the stock. Mix beans with onion, molasses, olive oil, garlic, savory, mustard seed, salt, cayenne and black
pepper. Stir in one cup bean stock.

Preheat oven to 250F. Put beans in oiled 2-quart pot. Cover and bake for three hours. Reduce heat to 200F and bake two hours longer.

After the first two hours, stir beans once an hour. Add remaining bean stock, 1/2 cup at a time, if the beans become dry. After four hours cooking time, season to taste. Serve beans hot from the pot.

Serves 8 to 10.

marjoram, summer savory is somewhat more fruity, like apples, and floral, with a hint of lavender and basil. Winter savory and its coarser aroma and flavor are nonetheless welcome when summer is past and a fresh herb is desired.

Summer savory reaches 4 to 15 inches high and can spread 7 to 30 inches wide. In early to midsummer pale lavender to pure white flowers literally cover the plant like so many drops of dew.

Planting and Care—Both species are easy to grow if given good soil drainage. Summer savory starts easily from seed in spring, or plant in fall in mild-winter regions. It self-sows if grown in full sun and given regular water. To encourage lush growth, cut bushy tops back regularly.

Winter savory is easiest to grow from cuttings or root division. With patience, it can be started from seed. Prune regularly to encourage fresh growth. Otherwise, stems thicken and knot and new leaves diminish. Plant in full sun. It requires much less water than summer savory and is cold hardy to -10F.

Harvesting and Use—Begin harvesting summer savory when the plant reaches 6 to 8 inches high. After blooming, the plant is not as vigorous so be attentive about snipping off buds. Once summer savory flowers, its leaves are at their most flavorful. The entire plant can be clipped and used. Harvest winter savory for fresh use anytime. Cut the fragrant branches before bloom if you plan to dry the harvest.

Winter savory blends well with many other dishes and herbs. It can be an alternative to sage in poultry dressing. Combined with basil, winter savory is a perfect replacement for salt and pepper in salt-free diets. Both winter and summer savory are traditional companions to all kinds of bean dishes, including soups, salads and spreads. (See recipe at left.) Milder summer savory sparks egg dishes, creamy soups and rich cheesy casseroles. Give cooked vegetables new life with a liberal sprinkle of fresh leaves of either species.

Caution: Pregnant women should not use either summer savory or winter savory.

Wormwood
Artemisia absinthium

Hardy shrubby perennial
Craft, Ornamental
3 to 4 feet high, 2 to 3 feet wide
Full sun
Rich, light, sandy, well-drained soil

(Also known as Absinthe, Common Wormwood, Green Ginger, Old Woman Wormwood)

In the Middle Ages, wormwood was strewn on the floors to control lice and release a fresh scent when trod upon. Its perceived insecticidal properties led to its use in granaries, hen houses, hospitals, sickrooms and clothes closets.

Native to the dry, rocky hillsides of the Mediterranean mountains, wormwood was carried by Roman soldiers throughout their empire. Later, Europeans brought the plant to the New World, where it has escaped and naturalized.

In the past wormwood was used to kill intestinal parasites. One of the strongest agents known, it was difficult to prescribe. If the dose was too strong, the patient experienced convulsions, insanity or even death.

A sturdy, shrubby perennial, wormwood grows to 4 feet high. Plants are usually heavily branched with downy stems and aromatic, divided leaves, silvery green on top, deep silver underneath. Spikes of yellow flowers appear in midsummer.

Three other *Artemisia* species are considered wormwoods.

A. frigida, fringed wormwood, grows as high as 1-1/2 feet in a dense mat of finely cut, silvery white leaves. Its color makes it an excellent accent plant.

A. pontica, Roman wormwood, is an erect, multibranched shrub 2 to 4 feet high, with aromatic, soft, silvery foliage. Its droopy white flowers rarely appear. It is an ingredient in sachets and vermouth.

A. stelleriana, dusty miller, also called old woman or beach wormwood, grows to 2-1/2 feet high. Leaves are whiter than those of common wormwood and have a feltlike texture.

Planting and Care—Sow directly where you want plants to grow in spring or early fall. Thin plants 1-1/2 to 2 feet apart. Locate in full sun and average to poor, well-drained soil. Accepts moderate water; provide regular irrigations for the most attractive plants. Does well in a container, providing a central accent or a silver backdrop for other colors. Do not plant wormwood near fennel, sage, caraway, anise or other culinary herbs. Rainwater or irrigation water washes a growth-inhibiting toxin out of the leaves, affecting neighboring plants.

Harvesting and Use—Harvest leaves, stems and flowers at peak appearance then spread on screens or hand to dry. Leaves have a strong, sagelike fragrance. Stitched into sachets, the scent is said to repel moths and ants. Also attractive in nosegays, bouquets and wreaths, and in dried arrangements. *Caution:* Most members of the genus *Artemisia*, including wormwood, are considered unsafe for internal consumption.

Yarrow
Achillea species

Hardy herbaceous perennial
Craft, Ornamental
2 to 4 feet high, to 3 feet wide
Full sun to partial shade
Almost any well-drained soil

From a genus named for Achilles, hero of Homer's *Iliad*, yarrow was reputedly given to soldiers to help stanch their wounds. Other names reflect this characteristic—soldier's woundwort, nosebleed, bloodwort, staunchgrass, staunchweed and sanguinary, derived from the Latin word for blood.

During the Middle Ages, yarrow was considered medically and magically potent. The fresh leaves were chewed to relieve toothaches, a tea soothed fevers and distressed stomachs and stimulated the appetite. A healing ointment made from yarrow was applied to man and beast.

Yarrows are tough, persistent, dependable plants for the sunny border or herb garden. Most bloom late in spring and well into summer, some later, especially if cut back. Plants form spreading clumps of gray-green, pungent leaves that are finely cut and sometimes ferny. Flowers on most species are flat or slightly rounded umbels of tiny, daisylike clusters carried on stiff stalks. Typical flower color is yellow, but white, red and pinkish red are also available. Recently introduced varieties of *Achillea millefolium* have red, orange-red and salmon flowers. 'Moonshine' has flat, pale yellow flower heads on plants 2 feet high. 'Red Beauty' is pinkish red. Plants are strongly aromatic.

A. m. X 'Coronation Gold' bears bright yellow flowers on 3-foot plants. Popular for cutting and drying.

A. ptarmica 'The Pearl' bears double, button-sized, white blossoms borne in loose, airy clusters. Fine substitute for baby's breath or filler in arrangements. Leaves are smooth, dark green spears. Note: Flowers tend to make people sneeze.

A. tomentosa, woolly yarrow, forms a dense mat of ferny, gray-green leaves with yellow or white flowers. Use as edging or ground cover for small areas.

Planting and Care—Most yarrows can be planted from containers in spring or fall, or start seed indoors. Space plants 12 inches apart, tallest varieties 18 inches apart. Cut plants back after main bloom (mid- to late summer for most varieties), and plants will often rebloom. Divide and transplant clumps (best done in fall) every one to four years—whenever clumps get crowded with shoots.

Harvesting and Use—To harvest yarrow, cut the blossom stalks just as flowers are fully open. Gather bunches of 6 to 12 stems and hang them upside down in a well-ventilated place out of direct sunlight.

Yarrow can be enjoyed as a reviving herb tea, tasting somewhat of cinnamon or nutmeg. Because of its astringent qualities, infuse yarrow for a toning skin wash. Begin by crumbling one cup of dried flowers and tops into a small glass dish. Cover with two cups boiling water. Allow the brew to steep 10 minutes, then strain. Apply this solution where desired with a cotton ball.

In the garden, we love yarrow for its persistent late spring and summer color and long-lasting arrangements.

Deer-Resistant Herbs

It's possible to limit the damage inflicted by deer, what some people refer to as "rats with hooves." Deer and their browsing habits vary according to geographical area, type of deer and availability of food in their native habitat. These herbs are known to be avoided by deer, but there are no guarantees.

Basil
Catnip
Chives
Garlic Chives
Germander
Lavender
Lemon Balm
Mexican Mint Marigold
Mints
Oregano
Rosemary
Rue
Sages
Salvias
Santolina
Silver King Artemisia
Silver Queen Artemisia
Southernwood
Tansy
Wormwood
Yarrow

Framework for a *garden*

Years ago, the planning and installation of the herb garden was primarily the domain of the woman of the house. It was her responsibility to decide which herbs to grow. Women weeded the beds, harvested the herbs and brought them to the kitchen to enhance the daily meals. Herbs were utilized for their household, cosmetic and medicinal properties, and were dried for potpourris, perfumes and tonics. Most early herb gardens were planted near the kitchen because most household work was done there.

Times have certainly changed. Traditional roles are now blurred and the making of an herb garden develops according to the needs and interests of the individuals involved. In our gardens at the Farm, Sylvia seldom gets her hands dirty. When it comes time to harvest, she is the one to instruct me which herbs to pick, and how much she needs for the recipes she's preparing.

As you begin to develop a framework for the herbs you want to grow, honestly access the time and energy you'll have to spend. If you are unsure of your gardening skills and you've never grown herbs (or anything) before, then clearly you should start out small.

It's wise to develop a plan even for a small garden. A simple design will provide unity and guide you in placing and spacing herbs properly.

Herb gardens can be as different as the people who design, plant and enjoy them. And any site can be transformed into a number of different gardens. But in many ways herb gardeners are remarkably similar. The majority of us plan and do most of the work and make the necessary decisions ourselves. We appreciate herbs and want to learn more about them.

If you're having trouble deciding on a design for your garden, review the photographs in this book, and look through gardening publications for additional ideas. Visit herb gardens and public botanical gardens and arboretums in your area. Many have well-tended display gardens that will provide inspiration.

"All my hurt my garden spade can heal."

--Ralph Waldo Emerson

Left: It's important to consider the growth habits and mature sizes of herbs when you make your planting decisions. This attractive combination includes lavender (background) and 'Silver Lace' society garlic. (foreground).

Above: An herb border planted against a wall makes a simple but effective garden.

Planning Your Herb Garden

Transforming an empty or overgrown spot into an herb garden can be one of life's most gratifying experiences. Time spent outdoors in your garden relaxes mind, body and spirit. However, facing a raw, undeveloped, what-did-I-get-myself-into site can be intimidating. Visions of a private herbal getaway do come true, but not before you make lots of choices and accept responsibility for a fair amount of planning, digging and planting.

In his classic book, *Herbs and the Earth,* Henry Beston wrote that an herb garden is "not difficult to plan, not difficult to maintain." Although the sentiment is wonderfully romantic, we do not agree. Hard work? Yes, but not unreasonably so if you enjoy herbs, gardening and being outdoors. What *is* difficult is developing a design that suits the site, looks great, expresses your style and meets your current and future needs.

The sample garden plans shown in this chapter will provide some options, ranging from simple to complex. Use them as guides to create gardens suited to your own unique circumstances. Keep in mind that the more formal your design, the more time you'll be required to spend maintaining the garden.

> *"He who sees things from the beginning will have the best view of them."*
>
> —Aristotle

Scope Out Your Situation

For most of us, the outdoor herb garden will be small in scale. Perhaps we'll include intersecting paths to form a cross and add interest. Some gardens will be raised to save our backs. Some will have paving stones and bricks with creeping thyme and low-growing mints planted in the cracks to soften the steps of visitors.

It's wise to start selectively and expand as your interest and experience with herbs grow. We began our garden with just a few clay pots and a large half-barrel on a pocket-size patio. The next planting season we added a couple of experimental garden beds. Five years later we bought our farm and began planting on a large scale. (See photos, pages 12 and 13.) Now we plan and plant one garden at a time.

As you develop your plan, be aware of natural features—trees, exposed rocks, sunny areas, shady and wet locations—as well as manmade items—sidewalks, fences, swings and swimming pools. Trees and buildings cast shade, which can affect the growth of your herbs. Most herbs need a minimum of 5 or 6 hours of direct sun each day to grow successfully.

Measure or pace off your intended garden spot to learn how much available space you have and what you'll have to work around.

The Add-A-Bed Herb Garden

This garden design allows you to start small with a single center bed, then add more beds as your time and interest allow. Use brick, railroad ties or other materials to designate planting areas.

Make beds as long as you like but keep to a maximum width of three to four feet to allow easy access for weeding, watering and harvesting herbs.

Bed A

A1 Prostrate Rosemary

A2 Bee Balm

A3 Garlic

A4 Chives

A5 Germander

A6 Lemon Thyme

A7 Lemon Verbena

A8 Caraway

A9 Creeping Thyme

Bed B

B1 Cilantro

B2 Lemon Basil

B3 Sweet Basil

B4 Parsley

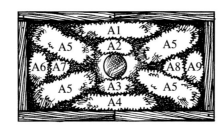

Bed C

C1 Marjoram

C2 Orange Mint

C3 Chervil

C4 Winter Savory

Bed D

D1 Dill

D2 Tarragon

D3 Lemon Balm

D4 Upright Rosemary

D5 Oregano

Bed E

E1 Pineapple Sage

E2 Fernleaf Tansy

E3 Lavender

E4 Southernwood

E5 Apple Mint

Make Plans to Prosper

Regardless of the size or style of the intended garden, we recommend you draw your design on paper. A bird's-eye view diagram will put your plan in perspective. A design also forces you to address the growth habits of the herbs you want to plant and give them the amount of space they need to develop. Too often, haphazard plantings become weedy and unattractive by the season's end. If your first herb garden is a disappointment, you'll surely wonder what all the fuss about herbs was about.

When it's time to designate plants in your plan, locate taller herbs in the center of a bed. Stagger shorter ones outward to the border. If a planting is against a wall or fence, locate taller herbs in the background, then the mid-sized, then the low-growers—much as you would for a flowering border.

Raised beds are excellent choices for herb gardens. To "raise" a bed, enclose a planting area with railroad ties, boards, bricks or native stones. These materials provide a container of sorts to hold the planting soil higher than the surrounding natural soil. A raised bed is a classic method for defining the shape of a planting area, plus it

> *"Try a thing you haven't done three times. Once, to get over the fear of doing it. Twice, to learn how to do it. And a third time to figure out whether you like it or not."*
>
> —Virgil Thomson

improves soil drainage. The borders of the raised bed also help contain invasive herbs such as mints, lemon balm, chamomile or thyme.

Put It In Writing

Measure your site and plot it on graph paper. Each square on the paper should represent a simple measurement, such as one square foot. Pencil in permanent features such as fences, buildings, trees and walls. Accuracy counts. Note variations in the ground level that may require steps, terracing or raised planting beds. After the base plan is complete, place a piece of tracing paper over it. Now is the time to experiment with different approaches. Remind yourself that you don't have to be precise the first go-round. We go through many sheets of tracing paper before we're satisfied with a plan. After you've created a design you like, add "dream details" such as statutes, fountain, lights and benches. (See page 135.)

Selecting Herbs for Your Garden

After you've made your design final, be prepared to choose which herbs you want to grow. The decision to

An Informal Border Garden

A naturalistic herbal border requires less maintenance than a formal garden and has a beauty all its own. Add in flowering plants for more color. Be sure to account for mature sizes when spacing.

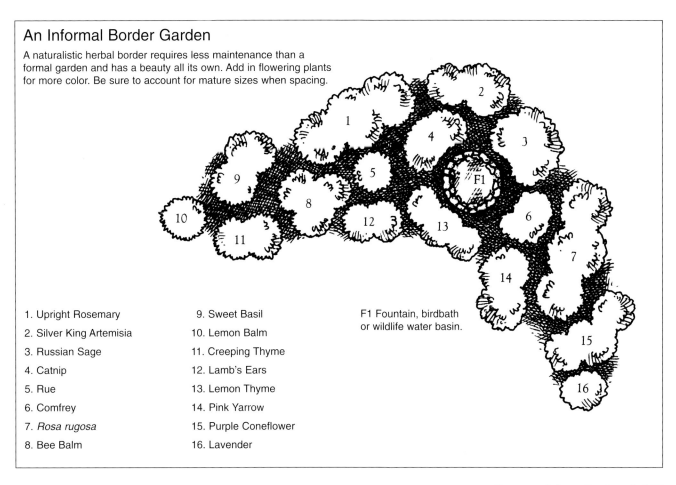

1. Upright Rosemary
2. Silver King Artemisia
3. Russian Sage
4. Catnip
5. Rue
6. Comfrey
7. *Rosa rugosa*
8. Bee Balm
9. Sweet Basil
10. Lemon Balm
11. Creeping Thyme
12. Lamb's Ears
13. Lemon Thyme
14. Pink Yarrow
15. Purple Coneflower
16. Lavender

F1 Fountain, birdbath or wildlife water basin.

Left: Rich green upright rosemary and feathery fennel creates an unusual but striking combination, effective as a screen.

Below left: Public gardens are great places to gain ideas for your own designs. This naturalistic herb garden is at San Diego Wild Animal Park in southern California.

Below: Consider *microclimates,* the small climates around your home, when locating your garden. This Phoenix, Arizona, garden planted with vegetables and herbs takes advantage of its sloped location for protection against intense sun and strong wind. Terraced planting beds are attractive; they contain improved soil for a better growing medium.

Opposite page

Top: Planting beds at the Fredericksburg Herb Farm are simple yet practical. Note depth of beds. They are narrow so it's easy to reach plants when watering, weeding and harvesting. Crushed granite makes appealing, low-maintenance pathways.

Bottom left: This oceanside home has no garden space. A narrow planter filled with culinary herbs becomes the garden.

Bottom right: Consider foliage textures of herbs when grouping them. This collection includes fluffy lamb's ears, fernlike tansy and purple-flowering lavender.

include one herb or another, or how many herbs to use in a given planting area, is not an exact science. One gardener may insist on 24 pots planted in a medieval knot pattern. Another claims that 10 or 12 pots will do, interplanted among tomatoes, onions and carrots. At the Farm, we prefer to create a garden design that supports a theme. For example, we may select herbs that have a symbolic relationship with saints, or grow herbs that are included in the Bible. Or we select herbs that will appeal to children, such as those having fragrant or touchable leaves. Other herbs may be chosen for their functional traits, such as culinary or cosmetic uses.

Planning and plant selection is the fun part of herb gardening. As architect of your garden, you become the master of its purpose and arrangement, deciding if it will be tasty or healthful, attractive or mysterious, planted in a row, circle, square or naturalistic theme.

For those herbs you select and plant, make a list of vital statistics: mature size (height *and* spread), whether they are *annual* (which means they live for one season only) or *perennial* (living year after year), and whether the plant is evergreen or deciduous. If an herb produces flowers, describe its typical bloom period and color. Note the planting locations on your final diagram. Record the full botanical names, if you know them. Many of us are so eager to get digging and planting that we don't follow through on this little detail. But a year or two after planting you'll be thankful you kept records. Despite our best efforts, the memory fails and name tags disappear or migrate.

The Stakeout

Time to transfer your ideas from paper to actual plot of ground. To gain an idea of the size, scale and appearance of the garden, lay a garden hose, rope or string on the ground to outline shapes and sizes of paths, beds and borders. Or drive stakes and use string or twine in dot-to-dot patterns to see if your paper-borne ideas are workable in real life. Examine the beds from all directions. Adjust now, before beginning the hard work of digging and planting.

Planting Time

Completely satisfied? If so, it's planting time. The following chapter, Putting Down Roots, will take you step by step through soil preparation, planting and care. But it is worth repeating here: Don't overplant. Setting plants too close together is one of the most common mistakes gardeners make. Perhaps it's because herbs just out of their potted homes look so dinky. Don't let them fool you. Most herbs are vigorous growers, especially when planted in good soil and given regular water. Refer to the Gallery of Herbs, pages 30 to 123, for typical height and spread, and space plants accordingly.

Utilitarian Garden: Four Gardens in One

Herbs for Fragrance

A1 Silver King Artemisia

A2 Lemon Balm

A3 Lavender

A4 Upright Rosemary

A5 Summer Savory

A6 'Coronation Gold' Yarrow

A7 Nasturtium

Herbs for Cooking

B1 Chives

B2 Common Thyme

B3 Lemongrass

B4 Spicy Globe Basil

B5 French Tarragon

B6 Curly Parsley

B7 Greek Oregano

Herbs for Medicinal Use

C1 Peppermint

C2 Chamomile

C3 Comfrey

C4 Hyssop

C5 Lamb's Ears

C6 Bee Balm

C7 Catnip

Herbs for Beauty

D1 Alba Rose

D2 Lemon Verbena

D3 Garden Sage

D4 'Coronation Gold' Yarrow

D5 Common Thyme

D6 Violet

D7 Pineapple Sage

Garden Design Options   E1 Sundial, birdbath, statue or fountain. Surround by benches.

Paths and Walks in the Herb Garden

Sixteenth-century English philosopher Francis Bacon used burnet in his "stepping garden," along with mint and other aromatics. The reason? As visitors walked through his garden, they stepped on the herbs to cause them to release their fragrances. Burnet's cooling green cucumber scent and mint's menthol would surely have lightened the step of any serious scholar.

In addition to their utility in allowing visitors to go from here to there, paths show off separate beds to their advantage, making your garden's design more evident. For an example, see photo, top of page 128.

Half the fun of arriving at a particular garden spot is in how you reach it. Crushed stone, pebbles, brick, flagstone and cross-sections of tree trunks are popular path materials. Several herbs also make attractive path covers; most are easy to grow and maintain. In addition, they smell wonderful and feel delightful between naked toes. Adding herbs to a walkway that's too difficult to reach with a mower and too tedious to hoe, or as filler between stepping stones, is a practical and pleasurable solution. Herbs such as rosemary and thyme do well in dry, sunny walkways that would otherwise not easily support green life. For damp, wooded areas that receive little sun, the bedstraws and mints thrive beautifully. Chamomile is another path cover worth considering. It can be trampled by foot traffic and even mowed yet it grows back, ready for more.

A final thought on herb garden design: Don't be discouraged if you don't have the time or money to follow through with all your ideas at once. Plant what you can afford to maintain. This is the principle behind the Add-A-Bed Garden on page 128. But do put all ideas on your master plan. Chances are you'll be able to develop them and increase the scope and beauty of your garden with each passing season.

Herb Gardens for Fragrance

By their nature, herb gardens are rich in fragrance—sharp, sweet or even richly pungent. It's a sensory delight to walk among herbs on a warm summer's evening, brushing against plants and pinching leaves, smelling newly opened flowers. Historically, the scents of each herb has its own special benefit: rosemary and marjoram cheer and invigorate; mint refreshes; southernwood increases awareness; hops and lavender are calming. Gardens rich in scent are among the most memorable.

The Site

If possible, select a location that provides shelter from wind. Exposed to wind, the fragrances are often swept away before we can fully enjoy them. A warm, sunny south or west exposure is also preferred. The higher temperatures encourage many plants to release their

A Celtic Cross Garden

1. Cabbage Rose
2. Rosemary
3. Aloe vera (in container)
4. Holy Basil
5. Santolina (gray)
6. Valerian
7. Sweet Bay (in container in cold areas)
8. Salad Burnet
9. Garlic
10. Tansy
11. Coriander
12. Hyssop
13. Mint (in container to control)
14. Lavender
15. Myrtle
16. Apothecary's Rose
17. Rue
18. Wormwood
19. Silver King Artemisia
20. Lemon Balm
21. Garlic Chives
22. Society Garlic

Above left: Iris planted among herbs adds color during the spring months.

Above: A single statue surrounded by mint makes a simple yet striking statement.

Left: Herb gardens can take on any size and shape. This is the Ichthus Garden at the Farm.

Below left: A traditional knot garden features low, trimmed hedges of boxwood and purple-leafed barberry, which define planting beds containing common thyme.
Also see knot garden planting plan on page 134.

Opposite page
Top: A formal garden at the Farm is more interesting when accented with statuary and a birdbath. See text, page 135.

Bottom: The Farm's Secret Garden is protected by native oaks. Once mature, the young hollies and other screening plants will enclose the garden. Angled planting beds add interest and make it easy to water, weed and harvest herbs.

aromatic bouquets. A screen of climbing honeysuckle, jasmine, hops or hedge of antique roses, lavender, rosemary or santolina help create a fragrant spot.

The Arrangement

Herbs grown for fragrance are best planted in small or narrow beds. Brushing past or touching these plants releases their fragrant oils. Many gardeners plant fragrant herbs around a bench or seat at the end or curve of a path, which provides a visual accent to the scene.

Although orderly rows may be suited to a culinary or medicinal herb garden, sweet-scented herbs are often best informally arranged—a romantic disorder if you will. For a more traditional landscape, plant small beds and divide them with paths or low boxwood hedges. Or create a formal shape such as a large wheel, divided square or ladder. (See drawing on page 135.) If a large herb garden packed with aromatic plants is not possible, arrange clusters of pots on a patio or balcony. Many herbs are content to grow in containers. Strawberry pots—large pots with planting holes in the sides—will accommodate several small stature herbs.

Selecting Fragrant Plants

If you like the scent of roses, grow rose geranium, *Pelargonium graveloens*. It is easier to grow than roses and has a more concentrated fragrance. As a bonus, you can count on a rich rose scent from the leaves anytime during its long growing season. When no substitute will satisfy, there are some powerfully

fragrant antique roses from which to choose.

Many herbs have lemony fragrances and flavors. *Aloysia triphylla*, lemon verbena, grows to 6 feet high or more, either from mother plants that survived the winter or from new cuttings set out in spring. Although plants of lemon verbena are leggy, they produce plenty of narrow three-inch leaves that will make you pucker.

Color Sense with Herbs and Flowers

A rose by any other name might smell as sweet, but would you be so quick to draw its scent deep into your lungs if its petals were rusty brown? Color can attract or repel, summon memories, energize, call out to others, define you as gardener-designer, perhaps even heal. Given the importance of color, it's amazing how little we consider its nuances or appreciate its potential, especially in our gardens. In the hands of a sensitive designer, color can be a creative tool for expression and illusion.

Color comes to the landscape from several sources. In addition to perennial and annual flowers and herbs, structural materials such as walls, fences, paving and buildings play a significant role. Trees, shrubs and groundcovers play their part, too, and pose challenges as each change though the seasons. Consider the following as you select and combine colors for your herb and flower gardens.

Yellow is the color your eyes see first. It can be startling, cheerful or alarming. Yellow is one of the most common colors in flowers. At its palest hue, yellow fades into silver and provides a strong contrast to dense backgrounds. Because pale yellows and grays are reflective, they offer sparkle and glitter. Yellow and grays require strong foliage support to heighten their daytime roles.

At the Farm, we have always loved blue-flowering herbs. Symbolizing honest intentions and mild passions, blue is a sedating color that calms. But blue can also depress if not lifted by complementing whites, pinks and yellows. In the garden, blues can be used to to create an illusion of spaciousness in cramped quarters. It recedes from the eye visually, lengthening perspective and giving depth. Groups of gray-blue plants provide harmony and cohesion in a garden otherwise going in many directions.

Red is a warning light that "buzzes" the brain, stimulating the heart and nervous system. In sunny spots, red can be joyful. Paired with other rich colors and textured backgrounds, it stirs up a fiesta of emotions. Visually, red is a dominating color that can tire the eye and mind, so avoid overusing it. Red can effectively supercharge a foreground bordering a monochromatic greenscape.

Unlike red, pink is warm and inviting, and it socializes with many colors. Pink is soft and restful. This is

Traditional Knot Garden

1. Germander hedge
2. English Lavender
3. Santolina
4. Common Thyme

particularly true when bedded down with gray herbs. Pink also holds its color as evening approaches. Select moderate pinks rather than optic pinks, common among modern hybrids, and anything but calming.

Orange is a challenge to use in the garden, but it can be extraordinarily warm and attractive. It elevates us with a rich, celebratory mood, especially when accompanied by purple or bronze foliage and forest greens.

The visual impact of flower color is almost always temporary. Foliage, however, is a constant throughout the growing season or year after year. Green is restful in all its variations. It neither advances nor recedes visually and is not tiring to the eyes. Gardens designed entirely around a thoughtful palette of green foliage can be subtle and peaceful.

Adding Personality to Your Garden

The ambience of your herb garden is created by its formal or informal layout, dominant colors (see preceding) and the plants themselves. Decorative accessories, garden benches, statues and pots can stimulate curiosity, amusement and memories. An anonymous writer once said that a garden should be "a place where the mind goes to seed." If you agree, garden accessories will fuel your flights of fancy.

More than just a home for plants, containers can serve as sentinels, marking the foot or head of steps, decorating entrances, exits and windows. For the gardener without a garden, herbs in containers add splashes of color and life when only patio or windowsill space is available. Pots, tubs, vases, urns with illustrations from classical mythology, old stone troughs, your grandmother's lead kitchen sink, all are suitable homes for herbs. These, plus other found objects or recycled family heirlooms, add a special quality to the garden.

Container gardening also provides a certain amount of control over certain unruly, invasive herbs. For the basics of how to grow herbs in containers, see page 146.

Garden Pluses

Statues suggest the presence of people, so visitors are often drawn to them. The statue should be in scale with the size of the garden so it does not overwhelm its surroundings. Animal figures such as rabbits, frogs and turtles nestled among the herbs bring out the child in all of us. An ideal place for a large, dominant work is at the end of a pathway, an intersection of paths or the focal point of two planted areas.

The reflected views of garden gazing balls make them attractive garden features. They can visually expand a garden and divert sunlight into unexpected places. Surrounded by herbs, a sundial reminds us of folklore, herbal medicine and simpler times.

In warm weather the splash of falling water can have a delightful effect on garden visitors. Something as simple as a hollowed bamboo spout dripping water into a shallow basin provides impact. Birdbaths are refreshing and provide a water source for wildlife.

Arbors covered in climbing roses or vines add a special intimacy. They give visitors a sense of passing from one area into another, with the promise of the unknown to explore.

A bench or chair adds a visual focal point and a reward at the end of a path. Weathered natural materials, cast iron pieces painted verdigris green, and cast concrete are always at home in the herb garden.

Ladder Garden
Easy to make from scrap lumber, each square of a ladder garden becomes a planting pocket. Select low-growing to moderate-size herbs. This ladder garden is planted with (from left) chamomile, oregano, sorrel, lavender and yarrow.

Putting Down

roots

At last, the time has come to plant your herb garden. You've decided which herbs you want to grow, have some ideas on how to put them to use, and have reviewed the information in the preceding chapter, Framework for a Garden. Perhaps you intend to grow herbs so you can use them in the kitchen for the tantalizing flavors they add to meals. Maybe you've got your eye on a few fragrant herbs and can imagine their pleasurable scents as you and your friends brush by them on the way to the front door. Or you may have decided on a small formal herb garden, and can envision how it will look after a few years growth.

These are wonderful reasons to grow herbs, but before you order seeds from a catalog or bring armloads of potted plants home from the nursery, we hope you will take a few moments to read through this chapter. Learning the basics before you plant will go a long way toward making sure your herbs will thrive rather than just survive.

In the following pages you'll learn how sun, soil, wind, rainfall and humidity combine to create the varied and unique growing conditions around your home. You'll see how to plant herbs from seeds and containers, step by step, as well as how to propagate existing plants. You'll also learn how to be a water-wise herb gardener, developing an efficient irrigation program. Instructions for making compost, protecting plants in winter, controlling pests organically, and reaping and keeping your harvest are also included here.

If you don't have space for a garden, we'll show you how to grow herbs in containers, outdoors and indoors. Raising herbs as houseplants becomes a sometimes-difficult balancing act of proper sunshine, heat and humidity but can be done successfully.

New to herb gardening? Be patient and start off with a small garden. In just one growing season, you'll be amazed at what your plants have taught you about putting down roots. With a little experience, you'll soon be looking for ways to make room for more herbs.

"When I go into my garden with a spade, and dig a bed, I feel such an exhilaration and health that I discover that I have been defrauding myself all this time in letting others do for me what I should have done with my own hands."

—Ralph Waldo Emerson

Left: Bill Varney replants a bed at the Farm.

Above: Ladybugs are welcome in the herb garden, feeding on many common pests.

The Big Picture of Gardening

The climate where you live creates the "big picture" of gardening, including growing herbs. Sunshine, high and low seasonal temperatures, rainfall, wind, soil and other elements create your unique gardening environment. Understanding your climate will help you select adapted herbs and locate them in the proper exposures and garden locations. This way you'll avoid serious problems such as cold damage or too much or too little sun.

Cold Temperatures

Every plant has a low-temperature tolerance. When the temperature drops below this point for a certain period of time, plant tissues are damaged. If the cold is severe or prolonged, the plant could die. How long cold temperatures last and how quickly they drop affect the extent of the damage. The faster they drop, the more severe the injury. Cold that lasts for an hour or less may not hurt plants, but if it stays cold for several hours, severe damage is likely.

To better understand herbs and their inherent ability to survive cold temperatures, it's helpful to be aware of their different life cycles. Most herbs can be categorized as *annual, biennial* or *perennial.*

Annuals are plants that last for one season. They are further characterized as *tender, half-hardy* or *hardy,* according to how well they withstand freezing temperatures. Tender annuals will not tolerate frost or cold weather; half-hardy plants will tolerate some frost; hardy annuals will survive heavy frost. Biennials normally require two growing seasons to complete their life cycle.

Perennials are plants that perform differently depending on the climate. In cold regions they die down in winter, then regrow from their roots in spring. In mild regions they may remain green throughout the year. Because perennials usually remain in the garden year after year, consider their cold hardiness carefully. Certain herbs are grown as annuals in cold-winter regions and as perennials where temperatures remain above freezing. They are noted in the Gallery of Herbs, pages 30 to 123.

You can help perennial herbs adjust to upcoming cold weather by inducing dormancy. In early fall, gradually reduce water and cease applications of fertilizer. This slows tender new growth and helps harden plant tissues for the oncoming cold weather.

Sunlight and Heat

Many of the aromatic, flavoring herbs are native to hot, sunny regions, such as mountainsides bordering the Mediterranean, or harsh scrubland. Thyme, rosemary, marjoram, savory and sage grow wild in the intense sun, heat and drying winds, developing their volatile oils and powerful flavors. The sun's heat draws oils from the leaves, surrounding the plant with a protective vapor. This, in combination with the often pungent flavor, sharp tips and leathery surfaces of leaves, make them less appealing to browsing animals. The toughness and grayish green colors of many herbs help them retain precious moisture that would otherwise be evaporated by the sun and dispersed by winds.

Bear this sun-loving habit in mind when selecting and planting herbs. Most herbs require a minimum of six hours of sunlight each day, although requirements vary from plant to plant.

Not all sunlight is equal. Much depends on your climate and time of day plants are exposed to the sun. Morning sun (eastern exposure) is much less intense than afternoon sun (southern or western exposure). In coastal gardens and cool-summer regions such as the Pacific Northwest, a lack of sunshine and heat can be a problem. Conditions are often too cool or too cloudy for basil, lavender, sage, thyme and santolina.

In hot inland valleys and desert regions, the sun and heat can be too intense for French tarragon, lamb's ears, dill, cilantro and caraway. High temperatures, intense sunlight and less-than-adequate water stress plants, making them more susceptible to pests and diseases. This is especially true for newly planted herbs. Check plant descriptions in the Gallery of Herbs for sunlight requirements, then select plants according to the availability of sunlight on your site.

Rainfall

If you live in a region that receives little rain, late summer is a sobering season. At the Herb Farm, we have one hour for watering before the pressure drops on our own well, then we must switch to a second well or to our city source to gain an additional hour of irrigation. We may be so busy watering potted plants in the greenhouse that the hottest areas of the gardens are sorely neglected. We make amends with mulches to keep evaporation of moisture from the soil at a minimum, but our Texas summers are usually long, hot and dry. Windy conditions during summer can threaten the survival of our plants. Fortunately, many common herbs, including rosemary, lavender, santolina and thyme, tolerate some dry spells. We planted the entire west side of our Star Garden with lavender mindful of its tough, sunny exposure and anticipating a lack of routine watering. The lavender has done remarkably well and served as a perfect "test patch" for us.

Too much rain may be as bad for plants as too little. Tiny roots in waterlogged soil die for want of air that is as necessary as water for life. If you live in a high rainfall area, be sure your soil is well drained. Avoid planting in low spots where moisture can accumulate.

Humidity

A certain amount of humidity is helpful and healthful to plants. (It's good for humans, too.) Humidity slows evaporation of moisture from leaves and reduces the need for frequent watering.

In a low-humidity climate, rainfall can evaporate

rapidly, to the extent that little moisture accumulates in the soil. Low humidity in combination with hot, dry winds and intense sunlight causes plants to dry out very quickly. During these conditions, pay close attention to the water needs of your herbs. Humidity can be increased by adding a coarse mulch around plants. Keep the mulch moist. As the moisture evaporates, humidity increases around plants.

In high-humidity regions—areas that typically receive a lot of rainfall—moisture is retained in the air and around plants. This decreases water need but encourages certain diseases, such as blackspot and mildew. In general, herbs that have shallow roots and delicate leaves require a lot of water, especially during periods of growth and flowering. Such herbs are best adapted to humid climates. Their leaves and roots are not adapted to store water or to resist evaporation. Herbs having waxy or leathery leaves generally perform better in warm, dry, windy climates.

Wind

Most herb gardens are relatively small, especially in cities, where home lot size is shrinking. Even larger rural gardens are often designed as a series of small linked areas, partly enclosed by hedges, fences or low walls. Herbs grow especially well in these kinds of enclosed spaces, where they are sheltered from winds and where their subtle, aromatic scents can be contained within the enclosures.

Strong winds, especially salt-laden winds of coastal gardens, can play havoc with herbs. Few plants thrive in salty air, and it can be difficult for even the sturdiest herbs to thrive in a strong prevailing breeze.

Before deciding on a garden location, observe the wind's direction and speed. If fallen leaves and last season's debris move and swirl in the wind, the wind is blowing approximately 20 mph. If large tree branches are swaying, the wind may be blowing 30 mph or more. Gusty winds will knock down tall-growing herbs such as bay, rosemary, lavender, roses, wormwood, southernwood, sage, fennel and dill. Leaves of lovage, valerian, comfrey, mugwort, tansy, catnip and mullein are easily tattered by strong winds.

If you notice that the wind generally blows from one direction, consider planting a hedge or screen to provide protection. Locate windbreak plantings perpendicular to the path of the wind.

When accompanied by high temperatures, wind will rapidly dry out plants. Watering "deep and wide" around the plant's perimeter encourages an extensive root system, which helps plants endure wind.

Microclimates

Many differences in climate exist around your neighborhood and your home. These small climates are called *microclimates*. If your general climate is the big picture, they are the "small picture." They vary from street to street, from the bottom to the top of a slope, and even in different areas of your own backyard. The lay of the land, paved areas, structures and size and placement of existing plants create a range of growing conditions, from full shade to reflected sun and heat. Every home lot is different, and conditions evolve as plants on site grow and create more shade.

Because most of us do not have ideal weather or perfect planting locations, we must study our gardens to find the best sites. Often, you can identify warm, protected spots that can shelter tender herbs. If none exist, you can "manufacture" microclimates. A garden enclosed by a wall or fence or modified by a building may be able to support plants that would not otherwise grow there. Be aware that such structures may block the sun, depriving herbs of necessary sunlight.

Where sunshine is lacking, a south or west-facing wall, particularly if it's light in color, will reflect heat and make a garden site warmer. If there is too much heat, it can be tempered by providing shade from trees, shade cloth or structures such as a lath panels.

One microclimate strategy is to plant herbs in containers and move them to a sunny, shaded or sheltered location as needed. This is often the only option for growing tender annuals and perennials in cold-winter regions. For more information, see page 146.

The Scoop on Soil

Most herbs survive in a wide range of soil types, as long as the soil is well drained. Poorly drained soils cause plant roots to become waterlogged. "Wet feet" will doom many herbs, including Mediterranean favorites such as rosemary and lavender. To find out if you have the right soil for the herbs you want to grow, do these few simple tests. (It is a good idea to test in more than one location; soil often varies from one location to another, even in a home landscape.)

Test Soil Drainage—Dig a hole 12 inches deep and fill with water. If the water takes longer than several hours to seep through the soil, there is a drainage problem, often caused by an impenetrable layer of rock or clay. One solution is to create your own drainage by building a raised planting bed at least two feet above ground level. Or select another site where the soil drains properly.

Herbs for Humid Climates	Herbs for Dry Climates
Basil	Chamomile
Comfrey	Costmary
Hoja Santa	Fennel
Lemon Balm	Hyssop
Mints	Lavender
Bog Myrtle	Mugwort
Rosemary	Rosemary
Soapwort	Sages
Garden Sorrel	St. John's Wort
Sweet Woodruff	Santolina
Valerian	Savory
Yarrow 'The Pearl'	Thyme

1. Planting a 6x6-foot herb garden, step by step. Check the soil to see if it needs improving. Some soils, particularly clay soils, are difficult to work and are slow draining. Most herbs need well-drained soil.

2. Watering the soil area well a day or two before preparing the soil makes digging easier. Wait to work soils when they are moist, not wet. Working wet clay soils will cause clods to form.

3. To improve the soil's drainage, workability and retention of moisture, add organic matter. Apply a layer 3 or 4 inches deep over the soil and blend thoroughly to 6 to 8 inches deep.

4. Position herbs according to mature height and spread. Place tallest herbs in center and low-growing herbs in the foreground. See the Gallery of Herbs, pages 30 to 123, for mature sizes.

5. Dig a planting hole the same depth and two to three times as wide as the container diameter. Carefully remove plant from container and place in hole, firming soil around roots.

6. Water well with light spray from watering can or garden hose. After watering check to make sure plant has not settled and rootball is at the same depth as it was in the original container.

Test Soil pH—Soil pH is a measure of *acidity* or *alkalinity,* expressed as a number between 1 (battery acid) and 14 (more alkaline than lye). It usually varies between 4 and 8; most herbs grow well in neutral soil with a pH between 6.2 and 7.0. If the soil is too acidic or too alkaline, nutrients can become chemically "tied up" so plants are unable to absorb them. Soil test kits are available at many garden centers. If your soil tests distinctly acid or alkaline, test again to be sure. If the pH is too high, adding elemental sulfur will reduce it. If the pH is too low, adding ground limestone will raise it. Modifications will be temporary, and in two to three years the soil will revert to its former pH.

Test Soil Texture—Pick up a handful of moist (not overly wet) soil. Sandy soil will feel coarse and gritty. Clay soil will feel slippery and waxy. Loam soil will feel spongy. Squeeze the soil into a ball, then roll the ball on the ground. A ball of sandy soil will fall apart; clay will keep its shape even when poked with your finger; loam will keep its shape but fall apart if poked. In sandy soil, water and nutrients drain through rapidly. In clay, tiny particles hold on to water, eliminating air and reducing drainage. Loam soil is ideal. It contains a mix of coarse and fine mineral particles and organic matter, which provides tiny spaces to hold air and water.

Improving Soil Structure

There isn't much you can do to change the *texture* of your soil, but you can improve the soil's *structure*—its arrangement of particles. The best way to do this is to add organic amendments. Packaged materials such as bark products or peat moss are commonly available at nurseries and home centers. Better yet, make your own amendment with a backyard compost pile, discussed below.

Dumping a load of amendments on the garden and raking it into a level "frosting" does little to improve the soil. You must blend organic matter into the existing soil, or the labor you spend digging and shoveling will be wasted. The soil will soon revert to its former state, whether "clay brick" or "sandy beach."

Shovel a 3- to 4-inch layer of compost or comparable organic material on top of the planting bed. Dig down and turn over the soil to a depth of 6 to 8 inches. Break up any large clods and mix well, fluffing up the soil to aid water and oxygen penetration. Don't spoil the preparation of your soil by walking across the bed; you'll compact it. Lay a board or plank across to hold and disperse your weight.

Backyard Compost

Think of your soil as a living dynamic system. Adding compost keeps it thriving. Two soil types benefit from the addition of compost, but for opposite reasons. Compost opens up clay soil, improving drainage and makes it easier for plant roots to penetrate. Sandy soils drain too rapidly. Adding compost increases retention of water and nutrients.

Compost is an ideal soil amendment. It's a crumbly, dark mixture of earth and decomposed plant materials. A basic compost heap consists of alternating layers of slightly moist vegetable matter (such as grass clippings, straw, sawdust, leaves, and kitchen wastes excluding meat) and sprinkles of garden fertilizer or manure and soil. Coarse materials (branches and stem clippings) should be layered 6 to 8 inches thick, finer ones (grass clippings) 2 to 3 inches thick. The fertilizer or manure provides nitrogen to feed the microorganisms that decompose the vegetable matter. The vegetable matter heats up as it decomposes. Shredding materials accelerates the decomposition process.

Do not add toxic substances—clippings from lawns treated with pesticides or herbicides, for example. Sunflower seed hulls and black walnuts are toxic to many plants and should be avoided. Dispose of diseased plants in your trash to avoid transferring diseases to the compost.

Most manures from plant-eating animals are acceptable. Add to the compost pile or allow to age for a year before adding directly to garden soil. If used fresh, the typically high ammonia content can burn plants. Do not use dog or cat droppings because they can carry diseases. Feedlot manures may contain large amounts of soluble salts, which also damage plants. Fresh animal manure and raw material such as sawdust require nitrogen for the decomposition process—nitrogen your herb plants could use.

If you live in a low-rainfall climate, spray compost materials with water to keep the pile moist. In a high-rainfall climate, cover compost materials with a tarp to keep them from getting too wet and to prevent nutrients from being leached out. Turn the pile after a few weeks, putting the raw materials on the inside, moistening it if it seems dry. The aeration and rearrangement will accelerate the decomposition. Eventually, the pile will be transformed into a pile of dark, crumbly, sweet-smelling compost—*black gold.*

Cultivating a "green manure" crop is another way of improving soil. This is a crop that's planted in the garden before you set out herbs. The crop grows and is tilled back into the soil. If your cover crop includes

---

Herbs to Match Your Soil Type

SANDY SOIL
Borage, Chamomile, Coriander, Fennel, Lavender, Tarragon, Thyme, Marjoram and Winter Savory

CLAY SOIL
Bee Balm, Comfrey, Mint and Wormwood
Working compost into clay soil makes it more hospitable to herbs that prefer loam and moist loam soils

LOAM SOIL
Basil, Bay, Caraway, Catnip, Chervil, Chives, Coriander, Dill, Fennel, Lady's Mantle, Lovage, Rosemary, Rue, Sage and Thyme

MOIST LOAM SOIL
Bee Balm, French Sorrel, Lady's Mantle, Lemon Balm, Mint, Parsley and Valerian

members of the pea family such as clover or alfalfa, bacteria on the roots will convert nitrogen from the air into a form that plants can use. Although effective, green manure takes time to break down.

Ready, Set, Plant

What to plant: seeds or small herbs from pots or containers? Certain herbs are easier to grow from seed than others. Some herbs, in fact, are best started from plants purchased at the nursery.

Planting Herbs from Pots, Packs and Containers

More kinds of herbs are becoming available in packs and containers at the nursery. Container plants are relatively inexpensive, are convenient and easy to plant. They can be planted almost any time, although depending on seasonal cold or heat, some periods are better than others.

Be selective when purchasing herb plants. Avoid a plant that has been growing in its container too long, with roots extending out the container bottom. Buy plants that have a robust, healthy appearance. As a rule, select a small plant with vigor rather than a large, less-robust specimen. For a step-by-step guide to planting from containers, see photos, page 140.

When to Plant?

Spring is the most common planting period. In cold-winter regions, plant in spring after the danger of frost has passed. If starting seeds indoors to set out as spring transplants, plan ahead and sow seeds several weeks before the last frost. See photos, page 144.

In warm-summer regions, plant early in spring so plants begin to establish before high temperatures come on. In moderate climates, planting can be done year-round. More water (and more time spent watering) will be required to establish plants set out late spring to summer due to the warmer temperatures.

Fall is a preferred planting time in mild-winter regions, with some exceptions. During fall the soil is still warm, which increases root growth, while air temperatures are moderate, decreasing stress and water need. By the time spring rolls around, the now-established roots respond to the warmer weather and produce healthy top growth.

It's a good idea to delay planting in summer to avoid the heat. High temperatures increase water need, and young plants will undergo serious stress. If you must plant in summer, be prepared to water diligently.

Watering

Learning to water correctly comes with practice. It pays to be aware of the changing water requirements of your plants as the mild temperatures of spring yield to the summer's heat. Miscalculate with too little or too much water and your herbs can suffer or die.

Watering Newly Planted Herbs

The most important watering period begins at planting time. Herbs planted from containers require moist soil, so regular irrigation is necessary. Plants are adjusting to an environment that is markedly different from their nursery growing grounds. Any prolonged dry period will prevent roots from developing uniformly and plant growth and performance can be permanently affected. If it does not rain, schedule daily irrigations for newly planted plants. If the weather is cloudy, you may be able to skip a day or two. If it is windy, the upper 1 to 2 inches of soil or mulch can dry out quickly, so monitor new plants carefully.

Young plants may need water once or even twice a day when it is hot. Temperatures higher than 90F take a toll on new plants. Adding an organic mulch—a 2- to 3-inch layer of material over the plant roots—cools soil temperatures and slows evaporation of moisture from the soil.

Apply water slowly around the plant's rootball. It helps to build a basin to hold the water. Avoid using a sprinkler to apply water, especially if it's windy. Water is wasted due to uneven applications and evaporation. Continue to monitor soil moisture by checking the soil regularly for several weeks.

It is just as critical to maintain a consistent watering program when starting herbs from seeds. Once seeds are planted and watered in, continue watering on a regular basis. Allowing the soil to dry out completely will cause the newly germinated seeds to perish.

Developing An Efficient Watering Program

After plants adjust to planting and produce new growth, gradually space out waterings, perhaps to one

Easy to Grow from Seed	Slow to Grow from Seed
Anise	Plant these herbs where they will not be disturbed while they take their time to germinate, grow and reach maturity.
Arugula	
Basil	
Borage	
Caraway	Catnip
Chervil	Coneflower (Echinacea)
Chives	Horehound
Coriander (Cilantro)	Hyssop
Dill	Lavender
Fennel	Lovage
Lemon Balm	Sweet Woodruff
Nasturtium	Winter Savory
Parsley	Wormwood
Rue	
Sage	
Salad Burnet	
Summer Savory	
Sweet Marjoram	
Thyme	

or two applications per week. Your prevailing climate and day-to-day weather are important factors. Irrigations will be far fewer in the cool, rainy Pacific Northwest and more frequent in the hot deserts and inland valleys of the Southwest. If temperatures reach 85F or more or if winds are excessive, check each day for moisture. Using a shovel or trowel, dig down into the soil to see how deep moisture has penetrated. The top few inches of the soil surface should be kept moist, but do not allow it to remain wet or soggy at any time. Most herbs, once they are past the new planting stage, prefer the soil to dry out slightly between waterings. This allows necessary oxygen to reach plant roots.

To water new plants efficiently, or to wean established plants from a high-water diet, gradually reduce irrigation frequency while increasing the duration of each irrigation. In other words, the number of days you water each week gradually become fewer, but you apply a greater volume of water with each irrigation. This helps develop root systems that are deep and wide spreading.

Propagating Herbs

Herbs can be propagated by several methods. If you want a few plants to season an occasional recipe, purchase plants in pots from a local nursery. If you need wheelbarrows of fragrant leaves and flowers for making potpourri, grow them from seed—the least expensive way to cultivate large quantities of herbs. New plants also can be started from stem or root cuttings, ground layering, division and offsets.

Starting with Seeds

The photos on page 144 show how to plant seed to grow transplants for your garden. If you collect seeds from your own plants, store them in a jar with a tight-fitting lid, fill with dry sand and keep in the refrigerator. This will help keep seed fresh for better and quicker germination. Refrigerating seeds causes them to overcome their natural dormancy and readies them for germination, a process called *stratifying*.
With a few exceptions, seed collected and planted from cultivated varieties of herbs, called cultivars, usually produce in inferior plants. Cultivated varieties are special forms of a species, so they have a mixed heritage. (Names of cultivars in this book are designated by being enclosed in single quote marks.) Plants started from seed collected from a straight species typically grow "true from seed." They will look and perform like the parent plant.

Cuttings

A large variety of herbs including lavender, lemon balm and rosemary can be propagated by cuttings, sometimes called *slips*. Cuttings from pineapple sage and mints are easy to root in water. Taking cuttings is sometimes faster than starting with seeds and it has the benefit of producing plants identical to the parent.

For rooting in soil, take 4- to 6-inch cuttings of stems from spring-flowering plants in midsummer. For plants that flower later in the year take cuttings before flowering. Fill a clean container with moistened sterile planting medium such as vermiculite (available at nurseries), sand or a combination of the two. Remove foliage from the bottom half of the cutting, wet it, then dip it in hormone rooting powder. Place cutting in soil to half of its length. Firm the soil around it. Enclose the cutting with clear plastic and set in indirect light; this creates an incubating greenhouse effect. Lemon balm, thyme and basil require 3 to 6 weeks to develop roots using this method. Woody herbs like rosemary, santolina and germander may require a few to several months.

Ground Layering

In ground layering, branches are rooted while still attached to the parent. It is a convenient, practically surefire way to start rosemary, santolina, lemon balm, thyme, sage and other perennial herbs. Select a branch that can be bent down until it touches the soil. Make a small slit on the underside of the branch tip and dust with hormone rooting powder. Scoop a shallow hole in soil under the branch. Peg branch down with a U-shaped wire and cover with soil. In six weeks, gently brush away soil to check branch for roots. When enough of a root system has formed, sever the new plant from its parent and pot up or replant.

Root Cuttings

Use this method when the parent plant is dormant. It works best with plants that have thick, fleshy roots such as comfrey, ginger and horehound. Dig up a section of root after the plant's bloom period has passed. If the rhizomes are massed, divide the mass into chunks. Each must hold a *bud*—a fan of leaves and root. Save the best ones then plant and water. Keep soil moist but not soggy.

Division

This is a good way to increase many herbs. In fact, some grow better after they are divided. It is important to divide at the proper time. As a rule, divide spring-flowering herbs in fall or directly after flowering. Divide fall-flowering herbs in spring (early spring in mild-winter regions). The reason for this timing? To provide several weeks of mild temperatures following the division so young plants have a better opportunity to become established.

Unless you have lots of garden space, don't keep every division. Replant only those pieces that have strong roots and healthy growth points or stems. Some perennial herbs, including tarragon, oregano and tansy, get woody or die out in the center. When dividing these, replant only the vigorous outer pieces. Set new divisions at the same soil level as they were growing. Water well, following the planting guidelines shown in the photographs on page 140.

1. Starting seeds indoors, step by step. Fill small pots with sterile potting soil. Be sure pots have drainage holes.

2. Tap a few seeds into each pot. Follow instructions on seed packet as to proper depth to plant seeds. Don't plant too deep.

3. Water with soft spray to avoid disturbing seeds and washing away soil. Label with herb name and planting date.

4. After 6 to 8 weeks, sage seedlings are ready to be planted in the garden. At the Farm we're fortunate to have a greenhouse, which provides the right amounts of light, heat and humidity. For windowsill-grown seeds, cover pots with a clear plastic bag and place in a window that receives 6 hours of sunlight each day. Check soil every few days. Keep it moist but not soggy.

Far left: Chives are among the easiest herbs to propagate. Dig up established clumps and carefully separate roots for replanting or give to friends or neighbors.

Bottom left: When propagating by cuttings, select a 4- or 5-inch-long stem from healthy parent plant. Make a sharp cut and dip end of stem in rooting hormone. Insert cut stem end into moistened sterile soil mix or sand. Keep in a warm, humid location receiving bright indirect light. These rosemary cuttings should form roots and be ready to replant in about two months.

Left: Seeds of many herbs and flowers can be collected and replanted the following spring. These are hollyhocks.

Below left: When planting, be sure to allow enough space between herbs for their mature spread.

Below: If container plants are rootbound, slice through rootball before planting to help plant roots spread and grow properly.

Offsets

Herbs with bulbous root systems such as chives, garlic and society garlic can be increased by separating offsets, which are immature bulbs or rhizomes. Plants are lifted from the ground, and small offsets are removed. They can then be planted at the appropriate time the same as new plants.

Growing Herbs in Containers

Apartment dwellers, urban home owners with limited yard space, and folks who just don't have time for a full-fledged herb garden can rejoice at the willingness of herbs to grow in containers. Without much rolling up of sleeves, anyone can savor the pleasures of fresh herbs grown on the patio, down the back steps or in a window box.

Selecting a soil mix suited to container culture is important. Often, plants fail because of poor drainage. Regular garden soil is almost always too heavy and drains much too slowly. Container soil mixes for herbs (and most plants) must be loose and fast draining.

Several kinds of mixes are available commercially at garden centers and home-improvement outlets. Some gardeners use a sterile potting mix, called a *soil-less mix,* straight out the bag. Others mix the potting soil with equal parts of sand and ground bark or peat moss. The added weight of the sand is helpful in windy regions, preventing plants from being blown over. For herbs in hanging containers, a lightweight house plant potting soil is recommended. Be sure there are holes in the container bottom to allow water to drain.

Container Types and Size

Choice of container size depends upon each herb's growth requirements. To learn the herb's mature size, see the descriptions in the Gallery of Herbs, pages 30 to 123. Containers having a soil depth of 6 inches or more are recommended. Generally, the smaller the container the more often you'll have to water. The root system must have enough soil space to draw sufficient moisture and food. Bay, rosemary, santolina, lemon verbena, sage and lavender do well in 10-inch pots. Herbs with strong tap roots, such as borage, dill and tansy, are more difficult to grow in pots.

Plant only cold-hardy herbs in large, immovable containers. Such herbs must be able to withstand the winter lows for your area. If tender perennials are planted in smaller, mobile containers (5-gallon or smaller), keep them near a front or back door. Then, when a freeze is predicted, it's easy to move them indoors.

It's not necessary to limit yourself to a one-herb-per-pot garden. Large containers, such as window boxes or half-barrel planters, allow for a healthy mixture of herbs. Place larger-growing plants in the center of the container and surround with a ring of lower-growing herbs. Upright herbs such as chives or garlic chives are at home in the middle, with trailing varieties of oregano, marjoram and savory around the container rim. To prevent center herbs from spreading and taking up too much space, plant them in a smaller clay pot or large coffee can. Punch drainage holes in the bottom and sides of the can. Sink the pot in the center of your container so that it will be hidden.

Some herbs seem to do better planted together than grown in separate pots. Strawberry pots are perfect for many small-growing herbs such as thyme, parsley and marjoram. Plant upright herbs on top and trailing ones in the pockets.

Container Care

Container gardens demand regular watering and fertilizing. The soil in a pot dries out and nutrients are washed out faster than garden soil. Container gardens often need daily watering during the growing season and dilute applications of fertilizer every 7 to 10 days. Porous pots, those that allow moisture to evaporate through the sides, such as unglazed terra cotta, dry out faster than glazed or plastic pots. Avoid letting container soils dry out completely or plants may die.

The Indoors-to-Outdoors-and-Back System

Freezing temperatures will kill cold-tender perennial herbs, so outdoor container plants must spend the winter indoors.

Moving any plant from a sunny, outdoor location directly indoors (or vice versa), greatly shocks the plant's system. Make the transition gradual and provide the best possible care after moving plants.

Allow about three to four weeks for the complete transition period, beginning before cold temperatures come on. First, move herbs to a location where they'll receive less direct sunlight. Leave for a week or two, then move them to a location where they'll receive even less sun. After another week herbs will be ready to move to a sunny location indoors. Unless you'll be keeping the herbs in a cool room, don't move plants after the weather turns cold and the heat is operating indoors. Moving outdoor plants into a warm, heated house can cause them to turn yellow and drop their leaves. Before moving plants indoors, hose off the foliage. If necessary, control insects now; pest problems will likely worsen indoors.

Repeat the gradual transition in reverse when moving herbs back outdoors in spring. Once outdoors for good, hose off foliage, water plants slowly and thoroughly to leach out salts that have accumulated in the soil, then fertilize.

Growing Herbs Indoors

Many herbs can be grown in a sunny window. A southern exposure is best for growing basil (remove flowers or seedheads as you see them), peppers, nasturtiums and thyme. An east or west window is suited for mints, parsley and scented geraniums, or any herb that will tolerate some shade. Others include catnip, chives, lavender, lemon balm, rosemary and sage.

Even with the best conditions, do not expect plants to grow as fast and become as lush indoors as they do outdoors. Too little sunlight, air that is too dry and containers that are too small reduce vigor and growth, and can cause plants to fail.

Provide a well-lit location that receives at least five hours of direct sun a day (more is preferred) and fresh air from an open window or door. Plant "grow-lights" can supplement sunlight.

Low humidity is a chronic problem indoors in winter. Place herbs on a large, waterproof tray covered with rocks or marbles. Fill the tray with water. As the water in the tray evaporates, it increases humidity around the plants. Indoor humidifiers and misting herbs also help.

Like their outdoor counterparts, herbs grown indoors thrive in a light, well-drained potting soil. Keep soil evenly moist and do not allow it to become soggy or dry out completely.

Garden Maintenance

Growing an herb garden should be a positive experience. As your gardening friends, we feel obligated to prepare you for some of the necessary evils of garden maintenance: pulling up weeds that threaten to overcome young plants; watering herbs diligently during periods of rainless weather; staking up herbs that become straggly; pruning unruly shoots during and especially at the end of the growing season; and fighting off crawly creatures that, like you, prefer to dine on the most-tender leaves and petals.

Weeding
Before planting, start off weed-free by cultivating the bed well, then watering it deeply. Wait one to two weeks for weed seeds to sprout. If possible, pull weeds to remove the roots. Try to disturb the soil as little as possible. If you use a hoe to cut off seedlings, go no deeper into the soil than 1 inch. Otherwise, more weed seeds come to the surface, where they, too, will germinate. After hoeing, lightly rake soil before planting.

Keeping ahead of weeds takes constant effort but there are a few simple methods to make this chore easier.

Attack weeds after a rain or an irrigation—any time the ground is soft. When you weed, get rid of the whole weed—especially its roots and seeds. Examine container plants carefully before planting. Often, weeds tag along with the herbs you are planting.

Feeding
Herbs growing outdoors in garden soil make few demands in terms of nourishment. Well-rotted garden compost mixed into the soil before planting, and at the end of every growing season, will provide most of the nutrients plants need. Apply an occasional dressing of an organic fertilizer, particularly if plants show signs of yellowing and lack of vigor.

Herbs growing in containers benefit from regular feeding. Liquid fertilizers work well. Follow label directions. If you live in a warm climate and container plants must be watered frequently, nutrients will be leached more rapidly from the soil. Reduce fertilizer application rates by half and apply more frequently.

Staking
Many herbs have a natural dwarfing habit. Others are cultivated specifically to form low-growing mounds. Even the tallest herbs, such as dill and fennel, usually can stand their ground on breezy days, especially if you have taken the precaution of planting them in a sheltered part of the garden.

If plants flop and sprawl, stake them as they grow to prevent damage to long stems and flowers. Keep them upright by inserting stout bamboo stakes, positioning three at intervals around a clump and secure with twine or plant ties.

Pruning
Most herbs benefit from pruning as a part of regular care. Pruning energizes dormant buds and helps develop strong, well-balanced plants.

At the end of the growing season, take stock of the health and appearance of your perennial herbs. Use sharp pruning shears to cut back any dead stems and to reduce long, straggly growth. Vigorous woody plants such as lavender, rue, sage and thyme should be cut back severely to reshape plants and encourage fresh new growth. Even though these plants are categorized as perennials, they are not everlasting. There will come a time (usually after a number of years) when they no longer have the vigor to renew themselves after being pruned. When plants reach this tired-out stage, replace them with new ones.

A wonderful way to recycle clippings (as an option to the compost pile) is adding them to your hot coals when grilling outdoors. Many herbs impart a flavorful aroma to foods. See page 163 for methods.

Pests in Your Herb Garden

Because of their strong pungent oils, many herbs are relatively free from problems with pests. This is even more the case with clean, healthy plants growing in well-drained soil. In fact, the overwhelming majority of plant problems are caused by incorrect cultural practices: overwatering or underwatering, overfertilizing, or planting too deep or too shallow. Soil type, soil drainage, incompatible plant mix and incorrect exposure to the sun add to the list of gardener-caused problems.

If problems do occur, chemical sprays are not the solution. Many herbs are grown to be ingested. Pesticides also kill beneficial insects that prey on pests. Your goal should be to eliminate these potentially harmful sprays around your home and garden.

Use natural or nontoxic control methods. Get to know which pests are common to your area and learn

Right: A mulch, a layer of material, often organic, has many uses in the garden. Use to cool the soil, conserve moisture and reduce weed growth around plants.

Below left: Half-barrel tubs are ideal for growing herbs. This is oregano.

Below right: A simple wooden planter with chives and thyme is handy if grown close to the kitchen door.

Left: An unusual form of pest control at work at the Farm. Guinea hens take a late-afternoon tour through the Star Garden, looking for insects.

Below left: Ladybird beetles, commonly called ladybugs, are good guys in the garden, eating aphids and other pests.

Bottom left: A worker adds lacewing eggs to herbs growing in nursery containers. Lacewings and their larvae feed on many garden pests.

Below: A companion planting of chives, rosemary and vegetables. Certain herbs are considered "good bedfellows," aiding plant growth and health. However, some herb-and-plant combinations are to be avoided. See text, page 151.

their life cycles. Most are vulnerable to control measures at certain stages of their lives. You should also learn to accept an occasional chewed leaf or flower.

As mentioned, keeping your herbs healthy with proper water and fertilizer prevents them from being bothered by many insects and diseases. Simply hosing off plants with a strong jet of water will control some common pests such as aphids or spider mites.

Providing shelter and food sources for beneficial insects in and around the garden supports an ongoing population of the "good bugs" such as ladybugs and lacewings. This is necessary for them to be effective over the long term. This means eliminating pesticides.

If control measures are required, use insecticidal soaps. These commercially available products interfere with the membrane activities of many types of pests, including aphids, scale and spider mites. You can purchase them premixed, or make your own spray by thoroughly mixing two tablespoons of dish soap to 1 gallon of water. (Additional recipes for organic sprays follow.) Thoroughly spray the soap solution on the entire affected plant. Allow it to remain for an hour or so, then rinse the plant with clean water. Do not use soap sprays on plants that are stressed for moisture, and do not spray when temperatures are over 90F; the spray can burn plant leaves.

Homemade Controls: "Bill's Bug-Buster Recipes"
Many homemade products can be used effectively to keep unwanted pests at bay. Unlike many chemicals, they are inexpensive and safe if used properly. This is especially important if herbs are grown for culinary use, or brought to the kitchen or other locations where food is prepared.

Garlic-Soap Spray

18 pureed garlic cloves
6 teaspoons mineral oil
1 quart water
8 tablespoons liquid dish soap

Soak garlic in mineral oil for 24 hours. Add water and soap, stirring well. Strain through cheesecloth or other filter to remove particles. Store this concentrate in glass jar until ready to use. Dilute at a rate of 1 part mixture to 30 parts of water to use as a spray. Effective on many common garden pests. See text above on how to use.

Hot Pepper Spray

1 cup cayenne peppers
1 cup water
3 tablespoons liquid dish soap

Puree peppers, mix well with water and liquid soap. Strain mixture through filter such as cheesecloth and store in glass container until ready to use. Dilute at a rate of 1 part mixture to 30 parts of water to use as a spray. Spray mixture directly on all leaf surfaces of infested plants.

Herb-Tea Spray

4 tablespoons pyrethrum
4 tablespoons wormwood
4 tablespoons lavender
4 tablespoons thyme
1 quart water

Blend ingredients together and make a "tea" by brewing 1 quart of hot water over herbs for 30 minutes. (Pyrethrum is available at at feed stores and nurseries.) Strain and pour into bottle with spray attachment. Helps control aphids, caterpillars and some fungi. See text at left for more detailed instructions on use.

Herbs in the Garden for Pest Control
Including selected herbs and herb combinations in the garden provides some measure of pest control. Damage by destructive insects can be minimized but don't expect eradication.

Some herbs help control insects by *repelling* or *confusing* them. If grown with vegetables or ornamental plants, the strong scent of these herbs masks the scent of the plants the egg-laying female is seeking.

Other herbs serve as *trap crops*. Insect pests are attracted to these herbs, which are usually planted well away from garden areas, including the herbs you want to harvest. After the pests have gathered on the host herb, it can be pulled and destroyed, along with the pests. Borage plants are sacrificed to control Japanese beetles. Mustard and nasturtiums attract aphids and squash bugs. Radishes attract cabbage maggots, and mullein is attractive to stinkbugs.

Herbs That Help Repel Pests

PEST	HERB
Ant	Spearmint, onion, tansy
Aphid	Castor bean, garlic, spearmint
Potato bean beetle	Marigold
Cabbage worm	Basil, chives, chamomile, dill, oregano, parsley
Carrot fly	Rosemary, sage, thyme, chives, onion, rosemary, sage
Colorado potato beetle	Green bean, horse-radish, marigold, tansy
Hornworm	Basil, eggplant
Japanese beetle	Garlic, tansy
Mexican bean beetle	Marigold
Nematode	Marigold
Striped cucumber beetle	Broccoli, nasturtium, radish, tansy
Whitefly	Garlic, marigold, nasturtium, spearmint, tansy

Dried herbs can be used as bug chasers. Wormwood and rosemary sprinkled around the garden deter snails and slugs, and southernwood and tansy discourage ants. Tansy combats fleas, mosquitoes and other parasites.

Good Bedfellows . . . Bad Bedfellows
Several herbs are believed to have positive effects when they are planted near vegetables or other herbs. They not only protect them from insects but are believed to boost their growth and improve their flavor. Chives, for instance, promote the growth of carrots; parsley or borage help tomatoes. Rosemary and sage thrive when planted in tandem, and yarrow is thought to increase the fragrance of most herbs. However, some plants decline because they cannot tolerate the particular chemistry of their companions. Basil, for example, hinders rue. Coriander retards the growth of fennel, tomatoes and beans.

Careful planning is the key to companion planting. Place good bedfellows close together. Use paths or walkways to separate foes. Alternate complementary herbs and plants in rows, locating them checkerboard-style in a bed. Or plant protective herb borders around pest-susceptible vegetables and ornamentals.

The most interesting aspect of companion planting is the cumulative benefit. When herbs, vegetables and flowers are grown together, food plants seem to be more flavorful, flowers and scented leaves become more fragrant. All the while the combinations and interactions help control insects.

Companion Plants: Good Bedfellows	
HERB	VEGETABLE
Anise	Coriander
Basil	Peppers, tomatoes
Bee balm	Tomatoes
Borage	Beans, strawberries, tomatoes
Chamomile	Cucumbers, onions, most herbs
Chervil	Radishes
Chives	Carrots, grapes, roses, tomatoes
Dill	Cabbages, onions, lettuces
Garlic	Roses
Horseradish	Potatoes
Hyssop	Cabbages, grapes
Lovage	Beans
Mint	Cabbages, tomatoes
Mustards	Beans, grapes, fruit trees, onions, beets, cabbages, lettuces, strawberries
Oregano	Beans
Rosemary	Beans, tomatoes, marjoram
Savory	Beans, onions
Tarragon	Most vegetables
Thyme	Eggplant, potatoes, tomatoes

Winter Protection

Unless you live in a frost-free climate, winter is time to put the garden to rest. There are a number of ways to ensure you'll have herbs the next spring. You may have to invite them inside, "winter coat" them or use their offspring to carry on the family name. Here are four common methods of increasing your herbs' chances of survival through winter.

1. Prevent damage by choosing growing locations carefully. Place cold-tender herbs in warm, protected locations. See Microclimates, page 139.

2. Mulch plants. A substantial layer (3 to 4 inches) of light, porous covering such as hay, pine needles, fir or hardwood bark or evergreen boughs insulates plants from the cold.

3. Overwinter plants in a cold frame. This box with a transparent cover acts like a mini-greenhouse, protecting plants against temperature fluctuations. Place cuttings and pots of lemon verbena, tarragon, pineapple sage and other cold-tender herbs inside.

4. Move herbs indoors. The challenge here is lack of space, the heated air, low humidity and insufficient light. See pages 146 and 147 for tips on growing herbs indoors.

Reaping and Keeping Your Harvest

Harvest time is traditionally associated with early fall, but herbs can be harvested as early as late spring and continue through fall. The growth of many herbs can be improved if plant parts are harvested and used regularly. Cut plants back by one-quarter to one-third; it will stimulate the plant, causing it to produce new, tender growth that is the best and most flavorful.

Here are some seasonal tips on when to harvest the most popular herbs.

Late Spring—leaves of arugula, borage, caraway, chervil, fennel, feverfew, rosemary, salad burnet, sorrel and sweet woodruff.

Early Summer—leaves and bulbs of chives, garlic chives, garlic and society garlic; basil leaves, bay leaves, calendula flowers, catnip leaves, dill leaves, lemon balm leaves, lemon verbena leaves, lovage leaves, mullein leaves and flowers, nasturtium leaves, parsley leaves, rose petals, sage leaves, tarragon leaves, thyme leaves and violet flowers.

Midsummer—anise leaves, chamomile flowers, lavender flowers, marjoram leaves and flowering herb, summer savory leaves, horehound flowering herb, yarrow flowering herb.

Late Summer—caraway seed, chervil leaves, coriander seed, dill seed, fennel seed, garlic bulbs, hop flowers, horseradish root, lovage seed.

Early Fall—anise seed, orris root.

Late Fall—chervil leaves.

For more information on preserving herbs, including salting, drying and freezing, see Herbal How-to Recipes, page 154.

Herbal How-to

recipes

M ankind has been concerned with desirable foods, and with the foods of desire, for as long as history has been recorded. Ancient manuscripts describe a pharmacopoeia used to incite passion in the hearts of the indifferent. As recently as a few hundred years ago it was widely believed that one could entrance, ensnare or sustain the love of another with the aid of certain leaves, petals, roots and fruits, blended to concoct love and fertility potions. It was common for people to pin their romantic hopes on the perceived magic of many familiar plants, including lettuce, pansies, bay, marigolds, thyme, marjoram, coriander, clove, cinnamon, ginger, lavender, rose, artichokes, parsley, carrot and dill.

Herbal lore carries reassuring prognostications of attraction, romance, marriage, happiness, fertility and protection from things that go bump in the night. Certain herbs were credited with strong feelings, humanlike personalities and spiritual powers, which were released when near certain people, their beds or their beloved. Honesty, *Lunaria* species, was said to thrive in a good woman's garden. Where rosemary flourished the mistress ruled. Sage would fade with the fortunes of the household and revive with its good luck, and earth dug from the footprints of a wandering lover and placed in a pot of marigolds would stop his or her roaming.

Could our forebears have been closer to the truth than we know? Although the reasons for attraction are almost as much a mystery today as they were in ancient times, we do know that the spur for love begins in the brain in the hypothalamus, which also governs our appetites for food and drink. Perhaps our epicurean activities are closely related and can influence the awakening of desire!

Cooking with herbs rekindles some of the charming rituals of the past. We hope our recipes impart the lure of uplifting fragrances, the hint of passion and an appreciation of subtle foliage, flowers and flavors provided by herbs. It doesn't matter whether the long history of herbal magic shows we are susceptible to suggestion, or that we simply believe in what has not yet been explained. Dining on herbs is a recipe for romance.

"Ceres presents a plate of vermicelli, For love must be sustained like flesh and blood, While Bacchus pours out wine, or hands a jelly: Eggs, oysters, too, are amatory food. "

—Lord Byron

Left: A picnic is that much more enjoyable when foods are enhanced with herbs.

Above: Herb vinegars allow the garden to keep on giving after the harvest season has passed.

Herbs in the Kitchen

"After a perfect meal we are more susceptible to the ecstasy of love than at any other time."
—Dr. Hans Bazli

Herbs as Healthy Seasonings

Herbs and spices make healthy eating less a matter of deprivation than of enchantment, offering delicious and nutritious alternatives to the salty, fatty and sugary foods many of us are used to eating. Most nutritious menus stress eating more fruits and vegetables, as well as increasing intake of fish, poultry and lean meats. Herbs are a perfect antidote when salt, sugar and fat have been reduced or eliminated from foods.

Mom's fried chicken won't be missed after you've sprinkled basil, garlic, marjoram, rosemary, sage, tarragon or thyme on your next roasted or broiled poultry dish. Fish seasoned with basil, a bay leaf, chervil, chives, dill, marjoram, parsley, rosemary, scallions, thyme or tarragon tastes fresher and more flavorful than when smothered in a cream sauce.

Serious dieters can spice up low-fat cottage or cream cheese with fresh chives or garlic. Homemade herb salts kept by the stove or table add extra flavor. Herb teas or unsweetened fruit juices can be flavored with mint or lemony herbs. Unsalted vegetable juices can be spiked with garlic, onion, basil, thyme or oregano.

Preserving Herbs for Kitchen Use

Fresh herbs are almost always preferred for use in cooking, but they are not always available. The good cook adjusts and takes advantage of bountiful harvests, preserving homegrown herbs so they will always be at hand after the growing season has passed. However you choose to preserve your herbs, have no doubt that they will be of higher quality (and

be much less expensive) than commercially available dried herbs. Plus you will have the great satisfaction of knowing that they are from your own garden.

Salting

One of the oldest preservation methods, salting works well with basil, dill and tarragon. Alternate layers of salt and herbs (Kosher salt is preferred) in a covered crock or jar. The middle layers of salt should just cover the herbs; the bottom and top layers should be slightly thicker. As a rule, use one cup of noniodized salt or sea salt for each cup of fresh herbs. This method also works using white sugar (instead of salt) with rose geranium leaves, mint, lemon balm, lemon verbena, roses and violets to make flavored sugar.

Drying

Herbs such as sage, rosemary, bay, spearmint, lovage, thyme, marjoram and oregano dry well, retaining their shape and flavor. One traditional way is to bundle several sprigs together, tie with rubber bands and hang upside down in a warm location away from light.

For short-stemmed herbs and flowers, *screen drying* is recommended. Lay herbs on a screen, wire rack or plastic tray with grid bottom, such as those found in plant nurseries. Spread leaves so that they barely touch each other in a single layer. Cover with paper towels, cheesecloth or muslin to keep herbs clean. Allow air to flow around herbs. Place in a cool, dry area out of direct sunlight, which spoils colors and dissipates oils.

Oven drying is a speedier method. Spread leaves on paper and dry in a preheated 100F oven. Leave the oven door open a crack to allow moisture to escape. With most herbs, 15 minutes should be sufficient to dry them. Allow to cool before storing.

The quickest way to dry herbs is in a microwave oven. Spread one layer of herbs over a paper towel on the bottom of the oven. Lay another paper towel on top. Operate the oven on low for about two minutes. If herbs are not fully dry, turn the leaves over and operate oven for another one to two minutes.
Caution: Don't leave herbs unattended when microwaving them; fires can occur.

Freezing

Many cooks prefer to freeze herbs that have fine or delicate leaves. The process is quick and, most important, the flavor of thawed herbs approaches that of fresh. Basil, chives, dill, fennel and parsley freeze well.

Freezing herbs in oil is equally convenient and flavorful. Be sure that herbs are air-dried. (Excess moisture promotes mold growth.) Strip leaves from branches and blend in a food processor. To two cups of fresh herbs gradually add about 1/2 cup high-quality oil; we prefer canola or olive. The mixture should be thick. Use only as much oil as is needed to bind the herbs into a spreadable paste. Pack the herb blend into small glass or plastic containers and freeze immediately. Later, spoon or scrape off the amount you need.

How Much Should You Use?

Herbs as seasonings should enhance foods, not cover up their natural flavors. Use them sparingly. Begin with 1/4 to 1/2 teaspoon of dried herbs for each four servings of food. Use three times as much of fresh herb as dry. If in doubt, add herbs in small amounts then taste, taste, taste.

The McCormick/Schilling Company tells us that "ground herbs and spices can be used in dishes with short cooking times while whole ones need a longer cooking time to release their flavor." Some cooks have found that herbs, whether dried of fresh, produce the best flavor when half the herb called for in a recipe is reserved and added to soups and stews during the last fifteen minutes of preparation. Garlic and bay are exceptions; they can be added at the beginning for best flavor development.

Herb Breads

"Bread deals with living things, with giving life, with growth, with the seed, the grain that nurtures. It is not coincidence that we say bread is the staff of life."

—Lionel Poilane

Caraway and Thyme Bread

Popular belief once held that caraway would prevent the theft of any item that contained it. This virtue gave it power as a love potion: Feed a person caraway and he or she cannot be stolen from you.

- 1 16-ounce package hot-roll mix
- 1 cup hot water
- 2 tablespoons butter, unsalted
- 1 large egg
- 2 tablespoons sugar
- 2 teaspoons caraway seeds
- 1 teaspoon thyme leaves, fresh
- 1 package (2-1/4 teaspoons) yeast

Combine all ingredients in large bowl. Stir until dough pulls away from side of bowl. With floured hands, shape into a ball. Dough will be sticky. Sprinkle frequently with flour and knead 5 minutes or until smooth. Grease a 9 x 5-inch loaf pan. Place dough in pan, cover with a damp dish towel and let rise in a warm place (80F to 85F) for about 30 to 45 minutes, or until doubled in size.

Preheat oven to 375F. Bake 20 to 30 minutes or until golden. When you tap the loaf with your fingers, you should hear a hollow sound. Cool on wire rack.

Fresh Herb Foccaccia Bread

"A pure soul starts with a pure body," advises our tea-room chef. She adds romance to meals with her aromatic version of foccaccia bread, a soft, thick, crusted pizzalike bread that teases the appetite.

- 2 cups lukewarm water
- 2 tablespoons yeast
- 1 tablespoon sugar
- 5-1/2 cups flour
- 1 teaspoon salt
- 1 teaspoon fresh chopped garlic
- 1 teaspoon fresh chopped rosemary (or herb of preference)
- 1 teaspoon chopped chives
- 2 tablespoons olive oil

Dissolve yeast and sugar in water in large bowl. Combine flour and salt. Add to yeast mixture, stirring well with wooden spoon. Add herbs and oil. Knead dough on lightly floured board until smooth, about five minutes. Place dough in oiled bowl and brush top of dough with oil. Let rest and rise until twice its original size, about 30 to 45 minutes. Punch dough down and shape into 10, 4 x 1-inch, oblong loaves. Make diagonal slashes with sharp knife across tops of loaves and place on ungreased baking sheet that has been lightly sprinkled with cornmeal. Let loaves rise for 10 to 15 minutes. Preheat oven to 400F. Bake for 10 to 15 minutes. Remove to wire rack to cool, and enjoy while warm.

Bread Baker Chocolate Bunny

Since the dawn of time, rabbits have been associated with new beginnings. They figure prominently in both human and agricultural fertility rites. What better way to celebrate the "spring" of a new relationship than with a rabbit-shaped loaf of bread? A French proverb claims, "Without bread, without wine, love is nothing." We add chocolate to this list.

- 2/3 cup warm milk (70F to 80F)
- 2 tablespoons unsalted butter, cut up
- 1 large egg
- 2 teaspoons vanilla extract
- 1/2 teaspoon salt
- 1/4 cup semisweet chocolate morsels
- 2-1/4 cups bread flour
- 3 tablespoons unsweetened cocoa powder
- 1/3 cup sugar
- 1 tablespoon yeast
- 3 medium rose-scented geranium leaves, finely minced

Add all ingredients to bread machine pan in the order listed. Process on dough/manual cycle. When complete, remove dough to floured surface. If necessary, knead in additional flour to make dough easy to handle. Divide dough in half. For bunny body, form dough into ball. Place on greased large baking sheet and flatten to 5-inch oval. For head, form one-third of remaining dough into ball and place above body. Flatten slightly and attach to body by pinching together. For nose, pinch off 1/2-inch ball from remaining dough and place on head. For arms and ears divide remaining dough into 4 pieces. Roll each to 5-inch rope. Arrange two ropes across body for arms, tucking ends under body. Shape remaining ropes into ears and arrange above head, tucking ends under head. Cover and let rise in warm place 30 to 45 minutes or until doubled in size. Bake at 350F for 35 to 40 minutes or until done, tenting with foil after 15 minutes to prevent overbrowning. Remove from pan and cool on wire rack. Decorate with fresh herbs and flowers as desired. See photo, page 156.

Sweet Coriander-Carrot Muffins

An herb symbolic of immortality, coriander was extolled as a lofty love charm in the Arabian romance, *The Thousand and One Nights.* In fact, the Arabs also considered carrots an aphrodisiac. Stewed in a milk sauce, carrots were believed to improve sexual performance. It was the Arabs who introduced the highly esteemed carrot to Europe.

Streusel Topping

- 1/3 cup brown sugar
- 1/2 teaspoon ground coriander
- 1 tablespoon unsalted butter
- 1/2 cup finely chopped walnuts

Mix sugar and coriander in a small bowl. Add butter and blend until ingredients look like coarse crumbs. Sir in nuts and set aside.

Recipe continued on page 157

Right: A whimsical Chocolate Bread Bunny, flavored with rose-scented geraniums.

Below: Sylvia Varney serves one of her herbal creations at the Farm's Tea Haus restaurant.

Bottom: Making salsa is a good excuse to sample the flavor of an herb you've never tried before. Cilantro, also known as coriander, enlivens this Mango Peach Salsa. See recipe on opposite page.

Muffin Mix

2-1/2 cups unbleached all-purpose flour
1 teaspoon baking soda
2 teaspoons baking powder
1/2 teaspoon ground coriander
Pinch of salt
1-1/3 cups light brown sugar, packed firm
2/3 cup vegetable oil
1 tablespoon minced lemon zest
1 large egg
1 cup buttermilk
2 teaspoons vanilla extract
1-3/4 cups grated carrot

Preheat oven to 400F. Lightly grease a 12-cup muffin tin (or 6-cup Texas-size tin). Whisk flour with next four ingredients. Stir next four ingredients in a large bowl; add buttermilk and vanilla. Gently combine dry ingredients with wet ones. Add carrots. Fill each muffin cup one-third full. Sprinkle streusel topping over batter. Bake 15 minutes, then reduce heat to 350F. Bake 10 to 12 minutes, until muffins are golden and spring back when lightly pressed with fingertips.

Herb Snacks

"Small cheer and great welcome makes a merry feast."
—Shakespeare

Americans are surely a society of confirmed snackers. Herbs give typical snacks a new twist, adding crisp, fresh flavors. You'll find these recipes a breeze to prepare.

Basil Cheese Snax

Basil leaves were once given as a token of love. Thomas Tusser, 1573, promoted this practice, claiming that basil "...receives fresh life from being touched by a fair lady." Italian girls wore basil in their hair to signal when they were ready to be kissed.

1 cup unsalted butter, softened
1 pound sharp cheese, grated
2 small sprigs of fresh basil
2-1/2 cups unbleached all-purpose flour
1 teaspoon salt
1/2 teaspoon ground cayenne pepper
1 cup toasted pecans, finely chopped

Preheat oven to 375F. Lightly grease a baking sheet. In a large bowl, cream softened butter and grated cheese together until smooth. In a mini-food processor, mince basil with 1/2 cup flour. Blend basil-flour and remaining flour, salt and pepper with cheese mixture. Add pecans and incorporate thoroughly. Dig in with hands to make a smooth ball. Divide dough into 12 to 24 pieces, depending on size of Snax desired. Roll each piece into a ball. Place the balls on the prepared baking sheet and flatten. Bake until Snax are puffy and slightly firm, 15 to 22 minutes.

Hot Artichoke Spread

The queen of France and renowned patroness of 16th-century art and literature, Catherine de Medici, included many artichokes in her diet. Paris street vendors of her time would cry, "Artichokes! Artichokes! Heats the body and the spirit!" Garlic, included in this dish, is another incendiary food and is universally celebrated as an aphrodisiac. As the herbalist Culpeper wrote, "Its heat is vehement."

1 14-ounce can artichoke hearts, drained, finely chopped
1 cup light mayonnaise
1 cup freshly grated Parmesan cheese
1/8 teaspoon Tabasco sauce
3 large garlic cloves, finely minced
Curry powder
Fresh basil, minced

Preheat oven to 350F. Combine all ingredients except the basil and spread in a shallow, lightly greased baking dish. Sprinkle with curry powder to taste. Bake 30 to 40 minutes. Garnish with minced basil and serve with crackers, chips or sliced French bread.

Salsas

If you've thought of salsas as just chopped-up tomatoes and peppers with a little cilantro thrown in, think again. Not exactly condiments, and not quite side dishes, salsas are a combination of fresh vegetables and fruits, herbs, chilies and spices. Although salsas vary widely in ingredients, taste, color and texture, they are similar in that their flavors are meant to be intense—whether sweet, sour, hot or earthy.

Salsas add flavor, lighting up our taste buds. Most salsas are healthy foods, containing little fat or cholesterol. Because salsas are typically made from simple raw ingredients, their recipes call for no more culinary equipment than a cutting board and a sharp knife.

Preparing salsa is a good excuse to sample the flavor of an herb you've never tried before. Salsa complements many dishes: scrambled eggs, steaks, pork or chicken, green beans, zucchini and summer squash, and, of course, with corn chips as an appetizer.

Mango Peach Salsa with Cilantro

This salsa contains little fat or cholesterol. It's simple, fast and flavorful.

1 small red bell pepper, peeled and seeded, then diced
1 cup chopped ripe peaches, peeled
1 cup chopped ripe mango, peeled
2 jalapenos, seeded and diced
2 tablespoons coarsely chopped fresh cilantro
1 cup freshly squeezed orange juice
1 tablespoon freshly squeezed lime juice
1 tablespoon fresh mint leaves, coarsely chopped
1 green onion, finely sliced
1/4 cup minced red onion

Mix all ingredients in a small nonreactive bowl (avoid using tin or aluminum). Allow to sit 30 minutes before serving to marry flavors. Use salsa the same day it is made. Enjoy it with warm corn chips, grilled chicken, fish or pork.

Rosemary-Thyme Salsa

1 medium tomato, diced
1/4 cup diced red onion
2 tablespoons chives, minced
2 small jalapeño peppers, seeded and minced
1 tablespoon fresh thyme leaves
1 tablespoon fresh rosemary, minced
1/8 teaspoon salt
1-1/2 tablespoons white wine
1-1/2 tablespoons olive oil
1 tablespoon Tabasco sauce

Combine in a skillet and simmer over moderate heat for 15 minutes. Serve warm at room temperature.

Substitute basil and tarragon, or dill and savory, for thyme and rosemary.

Avocado and Corn Salsa with Oregano

3 ears corn, husked (about 2 cups kernels)
2 avocados, peeled, pitted and diced
1 red onion, finely diced
1 red bell pepper, seeded and finely diced
2 tablespoons olive oil
1/3 cup red wine vinegar
1 tablespoon minced garlic
1 tablespoon ground cumin
1 teaspoon red pepper flakes
1/4 cup chopped fresh oregano
1/4 cup fresh lime juice (about 2 limes)
Salt and coarsely ground black pepper to taste

Blanch corn in boiling water for 3 minutes. Drain and cool under cold water. Cut kernels from cobs and place in medium bowl. Add remaining ingredients and mix well. Refrigerate. May be kept for one day for best flavor. Possible substitutions for oregano: marjoram, savory or thyme.

Herbal Vinegars

Vinegars have a sour reputation. They're considered afterthoughts for the diet-conscious, sprinkled sparingly on salads. The first vinegar may have been an accident. Its name, *vin aigre,* meaning sour wine, was first used in medieval France.

Today, vinegars flavored with herbs are prized for culinary, medicinal and even cosmetic use. Wine vinegars are made from all types of wine from many different countries, with balsamic vinegar considered the ultimate. Made in Modena, Italy, since the 16th century, balsamic vinegar was so valued that it was often included in a bride's dowry or family inheritance. Dark, rich, sweet, pungent balsamic is the fermented juice of trebbiano grapes. As with old cognac, wooden vats of oak, walnut, or cherry store the vinegar until maturity—traditionally ten years.

Some popular herbs for vinegars are basil, especially the purple varieties, which add a rosy glow to the infusion; chives, with blossoms; dill, garlic, lavender, mint, lovage, tarragon and savory. Try combining two herbs such as garlic and tarragon, onion and basil, garlic and marjoram or chives and dill.

Herb Vinegars as Flavor Boosters

Making herbal vinegars is a pleasure for the culinary herb gardener, and it's a simple simple way to concentrate a favorite herb's flavor and store it for use later on. Herb vinegar can give new flavor to any stew, vegetable dish, soup, marinade, sauce or salad dressing that normally calls for vinegar in the recipe. Here are a few pucker-up tips on using vinegars.

- Use an herb vinegar in place of one-fourth of the liquid when using a dry mix to make a sauce (such as spaghetti or taco) or gravy.
- After sautéing meat, pour a few tablespoons of vinegar into the same pan and combine it with any browned particles left from the meat for a quick, savory sauce.
- Use a tablespoon or less of herb vinegar to add moisture and lightness to cakes, cookie doughs, puddings and pie fillings.
- Use as part of the liquid, a spoonful per person, in preparing a favorite soup or stew.
- Choose an edible flower vinegar or balsamic vinegar to splash on sweetened fresh or frozen fruit.
- Use herb vinegar as a substitute for some of the fruit juice in jelly recipes that include pectin.
- Basil vinegar gives tomato juice a special zest.
- Tarragon vinegar can be added to a pot of beans.
- Mint vinegar is a compatible seasoning for lamb chops and ham.

Basic Herb Vinegar

Collect fresh herbs for vinegar in the morning after the dew has dried from the foliage, but before the hot sun has evaporated the essential oils from the leaves.

2 cups high-quality vinegar
1 cup loosely packed herbs of your choice

Gently clean the sprigs, if necessary, in cool water. Be careful not to bruise the leaves, which will cause them to release their oils prematurely. Pat-dry or use a vegetable spinner to remove excess water. Overly wet leaves will not affect the flavor but can make the vinegar cloudy.

Fill large, clean jars with the herbs and cover them with the vinegar to within 1 inch of the jar's top. With a wooden spoon, push down and bruise the herb leaves. Vinegar reacts chemically with metal and should not come in contact with metal containers, spoons or lids.

Allow herb-vinegar mixture to steep in a dark place at room temperature for three to four weeks. Taste to determine desired strength. If the flavor is too strong, dilute with unflavored vinegar. If there is not enough flavor, repeat the procedure, adding more fresh herbs. Remove herbs by straining the vinegar through a plastic colander and then through coffee filters until the liquid is clear.

Pour vinegar into small, attractive bottles, adding a fresh herb sprig, stopper and label. Store away from direct sunlight. Use within one year.

Seasonable Salads

Not sure lettuce is a food? Add herbs and a spiked dressing, and serve with chilled white wine and French bread. Sassy! Herb or vegetable? Fernlike fennel, featured in the recipe following, is an herb but its bulblike stalk is used more like a vegetable. Fennel's gentle anise-flavored leaves were lauded as a stimulant by the ancients. The Greeks in particular thought it contributed to long life, virility and bravado.

Pretty Fennel Salad

This crunchy, colorful creation features fennel, walnuts, mozzarella and other lively ingredients tossed in a tangy mustard vinaigrette.

    1/4 cup red wine vinegar
    2 cloves garlic, crushed
    2 teaspoons Dijon mustard
    2 cups chopped tomatoes
    1/2 cup walnut oil
    1 cup sliced, blanched green beans
    1/2 cup walnuts, chopped
    1 cup cubed mozzarella cheese
    2 cups sliced fennel bulb
    1/4 cup chopped fresh basil or celery leaves

In a small bowl, combine vinegar and mustard, then set aside. Heat oil over medium heat in large skillet. Add walnuts and sauté until they begin to brown. Toss in fennel and garlic. Cook, stirring constantly, about 2 to 3 minutes, until fennel begins to soften. Remove pan from heat and mix in remaining ingredients. Blend in vinegar-mustard mixture and toss gently. Serve while warm on large lettuce leaves.

Chicken Salad From The Garden

"Chicken salad has a certain glamour about it. Like the little black dress, it is chic and adaptable anywhere."
—Laurie Colwin

This is an excuse-proof version of chicken salad, and a favorite when served in our tearoom.

    4 cooked chicken breasts, diced
    3 tablespoons black olives, chopped
    1/2 cup mayonnaise
    2 tablespoons fresh parsley leaves, chopped
    1 cup sour cream
    1 tablespoon dry onion dip seasoning
    1 4-ounce can chopped, unsweetened pineapple
    1 tablespoon balsamic vinegar
    1-1/2 cups chopped celery
    1 bunch green onions, chopped
    1 tablespoon tarragon mustard
    1/4 cup pecans, chopped and toasted
    Salt and pepper to taste

Gently but thoroughly combine above ingredients. Keep chilled until time to serve.

Asparagus Bundles with Thyme Blossom Butter

Known as one of the favorite foods to ignite emotional embers, asparagus was much used in Europe, especially by Madame Pompadour for her King Louis XV. See photo, page 160.

    1-1/2 pounds fresh asparagus, trimmed
    8 scallion stems
    2 tablespoons butter, softened
    2 tablespoons grated lemon peel
    2 tablespoons fresh lemon juice
    1/2 cup thyme blossoms

In a saucepan, steam asparagus and scallion stems in a small amount of water. Cook until tender-crisp, then drain. Arrange asparagus stalks in four bundles and tie them with scallion stems. Place bundles on serving plate. Combine butter, lemon peel and half thyme blossoms in bowl and mix well. Spoon onto asparagus bundles. Garnish with remaining thyme blossoms.

Soups

"Only the pure of heart can make a good soup."
—Ludwig van Beethoven

It is difficult to imagine what soup would be like without the passionate flavors of herbs. Although they provide many options for the creative cook, certain herbs are known to enhance certain foods.

We believe that savory, both summer and winter varieties, is fundamental to soup seasoning. Blended with other herbs, it helps produce flavorful soups consistently. Consider our Savory Soup Blend: *basil, lovage, parsley, marjoram, thyme, savory* and *bay*. The herbs are listed in order of suggested volume; adjust proportions to suit your taste. Use fresh or dried herbs. The ratio of fresh to dried is about three to one.

Mucho Macho Gazpacho

Marjoram, symbol of joy and honor, and thyme, representing activity and courage, create the savory backbone of this cool, garden-fresh soup.

    5 to 6 large tomatoes, peeled and chopped
    1 tablespoon fresh lemon juice
    3 or 4 green onions, chopped
    1/2 cup light sour cream
    1 teaspoon salt
    Chicken broth (optional)
    1/2 teaspoon sugar
    1 teaspoon each fresh thyme and basil
      or 1 teaspoon each dill and marjoram
    Chives, parsley or dill, chopped, as garnish

Puree tomatoes in a blender. Yield should equal 4 cups. Add onions, salt, sugar and lemon juice, blending well. Pour into a large bowl and whisk in sour cream. Soup may thicken with standing. If so, thin with broth. Garnish with chopped chives, parsley or dill. Serve chilled.

Above: This picnic features Asparagus Bundles with Thyme Blossom Butter, recipe on page 159. Rose punch, creamy brie with crackers and a salad of fresh herbs, greens and edible flowers complete the menu.

Right: A good reason to pause for refreshment: Iced tea garnished and flavored with peppermint tastes that much better in the garden.

Opposite page

Top left: When placed on hot coals, the smoke from the stems and leaves of many herbs adds exquisite flavor to grilled foods.

Top right: Bill Varney with Herb-Skewered Kabobs, ready for the grill.

Right: Herb-Skewered Kabobs take advantage of the summertime garden, when many herbs have grown long and leggy. The stems of herbs such as rosemary, sage, many basil varieties and lavender hold and flavor foods. See recipe, page 163.

Oma's Chicken Noodle Soup

Every garden needs an angel, and ours is Carol Luckenbach, a longtime manager of our greenhouse and all that grows in the Farm's gardens. Carol's green-thumb talents touch the minds and souls of all who visit. Her creativity reaches beyond the garden's borders. Oma's Chicken Noodle Soup is Carol's culinary gift to our Farm.

    1 2-pound fryer chicken
    1 large potato, peeled and diced
    2 tablespoons salt
    1/2 cup rice, uncooked
    1/2 medium white onion, chopped
    1 tablespoon fresh parsley, chopped
    1 tablespoon fresh oregano, minced
    3 stalks celery, chopped
    1 tablespoon fresh basil, minced
    3 large carrots, diced
    4 ounces fine egg noodles, uncooked

Place chicken in a large Dutch oven and fill with water. Add salt and bring to a boil. Gently simmer for about 1 hour—until chicken is cooked and meat begins to fall off the bone. Remove chicken from broth and save for another use. Strain broth. Return broth to pot and add onion, celery, carrots, potato and rice. Bring to a boil, then simmer for 15 minutes. Sprinkle in parsley, oregano and basil, and continue simmering 15 more minutes. Stir in noodles and cook for about 5 minutes or until noodles are soft. Garnish with fresh sprig of parsley and enjoy hot. Serves 6.

The unused chicken meat is perfect for chicken salad. See recipe, page 159.

Cheddar and Chive Corn Chowder

With a lineage more than three thousand years old, chives in some form have always been part of our culinary heritage. The herb's name comes from the Latin word meaning "unity." The slender, dark green leaves of chives were pictured in the monuments of ancient Egyptians. In Shakespeare's play, A Midsummer's Night Dream, King Oberon's elfin troupe puffed on tiny pipes made of hollow chive leaves. Like a game of pick-up-sticks, Rumanian gypsies used the stems to tell fortunes.

    4 slices bacon, chopped
    1-1/2 cups milk
    1 medium onion, chopped
    1/2 cup evaporated milk or half-and-half
    2 cups diced potatoes
    2 cups water
    1 tablespoon butter
    2 cups cream-style corn
    Salt and pepper to taste
    Sharp cheddar cheese, cubed
    Chives and chive blossoms as garnish

Sauté bacon and onion and set aside. Boil potatoes in water about 15 minutes or until tender. Add remaining ingredients except cheese and chives. Simmer until heated through. Do not boil. Put cubed cheese in bowls. Ladle hot soup over cheese, garnish with finely snipped chives and blossoms before serving.

Savory Main Dishes

Vegetarian Lasagna

Adore lasagna but prefer your pasta without meat? This version features mushrooms, olives, carrots, onions, spinach and an assortment of luscious cheeses.

    10 lasagna noodles
    1/2 cup pitted ripe olives, chopped
    2 packages (10 ounces each) frozen spinach, chopped
    1/4 cup fresh oregano, chopped
    1/2 cup onion, chopped
    2 cups cream-style cottage cheese
    1 tablespoon olive oil
    1 cup raw carrots, coarsely grated
    1 pound Monterey Jack cheese, sliced
    2 cups fresh mushrooms, sliced
    1/4 cup grated fresh Parmesan cheese
    1 can (15 ounces) tomato sauce
    1 can (15 ounces) tomato paste

Place noodles in a pot of boiling, salted water and cook for 8 to 10 minutes. Drain. Prepare spinach then set aside. Preheat oven to 375F. Sauté onion in oil until soft. Add carrots and mushrooms to onion and cook until crisp-tender. Stir in tomato sauce, paste, olives and oregano. Oil a 13 x 9 x 2-inch pan. Layer in one-half each of noodles, cottage cheese, spinach and tomato-vegetable sauce mixture and one-third of the sliced cheese. Repeat, placing remaining third of Monterey Jack on top. Sprinkle with Parmesan cheese. Bake for 30 minutes or until bubbling hot. Serves 8.

Cumin-Black Bean Quiche

In the fourth century, Saint Jerome would not allow the nuns under his spiritual direction to eat black bean soup because of its reputation as an aphrodisiac.

    1 baked 9-inch, deep-dish pie crust
    5 large eggs
    1-1/2 cups evaporated milk or half-and-half
    1 16-ounce can black beans, drained
    2 cloves garlic, minced
    1/2 4-ounce can diced mild green chilies, drained
    1 tablespoon chili powder
    1 teaspoon ground cumin
    1/4 cup onion, chopped
    1/2 cup sour cream
    1 cup shredded Monterey Jack cheese
    1/2 cup guacamole
    1 medium tomato, chopped
    1 cup shredded sharp cheddar cheese
    Fresh oregano, minced, for garnish

Preheat oven to 350F. Combine cheeses, then sprinkle one-half over crust. Spread black beans evenly over cheese. Sprinkle chilies and onion over beans. Cover with remaining mixed cheese. Beat together eggs, evaporated milk, garlic, chili powder and cumin. Carefully pour egg mix into quiche. Bake about 45 minutes to 1 hour, until toothpick inserted in center comes out clean. Cover edges of crust with foil if needed to prevent overbrowning. Cool 10 minutes. Spread sour cream evenly over top of quiche. Spoon guacamole around inside edges of crust. Sprinkle chopped tomato over top. Complete with a garnish of minced oregano.

Grilling with Herbs

"Even an old boot tastes good if it is cooked over charcoal."

—Italian folk saying

Our taste buds tell us herbs and spices are not mere staples in the kitchen, they *spark* the flavors of grilled foods. Equally important to the actual grilling is how ingredients are marinated and assembled. From coast to coast, grilling defines the celebration of life that is all-American outdoor cooking. This is real food, perfect for a moonlit meal on a balmy summer night.

We prefer building a fire of natural hardwood such as mesquite, oak, almond or apple. Hardwoods burn longer and give a wonderful, true wood flavor to grilled foods. Shrubby herbs such as rosemary, thyme, winter savory and sage add their own flavors. Herbs may be placed over the coals of a gas grill but foods will not be as flavorful.

Herb-Skewered Kabobs

This meal takes advantage of the long and leggy herbs of a summertime garden. These branchlets present opportunities for harvesting an age-old piece of cooking equipment—the leaf and sprig.

1-1/4 to 1-1/2-pounds top sirloin steak, trimmed and cut
   into 16 cubes about 1 inch thick
or
1-1/2 pounds boneless chicken breasts cut into 16 cubes
16 cherry tomatoes or tomato slices
16 large garlic cloves, peeled
2 large green bell peppers, chopped into 16 pieces
1 red onion, chopped into 16 pieces
8 12- to 14-inch, leggy but sturdy sprigs of basil, lavender,
   rosemary, sage or thyme
Balsamic Herb Basting Sauce, recipe following

Strip leaves from all but the top two inches of herb sprigs to make skewers. Alternate pieces of beef or chicken, bell pepper, onion, tomatoes and garlic on each herb skewer. Place kebabs in 13 x 9 x 2-inch glass baking dish. Pour 1 cup Basting Sauce (see below) over kabobs. Let stand for at least 30 minutes, turning kabobs occasionally.

Prepare barbecue, heating to medium-high. Grill kabobs so beef or chicken is cooked medium-well, or to your preference. Brush Herb Basting Sauce frequently on each side. After meat is safely cooked, transfer to platter and serve.

Balsamic Herb Basting Sauce

1 cup vegetable oil
2 teaspoons chili powder
1/2 cup olive oil
1/2 cup mixed herbs, minced
(rosemary, thyme, sage, lemon verbena, basil)
1/2 cup red wine vinegar
1 tablespoon minced garlic
1 tablespoon black pepper
1 teaspoon salt
Combine all ingredients in a large, nonmetallic bowl.

Beverages

"Come quickly, I am tasting the stars."

—Dom Perignon, the moment of discovering champagne

Garden-fresh foods are inseparable from the drinks that accompany them. Homemade beverages featuring herbs are one of the most beautiful and personal ways to entertain. For a festive welcome to your guests, create one or more of these luscious libations.

Herb Teas

The method of making herb teas varies little from herb to herb. Teas made from bark and plant roots usually need a little longer brewing time. Bark and root teas are also higher in mineral content, especially iron and copper, so longer brewing extracts a maximum amount of their flavor and nutrients. Bring water to a boil, add material and reduce heat. Five to ten minutes of gentle simmering should be sufficient for seeds, roots and bark. For teas made from the leaves, petals and flowers, pour boiling water over the herbs and allow mixture to steep three to five minutes, or until the delicate flavors are released. Strain to remove herb leaves.

Blend your own flavors. Avoid mixing savory herbs with sweet-flavored herbs or you will suppress the flavor of one with the other. Also consider adding fresh garnishes to your herb tea for variety. A slice of lemon, a zest of orange peel, a stick of cinnamon or even a pinch of vegetable salt can make each cup a special occasion.

Basic Pot of Herb Tea

When we brew herb tea, we prefer to use more than the usual "1 teaspoon dried." Brewing too little of an herb often produces a weak, faintly flavored tea.

1 tablespoon dried herb or 2 packed tablespoons fresh herb
   for each cup
Add an additional 2 tablespoons fresh or 1 tablespoon dry
   herb "for the pot"
For iced tea, increase fresh herb to 3 tablespoons, dried
   herb to 2 tablespoons

Pour fresh cool water in a pan and bring to a rolling boil. Rinse out a nonmetalic (enamel) teapot with some of the hot water to warm the pot. Add herb leaves or flowers to teapot. Pour boiling water over herbs. Steep tea for at least 5 minutes.

Pour out a little to taste, repeating until the tea reaches the desired strength and flavor. Most herb teas are golden green in color when ready to drink. Don't steep too long. This may produce a bitter, grassy taste. If the tea is too weak, add more herbs for more flavor, but don't increase the steeping time. Strain leaves as you pour each cup. Serve with sugar, honey, rock candy or fresh lemon or orange slices. Milk is not recommended. Add a splash of brandy, rum or wine to make an enjoyable evening beverage.

Above: Buttermilk Pie, left, with Rose Geranium Shortbread, lower right, and Peppermint Shortbread, upper right.

Above right: Rose Geranium Pound Cake. See recipe on page 166.

Right: Lemon verbena adds a new twist to this margarita. See recipe, page 165.

Below: Container gardening is an excellent way to have fresh herbs handy for kitchen use. Lemon verbena is appealing as well as useful when grown in a half-barrel planter.

Sun Tea

For hundreds of years, people have used the sun as a source of heat to brew herbal beverages without boiling away natural flavors."Tea" is released from the herbs but not oils or acids, which can give overcooked teas their acrid taste. Try this blend; the measurements provided are "packed" fresh herbs.

1 cup fresh peppermint leaves
1 cup lemon balm leaves
1 tablespoon rosemary tops
3 sage leaves

Place all herbs in a 1/2-gallon glass jar, preferably one with a glass cover. Fill with fresh, cool water. Place in full sun. Move jar to follow the sun as the light shifts. Shake or stir occasionally. At the end of the day (or after 3 to 6 hours, depending on the sun's intensity), strain tea and add sugar if desired. Enjoy warm from the jar, or cool with lots of ice. The sun tea method does not work for seeds and roots, which require boiling water to release their flavors.

Selecting Tea to Suit a Mood

Apple mint and pineapple mint brew fruity teas and may be served hot or iced. Black peppermint tea is refreshing hot and soothing to upset stomachs and to treat headaches. It has the strongest flavor of the mints. Catnip, also from the mint family, has a bittersweet taste. Take before bed for its sedative effect. Lemon herb tea, either from lemon balm or lemon verbena, is stimulating and cooling. Lemon balm tea tastes like a sweet mint tea with a touch of lemon. Lemon balm is sometimes called "the scholar's herb" for its reputed ability to improve memory and clear the mind. Lemon verbena is stronger and cleaner in fragrance; it also has a mild sedative effect. Spearmint, essential to mint juleps, is pleasant by itself or added to black teas. It is also one of the best teas for counteracting flatulence after a large or rich meal.

Lemon Verbena Margaritas

An herb from hot Central America and South America, lemon verbena is believed to relieve nervous stomachs, depression, headaches and heart palpitations. Its intense, citrus-green scent makes it an ideal ingredient in a summer drink. A variation on an "ade," this herb-and-fruit drink makes juicy company for an open-air repast.

1 6-ounce can frozen limeade concentrate
3 tablespoons triple sec liqueur
3/4 cup tequila
3/4 cup water
1/2 fresh lime, juiced
2 tablespoons minced lemon verbena leaves
Lemon verbena sprigs for garnish
Ice cubes

Fill a 32-ounce blender-carafe with ice cubes. Add limeade, triple sec, tequila, water, lime juice and minced lemon verbena. Blend on high until all ice cubes are crushed to the point of being slushy. Pour into wide-mouth glasses, and garnish with sprigs of lemon verbena. Serves 4.

Minted Melon Potion

The Arabs have always believed that mint increases virility, and modern herbalists prescribe it for cases of impotence and decreased libido. Whether added to a glass of ice water or a tub of bath water, peppermint supplies pick-me-up vigor.

2 2-1/2-pound ripe cantaloupes
5 cups cold water
1/4 cup plus 3 tablespoons superfine sugar
1/4 cup fresh peppermint, minced
Peppermint sprigs and Johnny-jump-up blossoms as garnish
Ice cubes

Cut each melon in half. Scoop out and discard the seeds. Remove the rind and cut melon into 1-inch cubes. In a blender, blend half the melon with 1/2 cup water and half the minced peppermint until smooth. Repeat with remaining melon, 1/2 cup water and rest of peppermint. Transfer the puree to a large pitcher and add the final 4 cups water and sugar. Stir until the sugar is dissolved. Pour into glasses filled with ice. Garnish with a peppermint sprig and Johnny-jump-up blossoms. Makes about 12 cups.

Other fruits such watermelon, honeydew or strawberries can be substituted for cantaloupe.

Lemongrass Mimosa

Take two deep breaths of lemongrass and chances are its flowery citrus fragrance will create a cheery, party mood. The taste of lemongrass can be difficult to describe; its flavor is lemony but not the least bit acidic. We love its gentle pucker power.

1 lemongrass leaf, 6 inches long
1/2 teaspoon sugar
6 ounces fresh-squeezed orange juice
1 tablespoon fresh lemon juice
Champagne
Wedge of lemon and lemongrass leaf as garnish

Bruise lemongrass leaf with sugar in a 12-ounce glass. Add fresh squeezed orange juice and mix well. Add lemon juice and three or four ice cubes and mix again. Fill with chilled champagne. Garnish with a wedge of lemon and stem of lemongrass.

Party Cakes

"Once in a young lifetime one should be allowed to have as much sweetness as one can possibly want and hold."
—Judith Olney

Lemon Geranium Angel Food Cake

The fragrance of a single lemon-scented geranium leaf can invoke a sentimental journey, bringing back hand-in-hand walks through grandma's garden. Brush against a plant and you'll see what we mean. The sweet-tart, earthy scent is so addictive you'll go back again and again just to touch and take in another whiff.

Recipe continued on page 166

6 large lemon-scented geranium leaves
1-3/4 cups sugar, divided
12 large eggs, separated
1-1/4 cups cake flour
1/2 teaspoon salt
2 teaspoons cream of tartar
1 teaspoon lemon extract
1/2 teaspoon vanilla extract
2 tablespoons rose water
Strawberries and yellow pansies for garnish

In a mini-food processor, finely mince lemon-scented geranium leaves with 1/2 cup sugar. Set aside. Separate the whites and yolks (discard yolks or use in other dish) of refrigerated eggs. Allow whites to come to room temperature. Sift cake flour five times with 1/4 cup sugar. Stir in the lemon-geranium sugar, mixing thoroughly. In a chilled mixing bowl with chilled beaters, beat egg whites with salt at high speed until foamy. Add cream of tartar. Beat whites, gradually adding 1 cup sugar. Beat until sugar is blended and mixture is stiff enough to form peaks. Add lemon extract, vanilla extract and rose water. Slowly fold in flour mixture. Place batter in a clean, dry angel food cake pan. Bake in preheated oven at 375F for 35 minutes or until slightly golden. Invert cake pan and allow to cool. Serve with sliced strawberries and yellow pansies.

Rose Geranium Pound Cake

Men often present women with roses, chocolate, perfume, music and other pleasurable treats to put them in a romantic frame of mind. "Awaken her senses" seems to be the unstated motto of suitors. This cake certainly follows suit.

6 rose-scented geranium leaves
2-3/4 cups sugar
1 cup unsalted butter, softened
6 large eggs
2 teaspoons rose water
1/2 teaspoon lemon extract
1 teaspoon vanilla extract
3 cups unbleached all-purpose flour
1/4 teaspoon salt
1/4 teaspoon baking soda
1 cup sour cream
Zest from 1 small lemon
Powdered sugar, bittersweet chocolate, red roses,
  geranium leaves as optional garnishes

Preheat oven to 300F. Butter and flour a 10-inch tube pan. (We like to use a heart-shaped pan.) In a food processor, finely mince geranium leaves with sugar. Add butter and cream mixture until light. Mix in eggs one at a time. Add rose water and extracts. Blend well. Sift flour, salt and soda together three times. Add alternately with the sour cream to the butter mix. Add lemon zest and blend well. Pour into prepared pan and bake for 1-1/2 hours or until golden and firm. Loosen edges with knife and let stand for 15 minutes in the pan, then invert on wire rack to cool. Glaze or dust with powdered sugar. Drizzle with melted bittersweet chocolate. Garnish with roses and geranium leaves.

Rose Geranium Buttermilk Pie

Cookbook author Fanny Fern once said, "The way to a man's heart is through his stomach." Our buttermilk pie captures her claim of comfort food and adds a sexy little twist.

1-3/4 cups unbleached flour
1/4 teaspoon salt
2 teaspoons sugar
10 tablespoons cold unsalted butter cut into pieces
3 tablespoons cold shortening, cut into 1/4-inch pieces
1/2 cup (or less) of ice water
4 medium-sized rose geranium leaves
2 cups sugar
1/2 cup unsalted butter, softened
6 eggs
2 cups buttermilk
1/8 teaspoon nutmeg (or to taste)

Combine flour, salt and 2 teaspoons sugar in food processor. Add 10 tablespoons butter and shortening. Process until crumbly. Slowly add ice water with food processor running until mixture forms a ball. Turn out onto plastic wrap and shape dough into large ball. Chill for at least 30 minutes. Divide dough into two portions. Roll into circles onto floured surface. Fit dough into two 9-inch pie plates; trim and flute edges. Mince leaves with 2 cups sugar in food processor. Add remaining 1/2 cup butter and process until creamy. Beat in eggs, buttermilk and nutmeg. Pour into pie shells. Bake at 350F for 50 minutes or until center is almost set. Allow to cool completely before serving.

Spicy Kahlua Chocolate Cake

Chocolate contains mild central-nervous-system stimulants, as well as an amphetaminelike chemical similar to what the body produces naturally when we're in love. Montezuma was said to have drunk 50 cups of chocolate a day to boost his virility.

1 18.25-ounce box yellow cake mix
1/4 cup vodka
1/2 cup sugar
1/4 cup Kahlua liqueur
1 5.9-ounce box chocolate instant pudding
3/4 cup water
1 cup chopped pecans, toasted
2 teaspoons ground cinnamon
1 cup canola oil
4 extra-large eggs
Purple pansies for garnish

Preheat oven to 325F. Combine ingredients in a large bowl. Mix on low speed for 1 minute. Beat on high speed for 4 minutes. Pour mixture into greased and floured Bundt pan. Bake for 60 to 70 minutes.

Glaze Topping
1/4 cup powdered sugar
1/4 cup Kahlua liqueur

Combine ingredients and drizzle over warm cake. Allow to cool. Remove cake from pan and flip so that glazed side is facing up. Garnish with pansies.

Herbs in the Home

"Come, sweetheart, come, Dear as my heart to me
Come to the room I have made for thee...
Flowers for thee to tread,
Green herbs, sweet scented."
—10th-century song

Flowers and herbs are symbols—tangible, sweet-smelling markers for many of life's occasions, great and small. Consider the magic of the senior prom corsage as well as bridal bouquets and boutonnieres, exchanges of roses for Valentine's Day, baby carnations for Mother's Day, tree plantings to celebrate births, and wreaths and flowers to ease grief. To hold the beauty of the memories supplied by flowers and herbs, we have learned ways to preserve nature by drying petals, leaves, seeds and roots.

Herbal Bouquets and Centerpieces

"A flower unplucked is but left to the falling,
And nothing is gained by not gathering roses."
—Robert Frost

Herbal decorations and celebrations are old companions. In the late 19th century, creative hostesses abandoned traditional centerpieces and scattered flowers across table tops. Serious decorators attempted to recreate indoor gardens. Some went so far as to cut holes in the tables to allow palms or ferns to grow through, to stretch their green branches toward the chandelier! Whether consciously or not, people recognized that what is contained in a vase, bowl or pitcher isn't of primary importance. It is the combination of container, flower, leaf and imagination that counts.

Today, herbs (fresh-cut, growing or dried) take center stage, replacing floral bouquets. Abundant plants such as bushy mints, lush lemon balm or prostrate rosemary in a grapevine basket make a striking yet simple centerpiece. Why not invite guests to help themselves to a sprig to garnish their goblet of wine?

You can transport your guests to an English garden of perennial romance, where flowers and herbs are organized in groups rather than mixed together. Gather small assortments of nasturtiums, dianthus, petunias or roses, and fragrant green mints for each setting. When pansies are purchased in a flat and transferred to wide-mouth cups, they become delightful party favors for guests.

Combine culinary mainstays such as garden sage and golden sage, chives and garlic chives in flower, and purple basil with blooming dill. Dress up a table with petite creamers filled with edible flowers that also be used as dessert toppings, including borage, calendula, Johnny-jump-up and lavender.

A healthy arrangement of salad herbs and flowers, garlic chives, Italian flat-leaf parsley, lemon thyme, basil and tarragon becomes a get-well bouquet. When allowed to flower, basil produces delicate, spiky, spicy-scented blossoms that create a warm welcome. For a showy chorus of colors and scents, mix different flowering basils: bold purple opal, bright green sweet garden, variegated green and purple to pink cinnamon, and delicate, white-spiked lemon. Make the arrangement abundant and dense—it will invite people to bend down and drink in the fragrance.

Containers for Bouquets

The container you select for your gathering should reinforce the mood you want to convey. Choose a container in scale with the size of the table. The finished arrangement should not be too large or too high for seated guests to see over or around. If there is plenty of space, place plants in a container that will accommodate them without taking them out of their pots. If space is at a premium, transfer plants from their pots so they can be temporarily showcased. Handle plants gently so the soil around the rootball remains intact when moving them back and forth. Line the container with a plastic bag to protect the table from moisture damage. If gaps are noticeable in the arrangement, fill with Spanish moss. For a more fineshed look, cover edges of pots if they are showing.

Reading Between the Leaves

Herbs and flowers deepen the intimacy of our relationships. Their near perfection of form and their texture and fragrance make them the simplest and most elegant expressions of love. Their emotional qualities were particularly appreciated in Victorian times, when the language of love was flowers. Lady Wortley Montague noted that lovers could send their missives back and forth, telling volumes, ". . . without ever inking the fingers." Each flower not only conveyed a sentiment, but the manner in which the flowers were arranged in a "tussie-mussie" bouquet enhanced the communication. A flower inclined to the right meant the floral message was aimed at the recipient. Leaned to the left, the flower represented an admirable quality of the sender.

Desiccant Drying

A desiccant is a material that absorbs moisture when drying herbs. Cornmeal, borax and sand are useful household desiccants, or you can buy desiccants at craft stores. The basic process of drying with a desiccant is to pour the material carefully around plants in a wood or cardboard box, making sure it supports the plant and gets between its leaves and petals. When plant parts are thoroughly dry, after about a week or two, lift them carefully out of the desiccant and brush the particles away with a small, dry, soft-bristle brush.

Above right: Herbal bath bags are simple to make. Blend dried herbs such as mint, lavender, roses and rosemary, and place in muslin bag. See page 172.

Above: Hot bath water activates the bath bag's fragrances.

Right: Basic ingredients for making potpourri include dried herbs, essential oils (in glass container) and fixative (off-white granules) to prolong the potpourri's essence.

Below: A single, herb-laced candle makes a romantic statement.

Below right: Herb candles can be created in a range of shapes, sizes and fragrances. See step-by-step instructions on page 171.

Making an Herb Wreath, Step by Step

1. Make a circular frame using thick, sturdy wire, such as that of a coat hanger. Collect small sprays of sweet bay or artemisia leaves. The herb used in these photos is sweet Annie, an *Artemisia* species. Use thin floral wire to fasten sprays securely so each slightly overlaps the other, all around the wire frame. Your goal is to give your wreath a solid, leafy base.

2. A glue gun comes in handy to attach small bunches of dried herbs such as yarrow. Also consider using lavender sprigs, red rose hips, hawthorn berries or hops. Weave in sprigs or bunches of rosemary, purple basil, lemon verbena, southernwood, woodruff, chamomile, roses, statice or globe amaranth.

3. The completed wreath, ready to accent your home or to give as a gift from the garden. Spritzing lightly with hair spray will help preserve it.

Herbs and Wreaths

"Nothing is more the child of art than a garden."
—Sir Walter Scott

For some three thousand years, people have been using plants to make wreaths. As this botanical art developed, a crown of oak leaves came to adorn the honored warrior, ivy rewarded the poet and laurel elevated the statesman. Victorious Roman generals returning from war were crowned with the grasses and wildflowers growing in the battlefields they had conquered. It was unheard of for ordinary folks to wear such crowns of distinction.

Just about any public occasion was observed with wreaths. Wreaths were worn at festivals, sacrifices, weddings and banquets. Priests selected henbane, vervain and rue—plants associated with the other world and religious rites. Crowns for Olympic athletes were made of laurel, oak, olive, parsley, balm or poplar. Orange blossoms, myrtle and rosemary coronets (for purity and faithfulness) were fashionable for brides. Funeral wreaths were braided with daffodil and poppy flowers, as well as with amaranth, statice, tansy and yarrow, plants symbolizing remembrance and everlasting life.

In the Christian era, wreaths have come to be associated less with honor than with decoration and celebration, adorning a home's door, wall or table. Today, wreaths are often associated with Christmas and the Advent, literally "the coming."

Apart from their symbolism, wreaths have a charming innocence all their own. Their appearance, scents and flavors remind us of traditions and old-world beauty.

We've provided instructions and step-by-step photos on how to make a simple wreath on page 169.

Potpourri Potions

"Speak not, whisper not,
Here bloweth thyme and bergamot
Softly on thee every hour
Secret herbs their spices shower."
—Walter de la Mare

Generally speaking, a potpourri is a mixture of fragrant ingredients made up primarily of dried flower petals. To these are added aromatic herbs, seeds, spices and essential oils.

Aromatic herbs give potpourris their exotic and lasting touch. Sage, basil, marjoram, costmary, bay, lemon balm, eau de cologne mint, peppermint, bergamot, myrtle, rosemary, and lemon verbena leaves are popular choices.

Essential oils provide the dominating fragrance or strengthen the existing scent in the potpourri. Popular essential oils are rosemary, geranium, lavender, rose, peppermint, bergamot and patchouli. However, use oil with care. Too many or too much becomes over-powering and unappealing.

Most potpourris are made up of strong-scented flowers. Roses, violets, jasmine, lily of the valley, lavender, red bergamot, chamomile and mock orange are favorites. Color and texture are also important. Brightly hued petals and buds are included even though they may have little scent.

Materials called *fixatives* must be added to potpourri. Their function is to blend all fragrances together, absorb fragrant oils, retard the evaporation of essential oils and give the potpourri a longer, more aromatic life. Common fixatives include orris root, fiber fix, tonka beans and benzoin gum.

Making Potpourri, Moist and Dry

Potpourri is more an art than a science. Our noses and personal preferences help dictate the ingredients. Potpourri can be made dry or moist. Moist potpourri has a heavier fragrances than dry blends and retain their scent longer. Store moist ones in china jars that have perforated lids. This conserves fragrance and disguises the unattractive appearance.

To make a moist potpourri, allow flowers and

The Language of Herbs	
Basil	Love/Hatred
Bay leaf	I change but in death
Borage	Courage
Calendula	Uneasiness, grief
Carnation	Bond of affection
Chamomile	Energy in adversity
Chervil	Sincerity
Fennel	Worthy of all praise
Lemon Geranium	Unexpected meeting
Lavender	Distrust
Marjoram	Blushes
Mint	Virtue
Nasturtium	Patriotism
Pansy	Thoughts
Parsley	Festivity
Pennyroyal	Flee away
Peppermint	Warmth of feeling
Rose	Love, strength
Rosemary	Remembrance
Garden Sage	Esteem
Thyme	Activity
Yarrow	War

leaves to dry to the stage where they feel leathery but not dry. This takes about two days. Layer petals and leaves with dry, noniodized sea salt, half coarse, half fine, using 1 cup of salt to 3 packed cups of petals and leaves. Alternate every 1/2 inch of petals with salt in a bowl until it is two-thirds full. Place it in a dark, well-ventilated location for 10 days, and mixture has caked together. Break into small pieces and mix with whole spices, citrus peel and dried herbs as desired. Seal in an airtight container for 6 weeks to ferment, stirring daily. Add eight to ten drops (up to one teaspoon) of essential oil per quart of dried material. Seal again. Two weeks later, potpourri will be ready to enjoy.

Dry potpourris are less fragrant but more visually attractive than moist types. Dry potpourri is often placed in open glass or china bowls to show off its colors and textures. Lids can be placed on them when no one is in the room to help prolong their potency. Dry potpourris also make excellent sachets for scenting drawers and closets.

To make dry potpourri, gather petals, leaves, small flowers, buds and spices. Dry until they are crisp in texture. Combine all ingredients in a container. In another container, add a fixative and essential oil. Blend, cover and store for two or three days. As a guide your proportions should be one quart dry material to about three tablespoons fixative with up to one teaspoon essential oil.

Mix materials and the fixative–essential oil mixture together. Store in a covered nonmetallic container for 4 to 6 weeks, stirring occasionally. If the fragrance is faint after this period of time, add more essential oil. If it is too strong, add more dried ingredients.

After you reach the desired level of fragrance, your potpourri is ready to put into any pretty container.

Classic Rose Potpourri

3 tablespoons cut orris root (see page 94)
1 teaspoon rose oil
1 cup dried crushed rose petals
1-1/2 cups dried whole rose petals
1/2 cup dried lavender leaves and/or flowers
1/2 cup dried rose-scented geranium leaves
1/2 cup dried whole miniature roses
6 whole dried roses

Using a wooden spoon, mix orris root and rose oil in a covered quart glass jar. Shake the container to mix or "age" the ingredients a few times each day for three days. Pour the aged fixative into a large, nonmetallic bowl. Add all other ingredients (except the six whole roses), and mix well.

Place potpourri in the quart jar that was used to age the fixative. Let set for two weeks. If the scent is faint, add 1/2 teaspoon rose oil. In either case, leave mixture covered in a dark place for another two weeks. Every few days shake the jar or mix with a wooden spoon.

After the two weeks have passed, the potpourri is complete. Place in a favorite container and decorate the top with the six whole roses.

Creating a Little Candlelight

"To learn your luck for the year, they say
Burn a bayberry dip on Christmas Day
If the flame burns bright & the light shines clear
Good luck will be yours through the coming year."
—Ancient legend

Not long ago, before the work of Thomas Edison, evening light depended upon candles. Although the value of the candle as a practical source of illumination has greatly diminished, we continue to use it in festive and ceremonial ways. We light candles to decorate, create romance, worship and celebrate. The blessings of a candle are many: it provides a natural alternative light source; a soft, earthy glow of captivating beauty; a flattering decorative element; and a fragrant herbal air freshener.

It is not difficult to make your own candles. The candle itself can be composed of paraffin or beeswax. Both materials will accept color and fragrance, although beeswax is more expensive and is generally considered to have superior burning qualities. They may also be mixed together in any proportion.

Homemade Candles

2 pounds wax, broken into chunks
2 cups dried herb of choice, or 3 cups fresh
2 crayons or sticks of candle colorant, shaved
2 11-inch candle wicks
2 candle molds, 8 x 3 inches
silicone spray or petroleum jelly

Caution: Melting wax is highly flammable! Melt in a double boiler, never directly over heat.

Melt wax in a double boiler. Remove from heat and stir in coloring. Let wax cool slightly before adding herbs. As wax cools, stir occasionally to distribute herbs throughout wax. If wax sets, reheat. Prepare molds by lightly coating the insides with silicone spray or petroleum jelly. For each mold wrap one end of the wick around a pencil or stick. The remaining length of wick should extend to the depth of the mold. Center the wick over the mold. When wax has the consistency of almost-set gelatin, pour into molds. After about 45 minutes use a pencil to make a small hole in the crust near the wick. Fill this hole with hot wax. (A well forms around the wick as the wax hardens and shrinks.) Allow to set. When cool, remove candle carefully from the mold. Trim edges of the candle with a knife and polish with an old nylon stocking. Never leave burning candles unattended.

Beauty and the Bath

Herb-scented baths have been valued as relaxing beauty treatments since the time of Cleopatra. Citizens of ancient Egypt were once commanded to "perfume themselves" at least once a week. But this was not to disguise the odor of unwashed bodies, as was the case in Europe during the Middle Ages.

Egypt's elaborate baths were forerunners of the luxurious bathing establishments of ancient Greece and Rome. Egyptians soaked their skin in oils not only for the pleasure it gave them and their mates, but also to keep the skin supple and to protect it from the sun.

The early methods of using herbs as fragrances and disinfectants to "make the heart merrie" were lovely, but were they practical? The idea of curing my stuffy head by bathing with bundles of lemon thyme, marjoram and rosemary (herbs containing the antihistamine *thymol*), as did the ladies of long ago, intrigued me. Tossing fresh, aromatic bouquets of herbs into a tub of hot water did sound soothing and romantic. My fascination soon faded with the mess they made of the tub and me, and fear the herbs would clog the drain! I discovered these problems are easily solved by placing herbs, fresh or dried, in muslin bags.

Garden-to-bath tea bags, salts, scented antiseptic vinegars and tub oils are simple to concoct and make charming and caring gifts for family, friends or anyone who appreciates the magic of herbs.

Garden-to-Bath Tea Bags

The basis of this homemade product is the same as that of "mineral salts" available at many spas: Epsom salts, borax and baking soda. Aromatic salts make bath water feel silky, smell divine and soften the skin.

One handful each:
dried lavender flowers
dried rosemary leaves
dried rose petals
dried mint leaves
crushed comfrey root
medium ground oatmeal

Mix herbs and oatmeal together and spoon into a muslin bag. Place the bag in a large bowl, pour on boiling water to cover, and allow to infuse for 20 minutes. Pour this scented solution into a bath of warm water just before stepping in.

Time-Out Bath Salts

1/2 cup Epsom salts
1 tablespoon baking soda
1 tablespoon borax
1/8 teaspoon lavender essential oil
1/8 teaspoon geranium essential oil

Mix dry ingredients in a bowl, then add essential oils. Or put salts in a plastic zip-lock bag, add essential oils and seal tightly. Shake bag to distribute oils. Use about 1/4 cup for each bath.

"O! And I was a damsel so fair,
But fairer I wished to appear
So I washed me in milk
And I dressed me in silk
And put the sweet thyme in my hair."
—Old Devonshire song

MintZing Body Soak

1/4 cup castor oil
1/4 teaspoon peppermint essential oil
1/4 teaspoon lemon essential oil

Combine all ingredients. Garnish container with sprigs of dried peppermint for a decorative touch.

Herb Vinegars for Cosmetic Use

The most popular fragrant disinfectants in England and colonial America were herbal vinegars. Made of garden herbs, they were primarily used to scent bath water, perfume sickrooms and compensate for poor ventilation. They were also used as cosmetics, helping soothe muscles and keep the skin smooth.

Cling-To-Me Bath Oil

For relief of dry, itchy skin, splash on this layered bath balm made of vinegar and oil. The vinegar disperses throughout the water while the heavenly scented oil floats on the top. Layers form in the bottle, too.

1/4 cup apricot-kernel oil
2 teaspoons liquid lecithin
1/4 cup apple cider vinegar
1 teaspoon orange extract
1 teaspoon brandy extract
4 teaspoons rose extract

Combine all ingredients and allow to set. Mix will separate into layers. Shake vigorously just before using.

Herb Vinegar Bath Splash

2 ounces fresh or 1 ounce dried of each of the following:
Thyme sprigs and leaves
Lavender sprigs and flowers
Spearmint sprigs and leaves
Rosemary sprigs and leaves
Sage sprigs and leaves

Mix herbs together. Steep with 4 cups vinegar (apple cider or white wine) for several weeks. Strain. Mix until dissolved:
1/4 ounce gum camphor
1/2 ounce gum benzoin
3 tablespoons grain alcohol

Cover and let stand for three days. Strain, bottle and garnish with fresh sprigs if desired. Cap tightly and label.

Sources and Resources

PLANTS, SEEDS AND PRODUCTS

Antique Rose Emporium
9300 Leuckemeyer Rd.
Brenham, TX 77833-6453
800-441-0002. Catalog fee.

The Banana Tree
715 Northhampton St.
Easton, PA 18042
Free catalog.

W. Atlee Burpee Co.
P.O. Box 5114
Warminster, PA 18974-4818
Free catalog.

Carroll Gardens
444 E. Main St.
Westminster, MD 21157
800-638-6334
Catalog fee.

Companion Plants
7247 N. Coolville Ridge
Athens, OH 45701
Catalog fee.

Fredericksburg Herb Farm
402 Whitney St.
P.O. Box 927
Fredericksburg, TX 78624
1-800-259-HERB
Catalog fee refundable with
first order; newsletter by
subscription.
www.fredericksburg
herbfarm.com
email: herbfarm@ktc.com

Gardens Alive!
Highway 48
P.O. Box 149
Sunman, IN 47041
Free catalog.

Glasshouse Works
Church St.
P.O. Box 97
Stewart, OH 45778-0097
Catalog fee.

Goodwin Creek Gardens
P.O. Box 83
Williams, OR 97544
Catalog fee.

Greenfield Herb Gardens
P.O. Box 9
Shipshewana, IN 46565
Catalog fee.

The Herbfarm
32804 Issq.—F.C. Rd.
Fall City, WA 98024
800-866-4372.
Catalog fee.

Herbs, Etc.
1345 Cerrillos Rd.
Santa Fe, NM 78505
Free catalog.

Heronswood Nursery
7530 N.E. 288th St.
Kingston, WA 98346
Catalog fee.

Logee's Greenhouses
141 North St.
Danielson, CT 06239
Catalog fee.

The Cook's Garden
P.O. Box 5010
Hodges, SC 29653-9986
Free catalog.

Wayside Gardens Co.
1 Garden Lane
P.O. Box 1
Hodges, SC 29653-9990
888-222-3597
Free catalog.

White Flower Farm
P.O. Box 50
Litchfield, CT 06759-0050
800-475-0148
Free catalog.

It's About Thyme
P. O. Box 878
Manchaca, TX 78652
Free catalog.

Mellingers
2310 W. South Range Rd.
North Lima, OH 44452-9731
Free catalog.

Niche Gardens
1111 Dawson Rd.
Chapel, NC 27516
Catalog fee.

Nichols Garden Nursery
1190 North Pacific Hwy.
Albany, OR 97321-4580
Free catalog.

George W. Park Seed Co.
1 Parkton Ave.
P.O. Box 46
Greenwood, SC 29648-0046
800-845-3369
Free catalog.

Plants of the Southwest
Rt. 6 Box 11A
Santa Fe, NM 87501
Free catalog.

Johnny's Selected Seeds
1307 Foss Hill Rd.
Albion, ME 04910
Free catalog.

Rasland Farm
NC 82 at US 13
Godwin, NC 28344-2705
Catalog fee.

Renee's Garden
7389 West Zayante Rd.
Felton, CA 95018
888-880-7228
Catalog fee.

Richters Seeds & Plants
Box 26 Goodwood, Ontario,
Canada LOC1AO
Catalog fee.

Rosemary House
120 S. Market St.
Mechanicsburg, PA 17055
Catalog fee.

**Roses of Yesterday
and Today**
Brown's Valley Rd.
Watsonville, CA 95076
Catalog fee.

Sandy Mush Herb Nursery
316 Surrett Cove Rd.
Leicester, NC 28748-9622
Catalog fee.

The Scented Geranium
P.O. Box 123
Washington, KY 41096
Catalog fee.

Seeds Of Change
P.O. Box 15700
Santa Fe, NM 87506-5700
Free catalog.

Shady Acres Herb Farm
7815 Highway 212
Chaska, MN 55318
Catalog fee.

Shepherd's Garden Seeds
30 Irene St.
Torrington, CT 06790-6658
Catalog fee.

**Sunnybrook Farms
Nursery**
9448 Mayfield Rd.
Chesterland, OH 44026
Catalog fee.

Territorial Seed Company
P.O. Box 157
Cottage Grove, OR 97424
Catalog fee.

**Thompson & Morgan
Seed Co.**
P.O. Box 1308
Jackson, NJ 08527-0308
800 274-7333
Free catalog.

Well-Sweep Herb Farm
205 Mt. Bethel Rd.
Port Murray, NJ 08765
Catalog fee.

PUBLICATIONS

**The Aromatic Thymes
Magazine**
18-4 East Dundee Rd. #200
Barrington, IL 60010
email:
aromatic@interaccess.com

**Herb Companion
Magazine**
201 E. Fourth St.
Loveland, CO 80537-5655
800-645-3675

Herbalgram Magazine
P.O. Box 201660
Austin, TX 78720

**The Herb Quarterly
Magazine**
223 San Anselmo Ave. #7
P.O. Box 689
San Anselmo, CA 94960

The Herbal Connection
P.O. Box 245
Silver Spring, PA 17575
717-393-3295
email:
HERBWORLD@aol.com

**Herb Resource Directory
Northwind Publications**
439 Ponderosa Way
Jemez Springs, NM 87025

GARDENS TO VISIT

Caprilands Herb Farm
Silver St.
Coventry, CT 06238

Gilberties Herb Gardens
7 Sylvan Lane
Westport, CT 06880
203-227-4175

Golden Trowel Herb Farm
P.O. Box 449
Newalla, OK 74857

The Fragrance Shop
317 College Hill Rd.
Hopkinton, NH 03229

**Huntington Botanic
Gardens**
1151 Oxford Rd.
San Marino, CA 91108

**Miles Estate Herb
& Berry Farm**
4308 Marthaler Rd. N. E.
Woodburn, OR 97071

The Cloisters
Fort Tryon Park
190th Street
New York, NY

Biltmore Estate
Asheville, NC

**New York
Botanical Garden**
Bronx, NY 10458-9980

Hedgehog Hill Farm
54 Hedgehog Hill Road
Sumner, ME 04292

ORGANIZATIONS

**Horticultural Society of
New York**
128 West 58th Street
New York, NY 10019-2103

Herb Society of America
9019 Kirtland Chardon Rd.
Kirtland, OH 44094

Index

A

Absinthe, 122
Absolut Tarragon, 115
Absolute, 14
Achillea species, 123
  A. millefolium, 123
  A. ptarmica, 123
  A. tomentosa, 123
Acid soil, 14, 141
Acne, herb remedy, 21
Add-A-Bed Garden, 126
Air drying, 25
Air layering, 14
Alchemilla vulgaris, 77
Alecost, 57
Alkaline soil, 14, 141
Allergies, 111
Allheal, 118
Allium roseum, 66
  A. sativum, 66
  A. schoenoprasum, 51, 66
  A. tuberosum, 51
Aloe barbadensis, 33
  A. saponaria, 33
Aloe Hair Treatment, 33
Aloe vera, 20, 32, 33
Aloysia triphylla, 83
Alternate (leaves), 14
Anethum graveolens, 58
Angelica, 32, 33
Angelica archangelica, 33
Angelica Tea, 33
Angiosperm, 14
Anise, 21, 34, 142, 151
Anise basil, 38
Annual(s), 14, 26, 27, 130, 138
Ants, 150
Anthemis chamaemelum, 47
  A. cotula, 47
  A. nobilis, 47
  A. tinctoria, 47
Anther, 14
Anthriscus cerefolium, 50
Apex, 14
Aphid, 150
Aphrodisiac, 14
Apothecary, 14
Apothecary's rose, 99
Appetizers 91, 105, 110
Apple mint, 31, 86, 89, 126, 130
Aquatic, 14
Architectural, 14
Aromatherapy, 14
Aromatic, 14
Artemis, 34
Artemisia species, 28, 34, 35, 90, 169
  A. abrotanum, 111
  A. absinthium, 122
  A. annua, 111
  A. dracunculus var. *sativa*, 115
  A. dranunuloides, 115
  A. frigida, 122
  A. lactiflora, 87
  A. ludoviciana silver king, 36
  A. ludoviciana var. *albula*, 87
  A. pontica, 122
  A. purshiana, 87
  A. schmidtiana 'Nana', 87
  A. stellerana, 122

A. vulgaris, 87
Artichoke Spread, 157
Arugula, 35, 36, 142
Arugula Salad, 35
Asclepias tuberosa, 42
Asparagus Bundles with Thyme Blossom Butter, 159, 160
Avocado and Corn Salsa with Oregano, 158
Axil, 14

B

Backgrounds, herbs for, 28
Baked Beans with Winter Savory, 122
Ballota nigra, 75
Balm, 14
Balsamic Herb Basting Sauce, 163
Basil, 16, 19, 25, 35-39, 123, 139, 142, 150, 151, 170
Basil Cheese Snax, 157
Bath Oil, 172
Bath Salts, 172
Bay leaf, 170
Bay Rum Custard, 39
Beaked parsley, 50
Bedstraws, 131
Bee balm, 39-40, 41, 126, 127, 151
Bergamot, 39-40
Betony, 78
Beverages, 79, 115, 163, 165. See also Teas
Bible leaf, 57
Biennial(s), 14, 26, 43, 138
Bitter, 14
Black cumin, 93
Black horehound, 75
Blackwort, 51
Blender, 14
Blue balsam tea mint, 88
Body Scrub, 22
Bog myrtle, 139
Bolt, to seed, 14, 63
Boneset, 51
Borage, 40-42, 142, 151, 170
Borage Tea, 40
Borago officinalis, 40
Border garden, 26, 125, 127
Borders, herbs for, 28
Botany, 14
Bouncing Bet, 107, 110
Bouquet garni, 14, 95
Bouquets, 24, 167
Boxwood, 133, 134
Bract(s), 14, 59
Brassica species, 90
  B. hirta, 91
  B. nigra, 90-91
Bread Baker Chocolate Bunny, 155, 156
Breads and muffins, 46, 113, 155
Broccoli, 150
Bronze fennel, 62, 65
Bruise, 14
Bruisewort, 51, 107
Bud, 14
Butters, herb, 18, 51
Butterfly weed, 42-43, 44
Buttermilk Pie, 164

C

Cabbage rose, 99
Cabbage worm, 150
Cakes, 165-166
Calendula, 21, 23, 23, 43,

45, 170
Calendula officinalis, 43
Calendula Vinaigrette, 42
Caliche, 14
Calmative, 14
Calyx, 14
Camphor plant, 57
Canada root, 42
Candles, herb, 168, 171
Caraway, 43, 46, 126, 142
Caraway and Thyme Bread, 155
Caraway Apple Muffins, 46
Caraway thyme, 117
Carminative qualities of herbs, 34, 59
Carnation, 23, 170
Carrot fly, 150
Carrots, 61
Carum cavi, 43
Castor bean, 150
Catmint, 28, 46, 48
Catnip, 21, 45, 46-47, 48, 123, 127, 130, 142
Catnip Tea, 46
Celtic Cross Garden, 131
Centerpieces, 167
Centranthus ruber, 27, 118
Chamaemelum nobile, 47
  C. nobile 'Treneague', 47, 50
  C. nobile var. 'Florepleno', 47
Chamomile, 8, 21, 23, 47, 49, 50, 131, 135, 139, 150, 151, 170
Cheddar and Chive Corn Chowder, 162
Cheese snacks, 110, 157
Chenopodium ambrosioides, 59
Chervil, 50-51, 126, 142, 151, 170
Chervil Herb Popovers, 50
Chicken Noodle Soup, 162
Chicken Salad, 159
Chile-Peach Pesto, 38
Chive Butter, 51
Chives, 19, 28, 51, 52, 123, 126, 130, 142, 145, 148, 149, 150, 151
Chocolate mint, 88
Chrysanthemum, 130
Chrysanthemum balsamita, 57
  C. parthenium, 63
Cilantro, 19, 55, 57, 126, 142, 156
Cinnamon basil, 37, 38
Citronella grass, 82
Clay soil, herbs for, 141
Cleaner, herbal floor, 111
Climate, 138-139
Cold frame, 151
Cold protection, 151
Cold (medical) relief, 21, 54
Cold tender, 15
Colors, 26, 29, 134-135
Colorado potato beetle, 150
Comfrey, 21, 23, 51, 52, 54, 127, 130, 139
Comfrey Mask, 54
Common chamomile, 47
Common oregano, 94
Common sage, 105
Common wormwood, 122

Companion planting, 61, 149, 151
Compost, 14, 141-142
Condiment, 14
Coneflower, 54-55, 142
Coneflower, purple, 17, 29, 53
Containers, 29
  buying herbs in, 142
  designing with, 135
  for herb bouquets, 167
  growing herbs in, 146-147
  planting from, 145
  rootbound plants in, 145
Cookies, 55, 83
Cooking with herbs, 153-166
Coriander, 19, 53, 55, 57, 142
Coriander-Carrot Muffins, 155, 157
Coriander-Kissed Cookies, 55
Coriandrum sativum, 55
Corn chowder, 162
Corsican mint, 86, 87
Cosmetic herbs, 17, 22-23, 77, 114, 130
Cosmos, 24
Costmary, 56, 57, 139
Coughs, herb remedy, 21
Crafts, 167-172
Cream, 14
Creeping thyme, 117, 126, 127
Cucumber and Dill Soup, 58
Cudweed wormwood, 87
Culinary garden, 19, 130
Culinary herbs, 17, 18-19
Culpeper, Nicholas, 14, 39
Cultivar(s), 14, 143
Cumin-Black Bean Quiche, 162
Curled tansy, 114
Curly mint, 88
Curly parsley, 95, 97, 130
Curry, 25
Custard, bay rum, 39
Cut flowers, 25
Cutting back herbs, 147
Cuttings, propagating by, 14, 143, 145
Cymbopogon citratus, 82
  C. flexuosus, 82
  C. martinii, 82
  C. nardus, 82

D

Datura, 57-58, 60
Datura stramonium, 58
Deciduous, 14
Decoction, 14, 35
Decorative herbs, 17, 24-25, 167
Deer-resistant herbs, 123
Desiccant drying, 167
Designs, herb garden. See Plans, herb garden
Devil's-apple, 57
Dianthus, 23
Digitalis, 130
Dill, 19, 58-59, 61, 126, 142, 150, 151
Dioscorides, Pedanius, 14
Dittany of Crete, 59, 60
Division, propagation by, 14, 143, 145

Dormant, 14
Dragon's mugwort, 115
Dried herbs, 24
Drying herbs, to preserve, 25, 154, 167
Dusty miller, 122, 130
Dyer's chamomile, 47

E

Echinacea, 17, 53, 142
  E. purpurea, 29, 54
Eggplant, 150
Elephant garlic, 66
Elixir, 14
Enfleurage, 14
English chamomile, 47
English lavender, 79, 81
English sorrel, 110
English thyme, 116
Epazote, 59, 62, 64
Epazote Room Freshener, 62
Eruca vesicaria sub. *sativa*, 35
Essence, 14
Essential oil(s), 14, 168
Eupatorium purpureum, 77
European valerian, 118
Evergreen, 14
Everlastings, 14
Extract, 14
Eyes, tonic for, 22

F

Facial mask, 54
Fall planting, 142
False chamomile, 47
False tarragon, 85
Family, 14
Featherfoil, 114-115
Febrifuge, 63
Feeding, 147
Fennel, 19, 21, 23, 61, 62-63, 65, 129, 139, 142, 170
Fennel flower, 93
Fennel Salad, 159
Fernleaf tansy, 126
Fertilizing, 147
Feverfew, 63, 64, 130
Fines herbes, 50
Finocchio, 63
Fixative, 14, 168
Floor cleaner, herbal, 111
Florence fennel, 63
Florentine iris, 94
Floret, 14
Flower, 14
Flu, herb remedy, 21
Focal points, in garden, 135
Foccaccia Bread, 155
Foeniculum vulgare, 62
  F. vulgare 'Rubrum', 62
Foliage textures, 128
Follicles, 43
Formal garden, 132
Foxglove, 130
Fragrance, 22, 25, 131, 134
Fragrant herbs, 130
'Frau Dagmar Hartopp' rose, 100
Fredericksburg Herb Farm, 8, 10-13, 24, 26, 128, 132, 136, 156
Freezing, to preserve, 154
French lavender, 79
French oregano, 94
French parsley, 50
French sorrel, 56, 110

French tarragon, 19, 112, 115, 117, 130
Fringed wormwood, 122
Fuller's Herb, 107

G

Gabriel's trumpet, 58
Galium odoratum, 113
　G. verum, 114
Garden accessories, 135
Garden designs. See Plans, herb garden
Garden heliotrope, 118
Garden sage, 9, 104, 105, 170
Garden sorrel, 139
Garden-to-Bath Tea Bags, 172
Garlands, 24
Garlic, 19, 21, 64, 66, 126, 150, 151
Garlic-Baked Eggplant, 63
Garlic chives, 51, 123, 130
Garlic-Grilled Tomatoes, 66
Garlic-Soap Spray, 150
Garnish, 15
Gaspacho, 159
Genus, 15
Geraniums, scented, 19
Gerard, John, 15
German chamomile, 47, 49
German statice, 130
German valerian, 118
Germander, 69, 70, 123, 126, 134
Ginger, 70-71, 73
Ginger Baklava, 70
Gingergrass, 82
Ginseng, 71-72
Globe amaranth, 25
Glossary, 14-15
Glycosides, 43
Gold yarrow, 130
Golden lemon thyme, 117
Golden marjoram, 94
Golden sage, 104, 105
Gourmet parsley, 50
Grapefruit mint, 86
Great wild valerian, 118
Grecian laurel, 39
Greek marjoram, 94
Greek oregano, 94, 130
Green bean, 150
Green Bouquet Garni, 95
Green ginger, 122
Green manure, 141
Grilling with herbs, 161, 163
Ground layering, 143
Growing herbs, 136-161
Guinea hens, 149

H

Half-barrel planters, 29, 148
Half-hardy annuals, 138
Hangover, herb remedy for, 21
Hardy (plants), 15, 138
Harvesting herbs, 25, 151
Heat, effect on growing, 138
Herb Butter, 18
Herb, definition of, 6
Herb garden, planning, 124-135
Herb Rice, 103

Herb tea, brewing, 163
Herb Vinegar, 153, 158
Herb Vinegar Bath Splash, 172
Herb Vinegar, Four Thieves, 78
Herb wreaths, 169, 170
Herbaceous, 15
Herbal, 15
Herbal bath bags, 168, 172
Herbal bouquets and centerpieces, 167
Herbalist, 15
Herbal lore, 153
Herbal Salt, 59
Herb-Skewered Kabobs, 161, 163
Herb-Tea Spray, 150
Herbs
　climates, 139
　color, 29
　for pest control, 150
　history, 6-7
　organizations, 173
Herbs, growing
　companion plants, 151
　from seed, 142
　in containers, 146-147
　indoors, 146-147
　in planters, 128
　maintaining, 147-151
　that repel pests, 150
Herbs, in home, 167-172
　bath, 33, 172
　cosmetic, 17, 22-23, 77, 114, 130
　decorative, 17, 24-25, 167
　home care, 62, 111
　medicinal, 17, 20-21, 54, 130
　preserving, 154
　skin care, 22, 54, 77
　spiritual powers, 153
Herbs, in kitchen, 154-166
　as seasonings, 154
　culinary, 17
Herbs, in landscape, 17, 26-29
Hierba santa, 72
High humidity, gardening in, 139
Hippocrates, 15
Hoja santa, 72, 73, 139
Holy basil, 38
Homeopathy, 15
Hops, 72-74
Horehound, 74-75, 76, 142
Hormone rooting powder, 143
Hornworm, 150
Horseradish, 150, 151
Horsetail reed, 21
Hot Pepper Spray, 150
Humidity, effect on growing, 138-139
Humulus japonicus var. *variegatus*, 72
　H. lupulus, 72
Humus, 15
Hungarian chamomile, 47
Huntington Botanic Garden, 29
Hybrid, 15
Hypericum, 106
Hypericum perforatum, 106
Hyssop, 19, 21, 75, 77,

130, 139, 142, 151
Hyssopus officinalis, 75

I

Iced tea, 160
Indian cress, 91
Indian lemongrass, 82
Indoor seed starting, 144
Indoors, growing herbs, 146-147
Indoor-to-outdoors-and-back system, 146
Informal border garden, 127
Infusion, 15, 34-35
Insect repellent, 111
Insomnia, herb remedy, 21
Iris, 36, 95, 133
Iris X *germanica* var. *florentina*, 94, 96
Italian parsley, 95

J

Jamestown weed, 57, 58
Japanese beetle, 150
Japanese hops, 72
Java patchouli, 95
Jimson weed, 57-58
Joe Pye weed, 76, 77

K

Kabobs, herb-skewered, 163
Kahlua Chocolate Cake, 166
Knitbone, 51
Knot garden, 133, 134
Knotted marjoram, 94

L

Lacewings, 149
Ladder garden, plan, 135
Lady's bedstraw, 114
Lady's mantle, 76, 77-78
Ladybird beetles (ladybugs), 89, 137, 149, 149
Lamb's ears, 78, 80, 127, 128, 130
Landscaping with herbs, 17, 26-29
Language of herbs, 167, 170
Larkspur, 100
Lasagna, vegetarian, 162
Latherwort, 107
Laurus nobilis, 39
Lavandula species, 78
　L. angustifolia, 79
　L. dentata, 79, 81
　L. multifida, 81
　L. stoechas, 79
Lavender, 20, 21, 23, 25, 78-79, 80, 123, 124, 126, 127, 128, 134, 135, 139, 142, 170
Lavender cotton, 107
Leader, 15
Leaven, 15
Leaves, alternate, 14
Lemon balm, 19, 21, 29, 79, 82, 84, 123, 126, 127, 130, 139, 142
Lemon basil, 38, 126
Lemon geranium, 170
Lemon Geranium Angel Food Cake, 165-166
Lemon herbs, 79
Lemon thyme, 21, 116, 117, 126, 127
Lemon verbena, 23, 29,

79, 83, 84, 126, 164
Lemon Verbena Margarita, 164, 165
Lemon Verbena Sugar Cookies, 83
Lemon-Aid (recipe), 79
Lemongrass, 82-84, 130
Lemongrass Mimosa, 165
Lemony Lamb Chops 82
Lettuce-leaf basil, 38
Levisticum officinale, 83
Licorice basil, 37
Lift, 15
Ligusticum levisticum, 83
Loam, 15
Loam soil, herbs for, 141
Lovage, 83, 84, 85, 142, 151
Love-in-a-mist, 93
Low hedges, herbs for, 28
Low humidity, gardening in, 138-139

M

Mad apple, 57-58
Main dishes, 82, 122, 162
Maintaining herbs, 147-151
Mango Peach Salsa with Cilantro, 156, 157
Manures, 141
Marigold, 150
Marjoram, 21, 94, 126, 170
Marrubium incanum, 74
　M. vulgare, 74
Mask, facial, 54
Matricaria chamomilla, 47
　M. recutita, 47
May wine, 113
Mayweed, 47
Medicinal herbs, 17, 20-21, 54, 130
Melissa grass, 82-83
Melissa officinalis, 79
Mentha species, 86
　M. aquatica, 86
　M. pulegium, 86, 98
　M. requienni, 86
　M. spicata, 86
　M. suaveolens, 86
　M. X *piperita* var. *citrata*, 86
　M. X *villosa* var. *alopecuroides*, 86
Mexican bean beetle, 150
Mexican Black-Eyed Peas, 98
Mexican mint marigold, 84, 85-86, 123
Mexican Mint Marigold Vinaigrette, 85
Mexican oregano, 98-99, 100
Mexican purple garlic, 66
Mexican red garlic, 66
Microclimates, 129, 139
Microwave drying, 154
Mince, 15
Miner's lettuce, 110-111
Mint, 19, 89, 133, 151, 170
Mint, controlling, 86, 89
Minted Melon Potion, 165
Mints, 86-87, 123, 131, 139
　controlling, 86
MintZing Body Soak, 172
Monarda didyma, 39, 40
　M. fistulosa var. *menthifolia*, 40
Mother-of-thyme, 117

Mugwort, 87, 90, 92, 139
Mulch(es), 15, 148, 151
Mullein, 90
Musc de Bois, 113
Mustard, 90-91, 151

N

Nasturtium, 91-93, 130, 142, 150, 170
Nasturtium Hors d'oeuvres, 91
Nematode, 150
Nepeta cataria, 46
　N. mussinii, 46, 48
　N. X *faassenii*, 46
New Potatoes with Society Garlic, 110
Nigella, 93, 130
Nigella damascena, 93
North American ginseng, 71, 72
Nutmeg flower, 93

O

Ocimum basilicum, 35
Offsets, propagation by, 146
Oils, herb, 18
'Old Blush' rose, 99, 100
Old woman wormwood, 122
Onion, 150
Opal basil, 38
Oregano, 19, 93-94, 96, 123, 126, 135, 148, 150, 151
Oriental ginseng, 71
Origanum, 93
　O. dictamnus, 59
　O. heracleoticum, 94
　O. libanoticum, 94
　O. marjorana, 94, 113
　O. onites, 94
　O. rotundifolium, 94
　O. vulgare, 94, 98
Orris root, 94, 96
Oswego Tea, 40
Oven drying, 154

P

Panax ginseng, 71
　P. quinquefolium, 71
Parkinson, John, 15
Parsley, 19, 21, 28, 94-95, 126, 142, 150, 170
Pastries, 70, 166
Patchouli, 95, 96, 98
Paths, in herb garden, 26, 28-29, 131
Pelargonium, 66-67
　P. crispum, 67
　P. glutinosum, 67
　P. graveolens, 67, 134
　P. limoneum, 67
　P. quercifolium, 67
　P. tomentosum, 67, 68
　P. X *fragrans*, 67
Pennyroyal, 86, 87, 96, 98, 99, 170
Peppermint, 21, 86, 88, 130, 170
Peppermint geranium, 68
Perennial(s), 15, 26, 27, 130, 138
Perennial chamomile, 47
Perfume basil, 38
Pest control, 99, 102, 149, 150
Pesto, 38

Pest-repelling herbs, 150
Pests, 147, 150-151
Petiole, 15
Petroselinum sativum, 94
pH, soil, 15, 141
Pharmacognosy, 20
Phytochemicals, 55
Pimpinella anisum, 34
Pineapple mint, 86
Pineapple sage, 30, 105, 126, 130
Pink yarrow, 127
Piper auritum, 72
    P. sanctum, 72
Planning an herb garden, 124-135
Plans, herb garden,
    add-a-bed, 126
    Celtic cross, 131
    cosmetic, 130
    culinary, 130
    fragrant, 130
    informal border, 127
    knot, 134
    ladder, 135
    medicinal, 130
    utilitarian, 130
Plant sources, 173
Planters, 128
Planting,
    companion, 61
    from containers, 142
    spacing plants, 145
    step by step, 140
    timing of, 130, 142
Pleurisy root, 42
Pliny, 15
Pogostemon cablin, 95
    P. heyneanus, 95
Poliomintha, 98-99, 100
Poliomintha longiflora, 98
Pomade, 15
Poppy, 23
Pot marigold, 43
Pot oregano, 94
Potato bean beetle, 150
Poterium sanguisorba, 42
Potion, 15
Potpourri, 15, 57, 168, 170-171
Pots, buying herbs in, 142
Poultice, 15, 21
Preserving herbs, 25, 154
Product sources, 173
Propagating herbs, 143, 146
Propagation, suckers, 32
Prostrate germander, 69
Prostrate rosemary, 126
Protection, cold, 151
Pruning, 147
Publications, herb, 173
Purple basil, 36, 37, 38
Purple coneflower, 17, 24, 29, 53, 56
Purple ruffles basil, 38
Purple-leafed barberry, 133
Purple-leaved basil, 24

Q
Quiche, 162

R
Radish, 150
Rainfall, effect on growing, 138
Recipes, 152-172
Red valerian, 27, 118
Rhizome, 15, 94

Rice, herb, 103
Rock hyssop, 75
Roman chamomile, 21, 47, 49, 50
Roman coriander, 93
Roman wormwood, 122
Root cuttings, propagation by, 143
Rootbound plants, 145
Roquette, 35
Rosa species, 99
    R. damascena, 99
    R. eglanteria, 99
    R. gallica officinalis, 99
    R. rugosa, 99, 100
    R. X alba, 99
    R. X centifolia, 99
Rose, 23, 99, 102, 170
Rose geranium, 134
Rose Geranium Buttermilk Pie, 166
Rose Geranium Pound Cake, 164, 166
Rose Geranium Tea, 67
Rose hips, 100
Rose Potpourri, 171
Rosemary, 19, 20, 21, 23, 25, 36, 101, 102-103, 123, 129, 139, 149, 150, 151, 170
Rosemary-Thyme Salsa, 158
Roses, chemical-free, 102
Rose-scented geraniums, 156
Rosmarinus officinalis, 102
    R. officinalis 'Prostratus', 102
Rudbeckia, 45
Rue, 23, 101, 103, 105, 123, 127, 142
Rumex acetosa, 110
    R. scutatus, 110
Runner, 15
Russian comfrey, 54
Russian sage, 25, 127
Russian tarragon, 115
Ruta graveolens, 103

S
Sage, 9, 19, 21, 23, 25, 105-106, 123, 139, 142, 150
Sage and Cheese Torta, 105
Salad burnet, 42, 44, 142
Salad Burnet Sour Cream, 42
Salads, 35, 118, 159
Salsas, 157-158
Salt, herbal, 59
Salting, to preserve, 154
Salvia species, 105
    S. elegans, 30, 105
    S. leucantha, 127
    S. officinalis, 9, 105
Salvias, 123
San Diego Wild Animal Park, 129
Sandy soil, herbs for, 141
Santolina, 107, 123, 134, 139
    S. chamaecyparissus, 107, 108
    S. virens, 107, 108
Saponaria officinalis, 107
saponins, 107
Satureja hortensis, 119
    S. montana, 119
Savory, 119, 122, 139, 151
Scented geraniums, 19, 66-67, 68, 70

Scented mayweed, 47
Scopolamine, 58
Scorpioid cyme, 52
Screening plants, 132
Seasonings, healthy, 154
Seasons, harvesting by, 151
Seed sources, 173
Seeds, collecting for replanting, 145
Seeds, planting, 143
Seeds, starting indoors, 144
Self-seed (self sow), 15
Sepals, 15
Shade, herbs for, 28
Sheepwort, 107
Shoo-Fly Potpourri, 57
Side dishes, 50, 63, 66, 98, 103, 110
Sieve, 15
Silkweed, 42
Silver horehound, 74
Silver king artemisia, 36, 87, 92, 123, 127
Silver mint, 86
Silver mound artemisia, 87
Silver queen artemisia, 87, 123
Silver thyme, 116, 117
Simple, 15
Skim, 15
Skin care, 22, 77
Slippery root, 51
Slips, 143
Smoking foods, 161
Smoky fennel, 62
Snacks, 110, 117, 157
Soap spray, pest control, 102
Soapwort, 107, 108, 110, 139
Society garlic, 66, 109, 110, 124
Society garlic blossoms with new potatoes, 110
Soil, 139, 141
    acid, 14
    alkaline, 14
    drainage, 139, 141
    mix for containers, 146
    pH, testing, 141
    preparation, 140
    structure, 141
    types identifying, 141
Sorrel, 110-111, 135
Sorrel Cheese Spread, 110
Soups, 58, 159, 162
Sources, for herbs, 173
Southernwood, 109, 111, 123, 126
    Coat Hanger Insect Repellent, 111
Southernwood Fragrant Floor Cleaner, 111
Spacing plants, 140
Spanish lavender, 79, 81
Spearmint, 86, 88, 150
Species, 15
Spice, 15
Spicy globe basil, 38, 130
Sprays, pest, 147, 150
Sprig, 15
Spring planting, 142
St. John's wort, 106-107, 109, 139
Stachys byzantina, 78
    S. lanata, 78
    S. officinalis, 78
Staking, 147
Statice, 25, 130

Statues, in garden, 135
Stinking horehound, 75
Stinkweed, 58
Stolon, 15
Stratifying, 143
Strewing herb, 15, 57
Striped cucumber beetle, 150
Strobili, 72
Suckers, propagating with 32
Summer savory, 119, 120, 122, 130, 142
Sun, herbs for, 28
Sun Tea, 165
Sunlight, effect on growing, 138
Sweet anise, 63
Sweet Annie, 111, 112, 113, 169
Sweet basil, 36, 37, 38, 126, 127
Sweet bay, 39, 41
Sweet brier rose, 99
Sweet chamomile, 47
Sweet Joe Pye weed, 77
Sweet marjoram, 19, 94, 113, 142
Sweet Marjoram Cornbread, 113
Sweet mugwort, 87, 111
Sweet violet, 121
Sweet woodruff, 109, 113-114, 139, 142
Sweet wormwood, 111
Symphytum asperum, 54
    S. grandiflorum, 51
    S. officinale, 51
    S. tuberosum, 54
    S. X uplandicum, 54

T
Tagetes lucida, 85
Tanacetum balsamita, 57
    T. balsamita var. *tomentosum*, 57
    T. capitulatum, 114
    T. nuttallii, 114
    T. parthenium, 63
    T. vulgare, 114
    T. vulgare var. *crispum*, 114
Tansy, 25, 112, 114-115, 123, 128, 150
Tarragon, 115, 126, 151
Teas, 21, 163, 165
    angelica, 40
    borage, 40
    catnip, 46
    Oswego, 40
    rose geranium, 67
Temperatures, cold, 138
Tender, cold, 15
Tender annuals, 138
Terminology, 14-15
Testing soil drainage, 139, 141
Teucrium chamaedrys, 70
Texas tarragon, 85
Thorn apple, 58
Thyme, 19, 21, 23, 116, 117-118, 130, 133, 134, 139, 142, 148, 150, 151, 170
Thymol, 118, 172
Thymus, 116-118
    T. 'Argenteus', 116, 117
    T. 'Aureus', 117
    T. herba-barona, 117
    T. praecox arcticus, 117

    T. pseudolanuginosus, 117
    T. serpyllum, 117
    T. vulgaris, 116, 117
    T. X citriodorus, 117
Tincture, 15
Tisane, 15, 34
Topiary, 15
Torte, 15
Trap crops, 150
Tricolor sage, 104, 105
Tropaeolum majus, 91
True chamomile, 47
True valerian, 118
Tuber, 15
Tulbaghia violacea, 66, 109, 110
Turkish oregano, 94
Tussie-mussie, 15

U
Umbel, 15
Upright rosemary, 126, 127

V
Valerian, 21, 118, 139
Valeriana officinalis, 118
Vandalroot, 118
Variegated, 15
Variety, 15
Vegetable fennel, 63
Vegetarian Lasagna, 162
Verbascum thapsus, 90
Vinaigrettes, 42, 85
Vinegars, herb, 18, 78, 119, 153, 158
Viola odorata, 119
Violet, 119
Violet Salad, 118
Volatile, 15

W
Waldmeister, 113
Walnut, Thyme and Gorgonzola Crostini, 117
Water, in garden, 135
Water mint, 86
Watering program, 142-143
Weeding, 147
Whip, 15
White mugwort, 87
Whitefly, 150
Wild chamomile, 47
Wild marjoram, 94
Wild Sweet William, 107
Wind root, 42
Wind, effect on growing, 139
Window-box planter, 148
Winter marjoram, 94
Winter protection, 151
Winter savory, 119, 120, 122, 126, 142
Winter tarragon, 85
Woodruff, 113
Woolly mint, 86
Woolly thyme, 116, 117
Woolly yarrow, 123
Wormwood, 120, 122-123, 142
Wort (Wyrt), 15, 106
Wreaths, 24, 170

Y
Yarrow, 21, 23, 24, 25, 121, 123, 135, 169, 170
Yerba del diablo, 58

Z
Zingiber officinale, 70